HEROES, ROGUES, AND LOVERS

HEROES, ROGUES, AND LOVERS

Testosterone and Behavior

James McBride Dabbs
with Mary Godwin Dabbs

McGraw-Hill

New York   San Francisco   Washington, D.C.   Auckland   Bogotá   Caracas
Lisbon   London   Madrid   Mexico City   Milan   Montreal   New Delhi
San Juan   Singapore   Sydney   Tokyo   Toronto

McGraw-Hill

A Division of The **McGraw·Hill** Companies

1 2 3 4 5 6 7 8 9 0   AGM/AGM   0 9 8 7 6 5 4 3 2 1 0

ISBN 0-07-135739-4

This book was set in Berling by Tina Thompson.

Printed and bound by Quebecor Martinsburg

This publication is designed to provide accurate and authoritative information in regard to the subject matter covered. It is sold with the understanding
that the publisher is not engaged in rendering legal, accounting, or other
professional service. If legal advice or other expert assistance is required, the
services of a competent professional person should be sought.
        —*From a declaration of principles jointly adopted by a committee*
        of the American Bar Association and a committee of publishers.

This book is printed on recycled, acid-free paper containing a
minimum of 50% recycled, de-inked fiber.

To James, Alan, Geri, Haley, and Grace

CONTENTS

ACKNOWLEDGMENTS

Writing this book and conducting the research behind it has been challenging, and I am indebted to all the people who helped. My graduate and undergraduate students brought enthusiasm, creativity, and resourcefulness to the research. Many of the findings reported here came from experiments they initiated. The heroes, rogues, lovers, and others who allowed us to study them made the research possible. Friends and colleagues put me in touch with other researchers in the social and biological sciences who were studying testosterone. Georgia State University generously supported me, and the National Science Foundation, National Institute of Mental Health, and Guggenheim Foundation provided research funding. Olivia Blumer of the Karpfinger Agency and Griffin Hansbury of McGraw-Hill worked tirelessly to get the book into print.

My friends and family, including my sons James and Alan and my daughter-in-law Geri, read chapters and told me stories that I used in the book. Lynn Kerpel answered my questions about literature, history, and punctuation. Finally, many thanks to Mary, my wife and coauthor, who organized my notes, draft chapters, and stacks of articles into a coherent whole and translated academic language into plain English.

PROLOGUE

Beginnings

FARM ANIMALS

In *The African Queen*, Rose Sayer, a stern, puritanical missionary, objected to the uncivilized ways of her traveling companion, a hard-drinking riverboat man named Charlie Allnut. She said to him, "Nature, Mr. Allnut, is what we were put on this earth to rise above!" In 1951, when the movie came out, Miss Sayer was putting into words what almost everybody understood was a basic truth.

I was a teenager then, living with my family on a farm in South Carolina. We grew row crops and pine trees, and we had chickens, miscellaneous other animals, and a mule named Belle. I raised corn, lettuce, pigs and cows, on my own and as 4-H and Future Farmer projects. In those days before hi-tech pens, the animals were free enough to act natural, although we castrated the young bulls and boars. Castration reduced their boldness and their interest in sex. It also improved the flavor of their meat, which was the reason we castrated them. I didn't know the male sex hormone testosterone by name then, but I had a practical understanding of what it did.

On the farm, we were in a good position to see similarities between people and animals, but we preferred to see differences. We knew, or thought we knew, that all animals really cared about was food, sex, and danger. We, on the other hand, put a level of civilization between ourselves and all that. We had table manners, wore clothes, got married, and supported the sheriff with our tax dollars. Observing social decorum helped assure us that, unlike animals, people were blessed with souls.

The lines of nature seemed clear then. People were the children of God, and animals were, in the words of the Bible, "dumb beasts."

Perhaps we emphasized our souls because our bodies, washed and dressed up as they might be, were still animal bodies. Although we did not have horns and tails, we knew they would be part of the punishment package if we did not pay proper attention to our souls. We poked fun at people who reminded us of animals. I remember my mother's disdain for a neighbor who scratched his back against a doorjamb. She said, "He looks like a hog scratching his back on a fence post."

MONKEY GLANDS AND CULTURE

In 1955, I left the farm, went to college and then to graduate school, and became a social psychologist. I lived in cities, studied people, and didn't think much about animals until 1972, when I visited the Yerkes Primate Field Station, near Atlanta, Georgia. Scientists there were studying the social life of primates. They studied relationships, leadership, communication, sex, and aggression. Dr. Irwin Bernstein showed me around and told me about their work.

One part of the project involved redwood "totem poles" he had put up in the monkey compounds. Each pole had an electrically charged grid near the top, and the point of the study was to see how the monkeys would learn about the grids and tell the others about them. Not all monkeys responded the same way. One group ate their pole, and another never went near theirs. But in a group of stump-tailed macaques, the dominant male, called the alpha male, took the pole very seriously. Bernstein pointed him out to me. He was easy to identify by the way he strutted, fluffed out his fur, and stood with his front paws turned outward, making himself look bigger than he was. The alpha male had special privileges, including extra sex, but he also had responsibilities. He took it as part of his job to explore anything new or potentially harmful. It was he who climbed the tower first thing in the morning after it was put up and discovered it was dangerous. He braved a shock or two, pretending to feel no pain, but when the shocks continued, he let out a warning scream and jumped down. With the assistance of the beta male, his second-in-command, he chased the other monkeys into their indoor quarters. There they remained the rest of the morning, the alpha male leaning out the doorway, staring at the pole and threatening it. In the afternoon he let the group back outside, but he and the beta male continued to watch the pole and threaten it from time to time.[1]

The scientists at Yerkes were studying animal social activity, which turns out to be complex. Beyond caring about food, sex, and danger, monkeys have a primitive society and a capacity for altruism. Like people, they pass experience down from generation to generation. They learn from each other. They have friends and enemies, and they keep track of many relationships at once. A young female is likely to grow up dominant if her mother is dominant. A strong monkey will respect a weak monkey if the weak one has strong allies.

Although social activity was the focus of their studies, the scientists also paid attention to biological factors, including testosterone. In the world of monkeys, it was easy to see nature and nurture working together. Testosterone led to fighting, and to sex, too, which was often the point of the fight. Winning fights and having sex led to more testosterone. When a male monkey won a fight, his testosterone increased; when he lost a fight, it dropped. Defeated monkeys withdrew and looked depressed. Sex therapy helped them. Their testosterone levels returned to normal when they were moved away from other males and placed among friendly females. With less testosterone, the alpha male might not have been aggressive enough to fight and intimidate his way to the top of the hierarchy, or bold enough to protect his troop from the totem pole threat. Testosterone helps a monkey gain power, and the support of influential friends or a socially prominent family helps him stay in power.

The emphasis on biology made research at Yerkes different from most research on human behavior. Scientists studying people have tended to keep biology and behavior separate, perhaps because scientists, like most people, like to think their minds operate a rung or two above their glands and the rest of their bodies. After my trip to Yerkes, I thought about how the differences between animal and human research were consistent with the attitudes I grew up with on the farm. Maybe trying to rise above nature meant pretending nature was not important. I began to wonder more about physiological factors among people, particularly testosterone. Testosterone influenced the way farm animals and monkeys behaved. Could it play a role in human barroom fights, marital conflict, war, or national leadership? Did it change with winning and losing, as it did with the monkeys? Did it affect women as well as men? Babies produce testosterone before they are born. Could testosterone affect the behavior of newborn infants and children?

MANHOOD AND WOMANHOOD

Finally, the monkeys' concern for each other made me wonder about culture and the nature of manhood and womanhood. Manhood is not the same as masculinity, and womanhood is not the same as femininity. Masculinity and femininity are psychological characteristics that evolved to support the demands of being male or female. Masculinity is a frame of mind consistent with the need to compete with other males and attract females. Femininity is a frame of mind consistent with the need to acquire resources to support offspring. Most psychological literature describes masculinity in terms of competition and femininity in terms of nurturing.

Manhood and womanhood are masculinity and femininity acculturated and directed toward the needs of society. Manhood and womanhood are more culturally varied and less rooted in biology than masculinity and femininity. For men, with their high testosterone levels and combative tendencies, manhood varies as masculinity is harnessed and directed toward demands that differ from culture to culture, though manhood is always less self-centered than masculinity. Womanhood varies from culture to culture, too, but it usually involves nurturing, cooperation, and a degree of selflessness in the interest of offspring and the larger community.

It is generally assumed that animals can be masculine or feminine but only people can be manly or womanly. The more I learn about animal research, however, the less sure I feel about the uniquely human quality of manhood and womanhood. Animals are often selfless in helping their offspring and their groups. Hikers know to give wide berth to mother bears, who will risk dangerous confrontations to protect their cubs. Like a mother bear defending her cub, the alpha monkey places the safety of his group ahead of his own safety. The stump-tailed macaque alpha male did this in trying to protect his group from the strange totem pole. He seemed to understand that obligations go along with the perks of office. Among people, being willing to sacrifice personal comfort to help others and act for the good of the group is part of manhood, as it is of womanhood.

The culture of people differs from that of animals primarily in its complexity and in the training and initiation it requires of new members. Initiations, like the ones Masai boys must go through before they become warriors and Masai girls must go through before they marry, define the standards of manhood and womanhood in a society. Although initiation ceremonies sometimes force new members into rigid roles according to sex, they also channel the energy of testosterone into prosocial activities, as prosocial is defined by their particular cultures. While rigid sex roles have outlived their usefulness in most parts of the world, prosocial attitudes have not.

The Japanese are moving into the new century with initiation rites in place. According to T. R. Reid, author of *Confucius Lives Next Door,* "Every January 15th, in every little town, big city, hamlet in Japan, every person who's gonna turn 20 that year goes down to the town hall and is admitted to the rank of adulthood. This means now what—you can drink legally, you can bet at the race track, you can vote, and it also means you have a lot of responsibility. And these kids pack in there and get lectures about their responsibility."[2]

Unlike in Japan, there is no universal rite of passage in the United States. Bar mitzvahs, hell weeks, military basic training, sorority initiations, and society debuts define manhood and womanhood for selected groups of young people, but many others enter the adult world without ceremony. Partly out of a desire not to restrain our children too much, we often fail to teach them how to be responsible adults. Street gangs, deadbeat parents, and neglected children may be the price we pay for that. The animal qualities within us, including qualities associated with testosterone, require direction and control.

STARTING THE PROJECT

These issues seemed to me to deserve more study. Testosterone might tell us something important about how to deal with the problems of the world. I worked on a proposal and approached the National Institute of Mental Health and the National Science Foundation seeking money for research. These agencies were interested, I think owing both to a national concern with violence and an uneasy public tension between feminism and the men's movement. The time was right to try for a better understanding of testosterone in men and women alike, and the federal agencies and my own university provided the funds I would need.

In my lifetime, people have changed in how they view the world. Biologists write more about similarities among species. A new environmental awareness emphasizes the interrelationship of all life. We hear about the importance of links between people and the rest of nature. People seem close enough to other animals to share some of their qualities. In ancient Greece, an inscription at the Oracle at Delphi advised, "Know thyself." Most of us would like to know more about our roots, and our roots are biological as well as social and political. Our bodies are animal bodies. Our brains, as complex as they are, have animal origins. Our thoughts and emotions are nudged about by hormones that are the same as the hormones that affect other animals.

I do not believe people are like animals. I believe people are animals, of a special kind. They stand out as unique from other animals. But deep down, underneath human nature, people are understandable only if we consider the qualities they share with animals. That doesn't mean we have to become biological determinists. On the contrary, understanding human nature improves our chances for doing what needs to be done to make the best of it. Biology is only part of destiny.

UNDERSTANDING BEHAVIOR

Social psychologists study social relationships, which include our loves and hates, how we make friends and enemies, and how we make decisions about each other. Social psychologists explain people's behavior by their backgrounds, surroundings, and personalities. Over the past decade I have done this, but I have added testosterone and other hormones to the usual social variables. My students and I have studied testosterone measures from more than eight thousand men, women, and children, and I am convinced that what we and others are learning will fill a gap in our understanding of social behavior.

Testosterone is a small molecule with large effects, which can be moderated by environmental factors, including parenting and education. It is related to things as diverse as criminal violence and the way people smile. It affects our ability with language and our ability to navigate in space. It helps predict what occupation we will enter and whether or not we will marry, have extramarital affairs, or divorce. Testosterone is present in both sexes, and it affects men and women in similar ways. Although testosterone is considered a male hormone and the average man produces eight to ten times as much as the average woman, the average man is not necessarily eight to ten times more masculine than the average woman. Testosterone is only part of a complicated chemical profile that seems to result in women being more sensitive to small amounts of testosterone than men.

There is a great deal of variation in testosterone and its effect on personality and behavior among individuals of both sexes. Nevertheless testosterone, along with other biological factors and cultural influences, may explain why some personality traits and behavior patterns occur more frequently in men than in women. Researchers usually suspect that when a trait is found much more often among men than women, testosterone partly explains the difference. The role of testosterone is clearer, however, when a particular trait is found more often among higher- than lower-testosterone individuals of the same sex. This book is the story of what we know and what we are learning about testosterone, a part of the animal within us all.

This book is within the context of science, which is both creative and critical. Science is about the larger world. It examines phenomena inside and outside the laboratory. It works best by drawing ideas from many directions, keeping the ideas that bear up under scrutiny and letting the others go. Knowledge comes in small pieces that scientists slowly put together in a puzzle that is always growing and always changing.[3] The chapters that follow describe the pieces of the testosterone puzzle that are in place and offer a few educated guesses about where the next pieces might go. The chapters are both factual and speculative, and I have done my best to distinguish the two. The book presents the current state of knowledge about testosterone and behavior at the turn of the twenty-first century, speculates about how this knowledge might apply to as yet untested areas, and offers examples and anecdotes intended to animate the charts and statistics in the book. It is my hope that the material in its totality will convey the excitement of research that both draws upon and informs our everyday life.

Part One
HUMAN NATURE

1

The Animal Within

RASCALS, HEROES, AND COLORFUL PEOPLE

Sylvia Cross pushed her piano out into McLendon Avenue, smashed it apart with a hammer, and distributed the pieces among her friends who'd stayed for the grand finale of the last all-night party at Sylvia's Atomic Café. Business had been slow because a sinkhole had closed the street. Sylvia was bored and ready for a career change. She decided to go into art. She bought another piano and opened a new store, Sylvia's Art of This Century, an art supply boutique with musical entertainment in the evening. The last time I saw Sylvia, she was ready for another career change. She was planning to go on the Internet as an erotic storyteller.

Sylvia has a high-testosterone approach to life. She is a showperson and entrepreneur, and she deals with problems directly and flamboyantly. A few years ago she wanted to buy a house but didn't have money for the down payment. She solved the problem by having parties and selling tickets to her friends. Parties come naturally to Sylvia, and before the sinkhole, Sylvia's Atomic Café was an ongoing party in northeast Atlanta. It featured informal entertainment, often provided by Sylvia herself. One of the tricks she performed was fire-eating, which she'd learned from a circus performer.

While Sylvia was still in the restaurant business, a friend of mine who was a friend of hers told me Sylvia would make a good subject for the testosterone research I was doing. Sylvia told my friend she would be glad to participate if I let her know the results. When the lab finished her assay, I marked her score on a graph along with the scores of a group

3

of college women and a group of violent women from the local counterculture. Sylvia was higher in testosterone than the college students
and right in the middle of the violent group. My friend took the graph to
Sylvia at the café. Sylvia was delighted. She passed the graph around
among her customers, telling them that her testosterone level was as
high as that of most skinheads and devil worshipers. Sylvia seemed to
think a high testosterone level was an asset, and in this her opinion was
absolutely mid-American. My research assistants and I have found that
almost everyone—men, women, high school dropouts, college gradu-
ates, reporters, prisoners, and stockbrokers—wants to have a lot of
testosterone.

Construction workers are no exception. As a group, they do have
more testosterone than average, and they are proud of it. One of my former lab assistants, Denise de La Rue, had a friend, Mike Roseberry, who
was a construction supervisor. Mike agreed to ask his work crew to provide saliva samples to be assayed for our testosterone study. They were
enthusiastic about what they called the "Testosterone Olympics." They
wanted to know their scores. I made a graph showing all the scores, but
without saying who scored what. Intending to preserve their privacy,
I sent them their individual scores in sealed envelopes. They were
not interested in privacy; they were interested in competition. Pretty
soon everyone knew everyone else's score, and as would be expected,
because testosterone levels fall with age, one of the older men had the
lowest score. The others immediately gave him a girl's nickname. Mike,
like Sylvia, was pleased with his score. He called Denise and left a message, "Hey, Denise! I spit a ten. Not everybody can spit a ten."

The stereotype of a construction worker is muscular, tough, and
sexy. Mike does not question the stereotype. Although many women
give wide berth to construction sites, Mike doesn't see those women.
He sees the ones who stop by and leave their telephone numbers with
the men. Perhaps there is a difference in testosterone levels between
women who do and do not find construction workers attractive.

A few years ago, while I was studying construction workers and
testosterone, a living example of the stereotype appeared on the
Geraldo show. He was lean, muscular, bald, bearded, and tattooed. His
friends called him "Animal." With him were his ex-wife, his live-in girlfriend Michelle, and two of his eight other girlfriends. Michelle, who was

wearing a short skirt and white cowgirl boots, had met him at a construction site. She had a tooth missing from a fight with Animal, but she said she had injured him in the same fight as well, and neither of them seemed to be holding a grudge about it. She had one child who they agreed was his, but there was some animosity between them about who the father of her other child might be. She said it was Animal; he said it was somebody else. Another point of conflict between Animal and Michelle was Animal's ex-wife, whom he continued to visit each week. Michelle and the ex-wife did not like each other, but otherwise the various women got along well and were happy to share Animal. No one in the group was talkative, though they all answered questions when asked. My first thought was that Animal, and maybe his girlfriends, were suffering from what Alan Alda once called "testosterone poisoning,"[4] but on television they made a mostly peaceful scene.

Sylvia, Mike, and Animal, like many people who are high in testosterone, are confident, tough, competitive, bold, energetic, attractive to the opposite sex, and they are frequently outrageous. They have characteristics in common with James Bond, Kinsey Millhone, Night Man, Buffy the Vampire Slayer, Indiana Jones, Luke Skywalker, Sam Spade, and Xena the Warrior Princess. Fictional heroes and heroines let us experience life in dangerous times and on the risky edge of society. Every once in a while, a real macho hero makes the headlines and lifts the spirits of everyone. In the spring of 1999, Matt Moseley put good news on the front page. Moseley was the Atlanta fireman who, dangling from a helicopter line, rescued a crane operator trapped above a burning building. Then, two months later, a team of American women soccer players won the 1999 Women's World Cup and put good news on the front page again. Brandi Chastain kicked the winning goal and flexed her muscles on the cover of *Newsweek*,[5] and Women's Cup madness was in.

Most people have at least a vague idea about what testosterone is, and in spite of talk about "testosterone poisoning," they believe it is a good thing. When we ask people what testosterone is, they are likely to describe it in terms of football, the Marines, fighting, hunting, fishing, carburetors, tall tales, and sexual adventures. Sometimes they say, "You know, it's guystuff."

"Guystuff" is just part of the testosterone profile. Researchers have been busy adding new details to what is turning out to be a complex and intriguing picture. My students and I have found that whenever our work is mentioned in newspapers or magazines, we hear from people who think their testosterone is high and want verification from an expert, or who think it is low and want to know how to increase it. I get calls from people who want their testosterone measured. Not all the calls come from men. Quite a few women—an opera singer in Connecticut, a business entrepreneur in Texas, a telephone sex operator in Chicago, and lawyers in San Francisco, Washington, and New York— have called me.

Over the years, students approached me to study testosterone in lawyers, testosterone and violence in lesbian couples, testosterone and sexual intercourse, testosterone and the counterculture, and testosterone among fans at sporting events. Our research meetings took on a storytelling atmosphere, as students outdid each other in bringing new findings. We studied people ranging from ordinary to truly strange, and we began to uncover many links between testosterone and social behavior.

People who exhibit the qualities linked to testosterone are as varied as Bay and Pat Buchanan, O. J. Simpson, David Koresh, Madonna, Governor Jesse Ventura, Monica Lewinsky, Phyllis Schlafley, Eric Rudolph, George Steinbrenner, Clarence Thomas, and many members of the Kennedy family. Whether they are rogues or heroes, they are colorful people, and their exploits, escapades, and even their nefarious deeds capture our attention and fascinate us.

MEASURING TESTOSTERONE

In order to learn about testosterone, and to separate it from social, cultural, and other biological influences, we had to measure it in a large number of people. We needed a measure that was simple, painless, and reliable. The standard technique for measuring testosterone is called radioimmunoassay, or RIA. Until recently, RIA measured testosterone only in blood. That limitation was a roadblock to researchers who needed a large number of samples from the general population. People balk at volunteering their blood for science.

Fortunately, I learned that RIA could also measure testosterone in saliva. Saliva is a good substitute for blood as a diagnostic fluid.[6] Saliva originates in a network of blood vessels near the salivary glands, and testosterone passes from the blood into the saliva. Measurements of testosterone from saliva are as reliable as measurements from blood. Further, when we tried collecting saliva samples, we found that large numbers of people would volunteer for our studies. Occasionally we did have to reassure them that we were looking only for testosterone, because saliva tests can also indicate whether a person has been using alcohol, tobacco, or drugs.

Using salivary measures, my students and I set up procedures and began collecting data. Over the years we analyzed saliva samples from more than three thousand college students, prison inmates, trial lawyers, athletes, heroes, construction workers, sex offenders, strippers, actors, wrestlers, and various others. We measured people several times each, to examine changes across the day and around important events. We also examined data on blood levels of testosterone from government records of about five thousand military veterans.

People often ask me what a high testosterone score is. When Mike Roseberry said he'd "spit a ten," that meant the concentration of testosterone in his saliva sample measured ten nanograms (ng) of testosterone per deciliter (dl) of saliva. That was a high score in his particular assay batch. In our lab, we run assays in batches that range from thirty to fifty samples each. In another lab run, Mike's score might have been a little different, but still high in his particular assay. Radioimmunoassays often take two days to complete, and there is normal analytic variability in every lab that performs them. Variability in results from assay to assay are due to slight differences in chemicals, procedures, and lab personnel. Because of this variation, we include a high control and a low control sample in each assay. The comparison with known values tells us more about the testosterone level of a particular individual than his or her "number." That is why when I describe individuals, I say they are "high," "medium," or "low," rather than they scored a "two," "six," or "ten." Scores from blood samples are about a hundred times higher than scores from saliva samples, but the numbers are highly correlated with each other, which means that one measure is as accurate as the other.

Although testosterone is not visible to the naked eye, and there is no single marker to reveal its presence, we learned during the course of our research that testosterone is related to traits that are readily observed. For example, high-testosterone men, on average, are leaner, balder, more self-confident, more rambunctious, less likely to have friendly smiles, and more likely to favor tattoos than other men. That is not to say that we can look at a particular individual and know with certainty what his or her testosterone level is. Many characteristics and behaviors that are related to high testosterone levels are also related to social, cultural, and other biological factors. Nevertheless, my students who are familiar with testosterone research can often look at pictures of experimental subjects and tell which subjects are high or low in testosterone. As my students and I become more familiar with what high- and low-testosterone people are like, we get better at predicting which research projects will be productive.

Testosterone is a hormone, and understanding it requires a general understanding of hormones and how they work. Hormones are molecules, tightly bound clusters of atoms, that carry messages from one part of the body to another. Hormone molecules can be small, because all they do is carry simple messages, but they must be numerous enough to spread throughout the body. Each person, man or woman, produces just a few milligrams of testosterone every day, but each milligram contains a million trillion molecules.

Endocrinologists, who study hormones, group hormones into families, in which members of the same family have similar origins and do similar jobs.[7] For example, in the brain there is a family of hormones called endorphins that spreads feelings of pleasure and blocks feelings of pain. Elsewhere in the body there are families of hormones that control growth, metabolism, storage of energy from food, and release of stored energy in emergencies. Testosterone and estrogen are the major players in the sex hormone family. They start off as cholesterol, one of the building blocks of the body. Cholesterol is converted into testosterone by the action of enzymes, substances that change molecules from one form to another. This conversion takes place in the testes, ovaries, and adrenal glands. Testosterone can then be converted into a more potent form called dihydrotestosterone by the enzyme 5-alpha-reductase, or into estrogen by the enzyme aromatase (so named because its products sometimes have an "aroma" like that of benzine). Testosterone can be converted into estrogen, but estrogen cannot be converted back into testosterone. It is an oddity of sex hormones that estrogen in males and females comes from testosterone. Both sexes have testosterone and estrogen, although men have more testosterone and women have more estrogen. The same individual can have high levels of both hormones. Stallions have high levels of estrogen and testosterone, as do football players and rattlesnakes.[8]

Figure 1.1 shows the molecular structure of testosterone and estrogen. Testosterone molecules have twenty-one carbon and oxygen atoms. Removing one carbon atom changes testosterone into estrogen. The similarity of the two hormones is perhaps a metaphor for the similarity of men and women. Men and women are similar in many ways—in their bodies, their minds, their hopes and fears. We should remember this underlying similarity when thinking about the ways in which they differ.

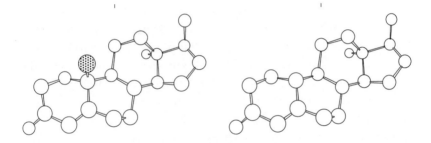

Figure 1.1. Molecular structure of testosterone *(left)* and estrogen *(right)*. The circles represent carbon and oxygen atoms in each molecule. Testosterone has one extra carbon atom, shaded gray in the figure. The molecules are so similar that you can merge them into a single three-dimensional image. If you cross your eyes slightly and look at the tick marks above the figures, they will gradually merge to form a new, third tick mark in the center. When the center mark is clearly in focus, move your eyes down to the figure below it, and a three-dimensional molecule will "pop out" into view.

Hormones operate by moving through the bloodstream from cells that produce them to target cells. When they reach the target cells they fit into receptor molecules, like keys into locks. What happens next depends on what the cells are designed to do. Cells are diverse, ranging from those that make up the brain to those that are parts of muscles, toenails, and eyelashes. In the nucleus of each cell, genetic material in the form of chromosomes—double strands of long DNA molecules—tells the cell what to do. Genes are sections on the DNA strands, and they contain information needed to build and maintain the body. Each cell has a complete set of genes, but it uses only a few of them. When a cell uses a gene, we say it "expresses" that gene. Gene expression begins when part of the double-stranded DNA unravels into a single strand, called RNA. The RNA moves out of the nucleus and into the main body of the cell, where it attracts small building-block molecules to form stable groups that make up new protein molecules. Creating the new protein is a step toward meeting the need of the moment, whether that need is to digest a meal, add a bit of muscle, attract a lover, or prepare for a fight.

Testosterone has many functions. Among other things, it signals cells to build muscle, make red blood cells, produce sperm, and release neurotransmitters in the brain. A testosterone molecule acts upon its target cell in one of two ways. It binds with a receptor at the membrane surrounding the cell and triggers action there, or it passes through the membrane to bind with a receptor inside the cell and triggers the expression of a gene. Action at the membrane can be completed within seconds. Action inside the cell takes minutes or hours.[9] Action inside the cell is complicated by the fact that testosterone, after binding with a testosterone receptor, is often transformed into estrogen (by aromatase) before triggering gene expression. Thus we have the interesting situation in which men, whose primary sex hormone is testosterone, convert their testosterone into estrogen before using it.

Testosterone is a sex hormone, and I think it is the most social of hormones. Other hormones indirectly affect the brain and mental function by affecting other organs of the body first. Testosterone makes direct contact with many cells in the brain. It stimulates activity in those cells, and that activity goes on to affect thinking. The major social effect of testosterone is to orient us toward issues of sex and power. This provides a background against which we act, encouraging some behaviors and discouraging others. It affects how we treat other people and how we react to the way they treat us. It makes us impatient with dull and boring aspects of school, but if we manage to sit through school and listen to our elders, the lessons we learn restrain and guide the effects of testosterone.

Testosterone has two different, but coordinated, effects on the mind and body. It is involved in both design and function. It first helps organize and develop the body and brain, beginning before birth and continuing through adolescence. It then helps direct activities in the body and brain throughout life. It is like a young automotive engineer who designs a fast, powerful car and then races it. The engineer designs a car with the capacity for power and speed, and then later he uses that capacity to race. Testosterone designs a fetus with the potential for power and speed, and when the fetus grows into an adult, testosterone encourages the adult to use this potential.

THE FETUS

Testosterone first appears *in utero*, where its job is to turn a neutral fetus into a male. Sex is determined by the X and Y chromosomes; females have two X's and males have an X and a Y. There is one gene, lying along the Y chromosome of every male, that determines his development as a male. The presence of this gene, like the flip of a switch, sets the stage for all that follows. The fetus starts off as a single cell, without a brain or body. Testosterone appears in the middle third of pregnancy, and it transforms the developing fetus into a male. When the gonads first appear, they are undifferentiated—neither ovaries nor testes. Left alone, they will become ovaries. Fallopian tubes will grow out of ducts in their sides, and a female reproductive system will grow out of the fallopian tubes. If the fetus is to be male, however, the gene on the Y chromosome will act to close these ducts and develop cells that produce testosterone and later produce sperm. Males and females are built from the same basic body parts. Organs that appear to be found only in one sex are in fact present in rudimentary or modified form in the other sex. Thus, in females, the gonads remain inside the body and develop into ovaries, and in males, they descend below the body and develop into testes. Dihydrotestosterone, a potent form of testosterone, causes external genitalia in males to develop into a penis and scrotum. Otherwise the same organs develop into a clitoris and the folds around the vagina in females.

Testosterone goes beyond determining the difference between males and females. The amount of testosterone affects the degree of masculinity within each sex. Regardless of whether people are male or female, they vary in how masculine they are. There are many examples, from animals and people, of how testosterone increases masculinity. Female hyenas are tougher than males because testosterone from their mothers affects them as fetuses.[10] Canary mothers put a little extra testosterone into the last few eggs they lay in each clutch. All the eggs hatch at the same time, and testosterone gives chicks from the last few eggs an extra toughness to compete with their "older" brothers and sisters.[11]

Hormonelike substances from the environment can sometimes affect the fetus. In the 1950s and 1960s, physicians prescribed diethylstilbestrol, or DES, to prevent miscarriages. DES is a synthetic estrogenlike hormone, but in utero it has some testosteronelike effects. The daughters of women who took DES were more masculine than other girls. They played with boys' toys and engaged in more rough-and-tumble "tomboyish" play. My wife's cousin took DES when she was pregnant, and she had a hyperactive, hard-to-handle baby girl, who grew up to be a supersalesperson in the cellular phone business. Unfortunately, the DES also caused reproductive disorders in many of the children of mothers who took it.

Pregnant women no longer take DES by prescription, but they can get it and similar chemicals from the environment. These chemicals are called "estrogenic," because they work like estrogen. Farmers give DES to cattle to promote growth, and some is passed on to people who eat meat from the cattle. A pregnant woman who encounters these substances can pass them on through her bloodstream to the fetus she is carrying. Later on, she can pass them on to her infant through her milk. Among some reptiles, birds, and fish, environmental pesticides and pollutants can feminize males. In 1980, there was a large pesticide spill in Florida's Lake Apopka. Following the spill, zoologists examined young male alligators from the lake and found they had low testosterone levels, high estrogen levels, and exceptionally small penises.[12]

Testosterone from human mothers affects their offspring. A recent study examined the daughters of mothers who were low or high in testosterone.[13] High-testosterone mothers tended to have high-testosterone daughters, and when the daughters grew up they were more masculine in their manner. Because testosterone exerts many of its effects after it is converted into estrogen, one might expect that estrogen from the mother would also masculinize the fetus. This does not happen, perhaps because female fetuses are protected by a substance called alpha-fetoprotein, which blocks the potential masculinizing effect of the mother's estrogen.

Testosterone that influences the fetus can come from another fetus sharing the same pregnancy. Among people, girls with boy cotwins are more tomboyish than girls with girl co-twins. This is partly due to the girls' experiences of growing up with twin brothers, but it is also biological. I once had a bold and forward female student assistant, an expert softball pitcher who married a football player, wanted to learn to box, and enjoyed going to prisons with me to collect testosterone measurements from inmates. She told me she was different from her sisters, who were more feminine, and she wondered why. When I told her about twin brothers, her mouth fell open. She said she had a twin brother who died at birth. He had not been around to affect her while she was growing up, but his testosterone could have affected her before she was born. We measured her testosterone level, and it was above the female average. When they share the womb with male siblings, females can get enough extra prenatal testosterone to masculinize them to varying degrees. The extra prenatal testosterone can increase the number of their testosterone receptors and make them more sensitive to testosterone in later life.

Testosterone from one fetus affecting another *in utero* has been studied more in animals than in people. Farmers have long known that when a cow has male and female twin calves, the female will be sterile. Such a calf is called a "freemartin," and the effect is presumably due to the testosterone she gets from her cotwin. In other animals, females born with males are not sterile, but testosterone from the males still affects them. During gestation, gerbil fetuses are lined up in the uterus in a row, like peas in a pod. A female gerbil situated between two males in the uterus will grow up to be more masculine than one between two females, and she will have more male offspring.[14] Among human beings, women who are more dominant are reported to have more sons. How this could happen is unclear, because it is the father's sperm rather than the mother's egg that determines whether conception will produce a male or a female. However, genetic factors or local chemical and physio-logical factors might affect a woman's reproductive tract so as to affect differentially the viability of x- and y-bearing sperm before conception, or the viability of male and female zygotes after conception.[15] The human studies have not measured the mothers' testosterone levels, though I suspect more dominant mothers are higher in testosterone. Some informal studies suggest that this may be the case.

A student at Georgia State University, Jonathan Bassett, has been exploring this area. Research shows that testosterone differs among occupations, so Jonathan used occupation as an indicator of testos-terone level, in lieu of actually measuring it. He thought that women trial lawyers, known to be a high-testosterone group,* would have more sons than daughters. He read the biographical sketches of the women trial lawyers listed in Who's Who and found that 58 percent of their children were boys. Findings from waist-to-hip-ratio research[16] sug-gested to Jonathan that curvaceous figures might be correlated with lower testosterone levels and thus that beauty queens, generally a cur-vaceous bunch, might be significantly different from trial lawyers in the sex ratio of their children. He read the biographical sketches posted at the Miss America Internet site, www.missamerica.com, to see if former Miss Americas had more daughters than sons. They did. They had twice as many.[17]

Extra, a syndicated television magazine show, ran a story about Jonathan's findings. *Extra* did some research, too. They thought the women working in the high-pressure atmosphere of the newsroom at *Extra* would be high in testosterone and, if Jonathan's hypothesis was right, they would have more boys than girls. Of the eleven women who had children, eight had boys, and three had girls.[18]

Researchers have paid more attention to how testosterone affects babies *in utero*, but there is some research concerning the effect of testosterone from the fetus on the pregnant mother. Gene Sackett, who studies monkeys, found that other monkeys bit pregnant mon-keys less often when the pregnant monkeys were carrying males than when they were carrying females.[19] Sackett suspects that hormones from the male fetus passed into the bloodstream of the mother and led

---

*Chapter 6 provides details on testosterone levels in different kinds of lawyers.

her to behave in a more masculine manner, which in turn made the other monkeys more cautious about biting her. Researchers have not studied how the sex of the fetus might affect a human mother, but some women report anecdotally that they can feel a difference emotionally between carrying a boy or a girl.

ADOLESCENCE AND ADULTHOOD

Effects of testosterone on a fetus are lasting, and they provide the background for further development. Receptors developed in the fetus allow the body to respond to testosterone later on. Further development comes in part from an unfolding of what was fixed before birth and in part from an increase in sex hormones during adolescence. Some effects of testosterone during adolescence are anabolic, a term derived from the Greek word for "building up," here meaning the building up of lean muscle tissue. Other effects are masculinizing, making organs more like those of a typical male. Testosterone and estrogen produce striking physical differences between males and females during adolescence, and these differences set the stage for differences in behavior.

Testosterone affects all parts of the body, especially the reproductive system, thyroid gland, blood, bones, skin, and brain.[20] It promotes faster, more intense action in males, in contrast with the slower, more durable action associated with estrogen in females.[21] Testosterone gives men more muscle, along with more red blood cells to carry oxygen to the muscle. Estrogen, on the other hand, gives women stronger immune systems and a greater ability to resist infection and disease.[22] Testosterone makes men store fat around their stomachs, where it can be easily burned off for energy in emergencies.[23] Estrogen makes women store fat on their hips, buttocks, and thighs, where it tends to stay unless needed to make up food shortages during pregnancy or breast-feeding.[24] Men have more body mass in their arms and legs, and women have more body mass in their torsos. Men, like other male mammals, have more development in their upper body areas, with stronger arms and shoulders, thicker skulls, and heads even larger than expected for their body size.

Figure 1.2 shows testosterone levels in both sexes across the life span. Boys have more testosterone than girls before birth. Boys also have a spike in testosterone in the first few months of life, when their levels rise briefly to the levels of adult females. From then until puberty, levels are low in both sexes. Testosterone increases in both sexes at puberty. By the end of puberty, males have levels eight to ten times as high as those of females, and then testosterone in both sexes begins a slow decline toward old age. The sexes become more alike as they grow older. Women begin to develop rougher skin and lower-pitched voices. This is because after menopause, women drop in estrogen more than they drop in testosterone, and it is the estrogen-testosterone ratio that matters.

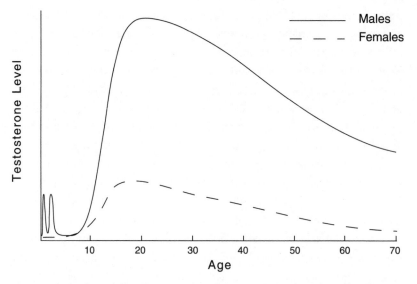

Figure 1.2. Male and female testosterone levels across the life span. The two small peaks among males occur around the midtrimester of pregnancy and a few months after birth.

Our average testosterone level is inherited from our parents, but physical and social conditions produce changes around this average level. Testosterone falls with ill health and physical exhaustion. It rises when we win important contests and falls when we lose (as described in more detail in Chapter 4). It changes with our status in life (Chapter 5 describes changes when men marry, divorce, or become fathers).

Changes in testosterone are usually temporary, riding along on top of a broad wave that rises and then declines across the life span.[25] Changes across the life span also differ among various populations around the world. Anthropologist Peter Ellison and his colleagues studied testosterone levels among Lese men in the Congo, Tamang men in Nepal, Ache men in Paraguay, and men in the United States from the Boston area.[26] Of the four groups, the Boston men dropped the most, going from highest in youth to lowest in old age. Figure 1.3 shows these findings.

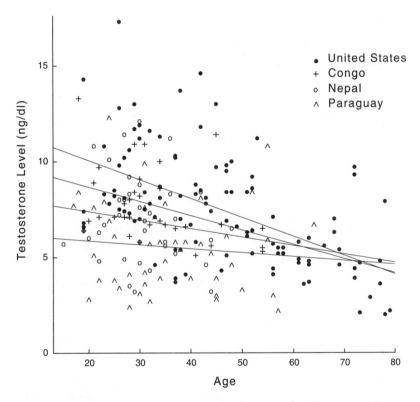

Figure 1.3. Decline in male testosterone levels across the life span in different populations. The graph represents men from Boston in the United States, the Lese of the Democratic Republic of the Congo, the Tamang of Nepal, and the Ache of Paraguay. The four sloping lines represent, from top to bottom, mean decline across the life span in the four groups, respectively. Boston men have the highest initial testosterone level and the steepest decline across the life span.

Many substances from the environment can affect testosterone levels. Plants and animals use hormones and other chemicals to control each other; the study of these chemical relationships involving plants is called "phytochemical ecology." Sometimes the chemicals are harmless, sometimes they benefit both parties, and sometimes they help one party and hurt the other. Testosterone and estrogen appear in animals, plants, and even bacteria. I discovered that cotton contains testosterone when I used cotton rolls to collect saliva. Suspecting that the cotton was affecting our test scores, I assayed cotton samples taken directly from a South Carolina cotton field. The cotton appeared to have testosterone levels about as high as those of adult women. I'm not sure what the testosterone in cotton does, but it could affect insects that eat the cotton. Alfalfa and clover produce estrogen. The estrogen helps the plants by acting as a birth-control substance, holding down the population of grazing animals. Alfalfa and clover produce enough estrogen to make sheep and cattle sterile. In Australia, a million sheep each year fail to have lambs because they eat too much clover.[27] Some creatures use the estrogen and other chemicals in plants to turn their reproductive cycles on and off.[28]

Like sheep grazing on clover, people are affected by what they eat. A mother may absorb estrogens from plants she eats and pass them on to a fetus she is carrying or a baby she is nursing.[29] Testosterone levels are lower among vegetarians, perhaps because plant estrogens, including dadzein, enterolactone, and equol, bind with androgen as well as estrogen receptors and "decrease androgen production by interference with the pituitary testicular feedback mechanism."[30] Soybean products are high in estrogen, and they are used in infant formula, food supplements, and tofu. Maybe the saying "Real men don't eat quiche" should be "Real men don't eat tofu." But maybe not. I wouldn't want to tell a Sumo wrestler that he wasn't a real man. Tofu and other soy products are dietary staples in Japan and are credited by some nutritionists for the low rate of prostate cancer there.[31]

Estrogen and estrogenlike chemicals, which are in our food, our water, and our cosmetic products, have become environmental pollutants. Estrogen from birth-control pills eventually passes into city water supplies, where it can affect people drinking the water,[32] and estrogens in hair care products may cause breast development in young girls.[33]

Sex-hormone molecules are busy chemical messengers. They hustle from place to place, like the Roman god Mercury, keeping their world in balance. They enable one organ or individual or species to affect another, and human beings are sometimes unwittingly caught up in the complex web of interactions. Recent reports of problems in male reproductive health, including an increased incidence of undescended testes, support this observation. In 1993, researchers reported a 50 percent drop in sperm counts over the past two generations, and they suggested that the drop may be caused by estrogenlike chemicals in the environment. More recent research indicates that the problem, while serious, may not be as extreme or as widespread as reported earlier.[34]

It is clear that testosterone affects our bodies in many ways, but some people reject the idea that testosterone has important effects on how we think and act. This latter view arises in part from the political philosophy that all people are created equal, at least in the eyes of God and the law. If we are created equal, it is said, then important differences among us must come from education and experience. In this view, biology and testosterone do not matter much, and studying them will only distract us from more important issues of human justice. I have a different view. I agree that education and experience are important, but I think biology is important, too. It is obvious to me that we are biological creatures who live and die according to the rules of nature. Illness wears us down. Bad food shortens our lives. Genetic disorders cloud our judgment. Chemicals affect our moods. When people say testosterone is unimportant in the study of human affairs, I think they are speaking more from bias than from evidence.

THE BRAIN AND THE MIND

A parent of a teenaged boy might say, "He's got sports cars on his brain," meaning "He's got sports cars on his mind." In everyday conversation, "brain" and "mind" are often used interchangeably, but they are not the same. The brain is a complex organ with many parts and many functions. The mind is one of the functions of the brain, especially of the frontal lobes. It is influenced by experience as well as biology, and it encompasses awareness, emotion, problem solving, decision making, memory, and introspection. We think of the mind as conscious, but there is an unconscious part. That part can be called into consciousness, sometimes with a struggle. Dealing with the almost conscious parts of our minds—remembering where we put things, understanding why we distrust a person, or making sense of feelings of déjà vu—can be frustrating. When we have brilliant insights, suffer emotional upsets, or make decisions, whether wise or foolish, both the conscious and the unconscious parts of our minds are working.

Testosterone acts on the brain and thereby influences the mind. When a man's testosterone binds with receptors in his brain and affects the way his mind works, especially when his thoughts seem to focus on inappropriate sexual conquests, we sometimes say, as many people said during President Bill Clinton's ordeal by sexual scandal, "He's thinking with his gonads." Testosterone works in tandem with the brain; it is produced by glands, but its production is controlled by the brain. Each testosterone molecule lasts at most only a few hours before being taken up by a target cell or broken down and discarded by the body. In the lower part of the brain, the hypothalamus works like a thermostat, monitoring how much testosterone is available and how much is needed. When the testosterone level in the bloodstream drops below a certain level called the set point, the hypothalamus signals the pituitary gland. In men, the pituitary signals the testes to produce testosterone, and about twenty minutes later the testosterone level begins to increase.[35] In men and women, the pituitary gland also produces a hormone called adrenocorticotropic hormone (ACTH), which signals the adrenal glands to produce testosterone. When the testosterone reaches the brain, the hypothalamus notes that the system is on track and stops further testosterone production until the level begins to drop again. While all this is going on, other parts of the brain can tell the hypothalamus to change its setting. For example, if a person is preparing for a fight, the brain will signal the hypothalamus to change its set point and increase the testosterone level.

This mechanical and regulatory activity is one aspect of the brain-testosterone relationship. Other aspects deal with thinking and feeling and the ways that the brain exerts control over the effects of testosterone. Testosterone is believed primarily to affect the lower and middle areas of the brain, including the hypothalamus and the limbic system. In the lower area, the hypothalamus regulates eating, drinking, sexual behavior, and hormone levels. In the middle area, the limbic system, including the amygdala, is involved with memory, sex, aggression, and emotion and with assessing social and environmental factors. Recent discoveries of testosterone receptors among subcortical glial cells in primates suggest a pathway in the upper area of the human brain whereby testosterone might affect the cerebral cortex, which handles perception, voluntary movement, language, thought, planning, and other advanced intellectual processes.[36]

An important role of the upper centers of the brain is the civilizing control they exert over testosterone. These centers of the brain are where we store our knowledge of learning and culture. They restrain our animal impulses. They keep us from eating every time we are hungry, scratching every time we itch, and losing our temper every time we are frustrated. They make us accommodate to others in small and large ways. They remind us that, as Robert Frost said, "to be social is to be forgiving."[37] They keep us from giving in to testosterone and seeking sex and power to the exclusion of everything else. At their best, these upper centers allow us to harness the strength of testosterone for positive social ends.

In discussing the brain we are quickly forced into guesswork, because we do not have a complete model of how it works. We know that signals go into the brain and thoughts come out. We are never exactly sure what happens in the middle. It is unclear how the activity of a few neurotransmitters can affect complex thinking and problem solving. We know that testosterone molecules signal some brain cells, which in turn signal other cells. One thing leads to another, and finally cascading patterns of nerve responses move us to think new thoughts and do new things. But we don't know all the details of this process, so it helps to have general models of the brain to guide us in our thinking about how the brain works.

A good model would summarize scientific knowledge about the brain into a metaphor that provides us with an image that goes beyond what is known precisely. The model may reflect our personal view of the world as well as objective reality. Today we compare the brain to a computer. We say people "process information" and have "memory banks." This sounds neat and orderly, but the idea that the brain functions like a computer is largely a modern fairy tale. Years ago, when people depended on steam for power, they used the steam engine as a model for the brain. When weaving was a major industry, they described the brain as "an enchanted loom where millions of flashing shuttles weave a dissolving pattern ..."[38] Where people once saw ideas weaving tapestries of thought, they now see electricity moving down the branches of neurons and jumping across switches to other neurons. But there is no electrical current in the brain, and there are no electrical switches. What moves along the neurons is a chemical change, and what crosses from one neuron to another is neurotransmitters. Modern computers provide us a handy metaphor, but they may not be much better than engines or looms as models in helping us understand what really goes on in the brain.

I think the brain is more like a soup than a computer. Its nerve cells float in a broth of supporting tissue, plasma, blood cells, nutrients, oxygen, hormones, neurotransmitters, and waste products. Its ingredients came, one at a time, from our ancestors and the world around us. It evolved over millions of years, stirred by many cooks struggling for survival and facing conflicting demands from the environment. Parts of the brain remain well suited to survival today. Other parts are random, leftover by-products of evolution, better suited to handling problems of the past. Some readers will find this view of the brain distasteful. The image of soup suggests an unseemly wetness about human nature. It is messy, organic, and subhuman. Surely, we think, people are better than that. But soup may be as useful a model as any for thinking about how the brain handles information.

Activity in the brain involves individual cells, and testosterone affects these cells. Regardless of the model we use, our practical concern is to discover the rules that link testosterone to our thoughts and actions.

TESTOSTERONE IS LIKE THE WEATHER

People differ in their testosterone levels, and testosterone is more important in some people than in others. For people near the middle of the range of testosterone, differences in testosterone do not matter much. These people are influenced more by other factors, and we would have to look at many such people to see the effects of testosterone. But for people with very high or low levels, testosterone can make a big difference.

A testosterone measurement is like a weather prediction. It gives a general idea of what will happen, but it leaves much unspecified. For example, August is usually hot in Atlanta, but it is sometimes extremely hot and sometimes pleasantly mild. Late-afternoon showers are common, and occasionally there is the edge of a hurricane. The weather can be affected by vagaries of the jet stream, local winds, fast-moving fronts, and moisture from the Gulf of Mexico. Knowing it is August tells us to expect summer weather, but there's no way to be sure what the weather will be on any given August day. Testosterone is like this. We can count on it to affect behavior in the long run. In the short run, on any given occasion, its effects are likely to be relatively mild, one of many influences on our behavior.[39]

With salivary assays, we can collect enough data to see how small effects of testosterone add up to general patterns. My students and I have been doing this, exploring ways in which individuals with high or low levels of testosterone differ from each other. We have also been exploring social and environmental factors that interact with testosterone, sometimes beneficially and sometimes not. Evolution offers a theoretical framework to examine the hormone's role in the survival of males, females, and their offspring, which we will describe in the next chapter. In later chapters we will talk more about men, women, and the social effects of testosterone, and finally we will consider how social forces and human values can modify the effects of testosterone and even channel them in ways that lead to altruistic types of behavior.

2

Two Sexes

TWO SEXES AND TESTOSTERONE

If a child asks us why there are two kinds of people, boys and girls, we are likely to say that is just the way it is, or God made us that way, or it is nice to have both kinds. These answers may miss the point of the child's question. Alun Anderson suggested in the journal *Science* that parents might try explaining why there are two sexes rather than a larger number or none at all. Two seems right to us, and we don't think about other possibilities, but in fact, there are a number of other possibilities. The prize goes to a lowly species of one-celled slime mold, *Plysarum polycephalum*, that has thirteen different sexes. A cell of one sex reproduces by joining with a cell of one of the twelve other sexes. This adds up to seventy-eight possible kinds of pairs, all different. For each pair there are rules as to what each party must do, including which one will pass on its mitochondria, the rod-shaped bodies that live within each cell and are essential to the host animal's metabolism. It is said that God must have loved beetles and other small bugs, or He would not have made so many of them. I think He may have picked the slime mold for special attention, or maybe experimentation, because he gave it such sexual variety. While variety could be the spice of slime mold life, thirteen sexes are an unnecessary complication in the wider evolutionary scheme, a complication that invites trouble. One problem involves the mitochondria. It is important that offspring inherit mitochondria from only one parent. If something goes wrong, and both parents pass along their mitochondria, the competing strains are likely to go to war, leaving the offspring with severely defective metabolism. In 1991, Shigeyuki Kawano of Tokyo University reported that aggressive mutant mitochondria were ignoring slime mold rules for mating. Competing mitochondria may be the beginning of the end for thirteen sexes.[1]

Well before evolution got around to people, two sexes, male and female, had become the standard, with only the females passing along mitochondria. The answer as to why there are two kinds of people is that more than two sexes are vulnerable to problems with competing mitochondria, and fewer than two are vulnerable to other problems. Some species reproduce without sex, in which case each offspring has one parent and inherits a set of genes identical to those of the parent. In this asexual reproduction, the genetic variability that allows for change and adaptability in each new generation is absent. Two sexes bring two sets of genes, which mix and match to produce variety among offspring.[2] Among large animals, including people, two sexes bring diversity without undue complexity. Human females produce ova, which are large enough to contain twenty-two autosomes (chromosomes carrying non—sex linked characteristics), one X sex chromosome, and many mitochondria. Males produce sperm, which are much smaller than ova and too small to carry mitochondria. Sperm have just enough room for twenty-two autosomes and either an X or a Y sex chromosome. The fertilized ovum ends up with twenty-two pairs of autosomes and one pair of sex chromosomes, including an X chromosome from the mother and either an X or Y chromosome from the father, and the mother's mitochondria. A fertilized ovum with two X chromosomes will be female and develop ovaries, while a fertilized ovum with an X and a Y chromosome will be male and develop testes. Later on, unless there is a genetic or congenital error, the females will produce more estrogen than testosterone, and the males will produce more testosterone than estrogen.

EVOLUTION

Two sexes and genetic diversity make evolution possible. Reproductive needs influence evolution's direction and partly explain human nature and the difference between the sexes. There are many places we can go to look for answers to questions about human nature. We can go to psychology, history, politics, religion, popular writing, our parents, or our friends. Most social scientists look to cultural history to explain human nature, but biology and evolution provide an equally useful way of thinking. Evolution molded us in the past and continues to mold us in the present. Life today can be understood in terms of its evolutionary past and offers clues about our evolutionary future. Examining the origins of human nature can make it clearer where the sexes are similar, where they are different, and what they have to disagree about.

Evolution is abstract, slow, and distant, with origins far into the past; it is one of many explanations for human nature, all of which may be true at once. Events have many causes. For example, a man may be alarmed when he meets a stranger on a dark street because of his earlier experiences, because of what others have told him, because of a release of neurotransmitters in his brain, and because evolution has shaped him to react that way. A boxer may fight because he has the ability and spirit of a fighter and because spectators pay to watch him fight. I exercise in a gym because it makes me feel good and constant messages from the fitness movement remind me that it's the thing to do. I eat a lot of rice, as do others from my home state, because rice once grew there and shaped the cuisine of the region. It is also true that my species evolved with muscles that need exercise and a stomach that digests rice.

People interested in evolution distinguish between "proximal" explanations, which are immediate and close at hand, and "distal" explanations, which are remote and far away. Evolution is a distal explanation. Long ago evolution shaped the structure of our bodies, brains, and behavior. It remains an invisible force, nudging us along and emerging at moments to arouse us or trip us up. Distal explanations are useful in understanding overall patterns. They allow us to put many facts into perspective and comprehend their significance.

We act as a result of immediate causes, while in the background other causes have led us to the moment. Evolution is in the background, and it influences us without our awareness. It works as in Lewis Thomas's description of a male moth flying toward pheromones released by a female miles away. The moth does not know why he flies. For all he knows, it is a good day for a flight and a pleasant direction in which to fly. If he does meet the female, then it's a nice surprise. In Lewis's words:

The messages are urgent, but they may arrive, for all we know, in a fragrance of ambiguity. "At home, 4 P.M. today," says the female moth, and releases a brief explosion of bombykol, a single molecule of which will tremble the hairs of any male within miles and send him driving upwind in a confusion of ardor. But it is doubtful if he has an awareness of being caught in an aerosol of chemical attractant. On the contrary, he probably finds suddenly that it has become an excellent day, the weather remarkably bracing, the time appropriate for a bit of exercise of the old wings, a brisk turn upwind. En route, traveling the gradient of bombykol, he notes the presence of other males, heading in the same direction, all in a good mood, inclined to race for the sheer sport of it. Then, when he reaches his destination, it may seem to him the most extraordinary of coincidences, the greatest piece of luck: "Bless my soul, what have we here!"[3]

Like the moth, we are aware of only the more proximal reasons for our behavior. And, like the moth's pheromones, these reasons have the appealing fragrance of ambiguity. They obscure the importance of other reasons. Testosterone has distal origins. It is a legacy of evolution, and evolution stands in the background linking testosterone to our current interest in sex and power.

Simply put, evolution is a process whereby life adjusts to changing pressures and opportunities. New characteristics appear from time to time. Some are helpful, and others are detrimental. Characteristics that help survival increase in each new generation and become more prevalent. Characteristics that hinder survival diminish or disappear. Evolution involves two processes: natural selection and sexual selection. Natural selection explains how people as a species acquired the characteristics of human beings, which include having some amount of testosterone. Sexual selection explains how men and women became different, including being different in their testosterone levels.

NATURAL SELECTION

The principle of natural selection is simple. The world changes, and creatures change with it or disappear. A meteor impact wipes out a whole group of species. Forests turn into grasslands or an ice age begins, forcing old species out and making room for new ones. New neighbors arrive on the scene, making old ways of life less tenable. The ancestors of modern people appeared from one to four million years ago, and the world since then has changed in many ways. In adapting continuously to the world, including the physical and social aspects they themselves created, people changed over time in size, strength, intelligence, longevity, brain structure, and, undoubtedly, testosterone levels.

Evolution goes mostly unnoticed over the short run, as species adapt to small environmental changes. There are clues, though, that changes are in progress. Wisdom teeth have become a liability, and there are people who have genes for less than four of them. Many generations will pass before wisdom teeth become extinct, if they are in fact beginning the slow process of becoming extinct. Over the long run, the effects of evolution are more dramatic, as species change or disappear. Some species split and branch into many subspecies, and some remain largely untouched. Some species are more flexible than others. Horses are well suited to running at high speeds and carrying human riders, but the fact that there are few other animals like horses suggests their unique characteristics are of limited evolutionary value. Horses as a species are almost alone, and if their environment changes drastically, they almost surely will disappear. Ants, on the other hand, have thousands of species, adapted to thousands of niches all over the world. Ants in this way are more resourceful, and they will likely be here long after horses are gone. We never are certain until after the fact whether or not evolution is working well for a given species. Much of the outcome depends on chance and luck.[4]

Evolution has brought remarkable adaptive features to people, including the upright posture, complex hands, and large brain that enable standing, carrying, organizing, and building for the future. These adaptations support human culture, which evolves in much the same way as biological organisms evolve.[5] People everywhere have developed language, elaborate kinship reckonings, and the politics of marital exchanges among families. Universal human practices include cooking, mealtimes, family feasting, dancing, funeral rites, gift-giving, law, and religious rituals.[6] Testosterone influences human culture in many of the same ways that it influences the social life of other animals. Humans evolved with testosterone levels similar to the levels of many other animals, including our closest living relatives, the chimpanzees. The evolution of testosterone in human beings resulted in the muscles, energy, sexual interest, and combativeness needed for survival in a primitive world. Whether these levels are suitable for survival in the modern world, where a few people can hold enormous power and whole nations are balanced between success and disaster, remains to be seen.

Natural selection deals with changes in the species as a whole. Males and females evolve as members of the same species, reacting to the same physical environment. Every species must fit into an ecological niche, and males and females alike must meet the demands of the niche. If the niche changes or disappears, both males and females will be in trouble. Both need to avoid predators, resist parasites and disease, and find food and protection from the elements. Natural selection leads to characteristics that the sexes have in common, and in the world of our ancestors, everyone needed a certain degree of toughness to survive. Both sexes needed testosterone. Both sexes also needed variability in testosterone levels, to take advantage of strategies that called for more or less toughness.

SEXUAL SELECTION

Males and females each have their own specialized needs, as well, and evolution works so as to select members of each sex who are best suited to get what they need. Sexual selection is the evolution of sex-linked traits, and testosterone differences are one of the main outcomes of this type of evolution. It is testosterone in the fetus that brings out the traits that have been most useful and most adaptive to males; and at puberty, the sex hormones in both girls and boys determine secondary sexual characteristics and lead to sexual maturity.

Sex hormones interact with certain genes that lie on the twenty-two autosomes that males and females share. Without male levels of testosterone, some genes may have less effect or no effect at all. For instance, both male and female impalas have genes for horns, but only male impalas actually have horns. That is not true of gazelles, a species in which both males and females have horns. Similarly, in birds, bright feathers may or may not be a masculine trait. Cardinals have them; wrens do not. Testosterone does not always affect the same genes in one species as in another. Sexual selection, like natural selection, is flexible.

Estrogen, too, is necessary for the expression of some genes. Boars have nipples but no breasts, which do not develop without female levels of estrogen. Nevertheless, farmers who raise hogs do not use boars for breeding unless they have the correct number of properly placed nipples, making sure they will pass on good genes to any female offspring. With a great deal of sorting out, sexual selection results in each sex having characteristics that promote reproductive success, and those characteristics vary among the species.

To achieve reproductive success, members of a species need to produce offspring that live, thrive, and produce further offspring. Among mammals, females jockey for position to gain resources for their offspring, and males jockey for position to mate with females and father offspring, sometimes showing as much interest in keeping other males away as in mating. Females need to carry the fetus, give birth, and nurse the young. The female invests heavily in her offspring and needs to protect and nurture them. The male's role is more variable. In some species, males lose interest in family matters immediately after mating, while in others, males help raise their young.

Sexual selection is especially relevant to our concern with testosterone. If we understand the origins and consequences of the large and consistent differences in the levels of testosterone between the two sexes, we will be in a better position to understand variability within each sex, and to contrast low- and high-testosterone males and low- and high-testosterone females.

Males and females live in the same environment and are affected the same way by the forces of natural selection, but other forces affect each sex differently. The characteristics of men and women originated in prehistoric times in response to these other forces. The details of the everyday lives of our prehistoric ancestors are mostly lost to us, but archaeological digs have yielded clues about how our ancestors lived. We have skeletons of ancient people, bones of the animals they hunted, and some of the tools and weapons they used, but we can only make educated guesses about their social structure. We know more about our forefathers than our foremothers because, until recently, research has focused on the way men lived. Now researchers have begun to pay attention to our female ancestors,[7] probably because during recent years more women have become involved in archaeological research.

The generally accepted view among researchers is that prehistoric men and women lived different lives. Men traveled widely, hunted, and dealt with politics, authority, and quasi-military activity, while women stayed closer to the home base, gathered food, took care of children, and worked together to maintain their community.

The remains of a Neanderthal settlement of a hundred thousand years ago support this view.[8] Neanderthal people had bodies similar to ours, and they undoubtedly acted in many ways as our direct ancestors did. The remains of bones, tools, and fireplaces in the settlement show differences between males and females. Females stayed in the local area near a home base. They tended slow-burning fires and used plant foods and materials from nearby. Males traveled and hunted widely, used tools made from stone from far away, built small, hot fires, and brought occasional food back to the cave.

Both sexes need children for evolutionary survival, but only females can give birth. Although they need mates to impregnate them, females bear their own offspring and must be able to provide them with food and safety. Thus through sexual selection females have evolved with resources males do not have. For example, human females evolved with extra body fat on their hips and thighs, which provided our maternal ancestors with the extra calories they needed to survive pregnancy and lactation, especially during hard times. In some environments food is easy to find, and mothers do not have to leave their young unprotected for long periods of time to hunt for food. In harsher environments and in species with prolonged infancy, mothers find it more difficult to support their young without help from relatives and mates. Over periods of many generations, evolution selected females who were tough enough to take care of themselves and their offspring, and clever enough to enlist the help of others when needed.

Males need mates to bear their children. Sex-linked traits enable males to compete with other males for mates and attract the attention of females. Males of different species use different courtship strategies. Many give gifts: male bower birds present females with gifts of colorful pebbles and shiny treasures, and hornbill males bring lizards to prove they are good hunters and therefore will be good providers. In other species, males win mates through force, as hamadryas baboons do; they bite females who try to get away.

Human males approach potential mates using a variety of tactics, including love, support, seduction, and rape. An interest in sex and power, the hallmarks of testosterone, are still important to males in competition for mates and offspring. Generally males succeed by being dominant, which means having power and using it to get what they want. Fighting is a way to be dominant, but not the only way. Males also strut, and they use bluff and bluster to good advantage in scaring off other males and attracting females.

The men in primitive times most likely to have many children were those who had won positions of leadership in the male hierarchy by being good hunters and fighters. As with the hornbills, hunting was as much about getting mates as about getting food. There was usually enough vegetarian food for everyone to eat. But meat was a useful supplement, and men who brought it home had a better chance of attracting women, who knew that babies fathered by powerful hunters had the best chance to thrive. High levels of testosterone contributed to the physical and mental traits that enabled our male ancestors to hunt, fight, and reproduce. These traits included a proclivity for action, sometimes violent; strong physiques characterized by broad shoulders and heavy muscles in the arms and legs; fat stored around the stomach, providing ready calories on long trips;[9] and the skills necessary to track game and make weapons.

The physical characteristics of males are not easy to maintain, and come at considerable cost. It is physically demanding to forage for the calories to support a male's extra size and strength. Furthermore, extra testosterone leads to earlier death, which will be explored in more detail later. Females live longer. Just as they are the basic models *in utero*, females are the basic adult models for the species.[10] Females have the appropriate body size and other characteristics needed to survive in the species' ecological niche. Characteristics that go beyond the basic model—like big muscles and bright plumage—are associated with male reproductive needs.

What we know about our female ancestors and their Neanderthal cousins suggests that women in prehistoric societies did not need heavy muscles and combative dispositions to attract mates. Women were sometimes aggressive, but less often than males, and their average testosterone levels were lower. Women evolved with temperaments that were conducive to long friendships with other women and a cooperative approach to other relationships. We see a similar pattern today. Men tend to drop what appear to be strong loyalties when they change work assignments, jobs, or sports teams.[11] Women maintain lasting relationships around their home communities.

There is strong evidence that the female capacity for friendship is the result of sexual selection. For instance, researchers have noticed sex differences in friendships among other primates. Irwin Bernstein, of the Yerkes Primate Center, can disrupt the hierarchy in a group of male rhesus monkeys by moving the animals to a new setting. When I asked whether he could do this with female monkeys, he said, "No. They would remember their friends."

Modern men live an average of seven years less than women. They would probably live longer if they spent more time appreciating their friends than fighting their rivals. Men pay a price for having high levels of testosterone and the heavy physical apparatus and aggressive temperament that go with it. The fact that these costly characteristics survived the evolutionary process indicates that they are important to reproductive success, or at least have been important until recent times. When traits cease to be important, they wither and disappear over time, like the eyes of fish who live beyond the reach of light in the ocean depths, or the pigmentation of insects who live in dark underground caves and pools. Unessential characteristics that cost nothing to maintain can remain indefinitely, but those that are expensive will begin to disappear when they no longer contribute to survival. Something as expensive as testosterone must have contributed a great deal recently in our evolution.

LARGE TOOLS AND HEAVY EQUIPMENT

The dissimilarities between men's and women's bodies in size, shape, and development, which have emerged from sexual selection, add up to sexual dimorphism, and sex hormones control the process. It is easy to see why sex differences were important in ancient times. Men and women faced disparate survival requirements, and their bodies and behavior evolved to meet those requirements. But do the differences matter today? Is the way men and women act still related to differences in their bodies? Sexual dimorphism is not static. The characteristics that define masculinity and femininity have changed over time, as environmental demands changed and men and women used more or less similar strategies to survive and make a living.[12] But physical dissimilarities between the sexes continue to exist today, as do dissimilarities in behavior.

One popular view is that these dissimilarities are not important and should be ignored. Another popular view is that culture and history have arbitrarily grouped traits into what we call "masculine" and "feminine," and that these terms do not refer to anything natural or basic about the sexes.[13] It is true that natural tendencies can be overwhelmed by learning and culture, but it is also true that some characteristics of the sexes, including those involving pregnancy, lactation, language ability, health, and longevity, are profoundly important and resistant to change.[14] Sexual dimorphism may matter less than it did a hundred thousand years ago, but it still matters. It is well to recognize that average differences exist between the sexes, even though people within each sex are quite varied.

Research indicates that ancient behavioral tendencies related to testosterone persist. Many male animals, including men, are stronger and more violent than females. Sexual selection resulted in those males having traits that go along with high levels of testosterone and a propensity for fighting. Not all male animals fight the same way, and sexual dimorphism often explains why. For example, males of many species fight with their teeth and have larger teeth than the females of the species. But among orangutans, where males are aggressive and would appear to have dangerous bites, the teeth of males and females are similar. It turns out that male orangutans threaten each other with bluff and bluster more than they bite each other. The fierce male orangutan face that gives us pause at the zoo also gives pause to a competitor in the wild.[15]

Men, too, have evolved without large fangs and much of the equipment the males of many other species still use for fighting. By the time our ancestor *Australopithecus* appeared in east Africa a million years ago, human male bodies had begun to evolve away from the muscular head and heavy jaws other male primates used for fighting. Nevertheless, even without so much built-in weaponry, men have remained more aggressive than women. *Australopithecus* men were still competing, but not with their jaws. They were relying on upper-body strength, the temperament associated with high testosterone, and the ability to make and use tools and weapons. Men today build bigger and better weapons and continue to fight each other, and for much the same reason they have always fought: they fight to show they are of more consequence than their fellows. Large tools and heavy equipment have replaced sharp teeth and claws in sexual competition.

THE TRUCE BETWEEN THE SEXES

This discussion of sexual selection and male competition brings us back to considering the range of testosterone in each sex and the average difference in levels of the hormone between males and females. It makes us ask whether men's testosterone leads to violence toward their mates, or to energy for supporting their mates. In *The Selfish Gene*, Richard Dawkins describes a "war between the sexes."[16] He believes men and women are in basic conflict with each other. When we examine the many differences between men and women in testosterone levels, physical characteristics, and reproductive needs, it is easy to see why there is conflict. But conflict is only part of the story. The sexes live together, and their fates are intertwined. They evolved together out of a process of mutual influence sometimes called "coevolution." Men and women do have occasional skirmishes, border raids, and outbreaks of domestic violence in households throughout the world, but mostly they accommodate each other. The war is limited. There is a truce between men and women, and within the truce there is much room for affection.

Some people, when they think about sex differences and evolution, conclude that testosterone drives men toward competition and success. In this view, men who are better at fighting each other and chasing women have more children, which gets their genes into the next generation, where the same thing happens again. But the value of high testosterone levels is not the whole story. If it were the whole story, testosterone levels would rise higher and higher with each generation, as more and more fighting and sexual activity led to more and more success in having children. But there is no evidence that men today have higher levels of testosterone than did men in the past. In fact, men are quite varied in their testosterone levels, and presumably they always have been. Even those who are low in testosterone manage to reproduce quite well, and low-testosterone men appear in every generation. What is missing from the view that testosterone brings success is the fact that high testosterone also carries a heavy cost.

The problem is that individuals with extremely high levels of testosterone are likely to die before they have offspring. Studies with animals illustrate this. Male birds injected with testosterone sing more, patrol larger areas, have more fights, and are less likely to live out the year. Those that do live end up with more injuries.[17] When male lizards are given extra testosterone, they fight more, move around more, and can be seen more easily in the wild, all of which makes them less likely to survive.[18] Evolution maintains a delicate balance between producing enough testosterone to compete successfully and producing so much that one's own survival is at risk. Among many animals, castrated males live longer. This is true of sheep, cats, rats, and moths. It is also true of men.[19] Even normal levels of testosterone put men at risk, though most men would reject castration as a way of gaining a long life.

Just as high levels of testosterone make men as a group more combative than women, men with more testosterone are more combative than men with less testosterone. Higher-testosterone men have more problems in relationships with their mates. Higher-testosterone men are less reliable as mates and fathers, and men who ignore their wives and children will have fewer viable offspring. Females seem to recognize both the good and the bad aspects of masculinity. In general, they find men attractive who are high in testosterone but not too high, men who have a good build but are not muscle bound. Despite the effort men put into developing their muscles, most women do not find highly muscular men especially attractive.[20] Perhaps male bodybuilders are more interested in competing with other men than in attracting women. The preferences of females, along with the hazards of high testosterone levels, explain why the males of many species, including male vervet monkeys and men, do not have higher levels of testosterone with each new generation. Vervet monkeys are good-natured ground dwellers that live on the African savanna. The females take part in selecting leaders from among the males in the troop. The females, who do not like overly excitable or combative males, promote calm and peaceful leaders.[21]

In harsh environments, females need helpful mates to raise viable offspring, with the result that the genes of the most negligent males tend to die out. Men vary in the amount of attention they give their families, but as with other animals, sexual selection has worked in favor of men who meet the needs of their particular environment. Thus it is not surprising that research shows that men who live in colder climates tend to be more monogamous and reliable than men who live in warmer climates.[22] Nevertheless, whatever the climate, human infants are dependent for a long time and need a great deal of parental attention. Evolutionary pressure to be responsible mates and good providers has affected both men and women. It has restrained male competition and kept men from becoming too brutish a bunch, at least most of the time.

There remains an uneasy relationship between men and women, who are often at cross purposes with each other. This uneasiness is part of folklore. In T. S. Eliot's poem "The Love Song of J. Alfred Prufrock," Prufrock shies away from talking with his lady friend because he is afraid they'll misunderstand each other.[23] Eliot stated the problem poetically and offered no solution. The sociolinguist Deborah Tannen and the actress Katharine Hepburn both offer solutions. In *You Just Don't Understand,* Tannen writes that men and women have different conversational styles. She believes that men and women who understand this will "accept differences without blaming themselves, their partners, or their relationships."[24] Hepburn has another strategy for harmony between the sexes. She says, "Sometimes I wonder if men and women really suit each other. Perhaps they should live next door, and just visit now and then."[25]

Tannen and Hepburn live in different social circles, and their ideas show it. Tannen works with literary and academic people. Their well-developed verbal skills indicate that the men in the group would often be lower than average in testosterone. Hepburn, on the other hand, works with actors, generally a high-testosterone group whose success depends on a charismatic way of speaking the words that other people write.* Tannen is trying to overcome the gap between men and women. Hepburn has accepted the gap and come to terms with it.

---

*Other differences in testosterone between these occupational groups are discussed in Chapter 6.

As is often the case with opposite points of view, both Tannen and Hepburn are right. Men and women do misunderstand each other. Better communication would help, but it will not solve everything. Whether or not disagreements are resolved will depend on how hard the parties try and how different they are. The parties can differ in temperament, interests, and commitment to a relationship. Tannen's strategy succeeds with people who share interests and enjoy each other's company, but for others, even Hepburn's "next door" is too close. Jack Nicholson bought a house ten minutes away from his own house for his girlfriend and their two children. Nicholson sympathizes with the male who is in danger of becoming obsolete because he has "too much testosterone for society to control." Still, Nicholson is not totally beyond help from Tannen's solution. He has periods of what he calls "intermittent monogamy." He says, "It's a matter of communication."[26]

Some couples combine the Tannen and Hepburn strategies. Carolyn, my sister, and Rick, her husband who died a few years ago, were married over forty years and had many common interests. They were committed to their family and to their relationship; nevertheless, they had what Tannen calls "different conversational styles." Carolyn likes to explore a topic from every angle and may change the angle in midsentence. Rick, on the other hand, had a legal and military background and liked to go to the main point without being distracted along the way. Their marriage thrived on alternating togetherness and separation. During the last twenty years of their marriage, she lived in Tennessee, where she still lives, and he lived in North Carolina. They visited often and took trips together. They came to terms with their differences, accommodated to them, and had a happy marriage.

INDIVIDUAL DIFFERENCES

This discussion makes it sound as though there is a clear line between men and women. In fact, the line is often blurred. It is most blurred when there are genetic or congenital abnormalities. For instance, men with two X chromosomes and one Y chromosome have abnormally low levels of testosterone, and they do not develop normally during adolescence unless they receive extra testosterone. On the other hand, some people have one X and one Y chromosome, the usual male pattern, but lack testosterone receptors. These people are genetic males, but they are sterile, and they look like women, sometimes exceptionally attractive women. There is another condition, a genetic disorder, mostly identified with the Dominican Republic, that causes boys to look like girls, but only until they reach puberty. Then they suddenly start responding to testosterone; their testes descend and they develop male bodies.[27]

People who have undergone male-to-female sex-change operations often say they have always known deep down in their hearts that they are really women. There appear to be biological reasons for these feelings. Research at the Brain Institution of the Netherlands indicates that some male-to-female transsexuals have a nucleus in the hypothalamus, a regulatory part of the brain, that is more typical of females than males.[28] Some people mistakenly identified as transsexual are really genetic females with an enzyme disorder resulting in excessive testosterone, which causes their external genitalia to appear masculine.

One such case was Gordon Langley Hall, a socially prominent white man in Charleston, South Carolina. In 1968, Hall had an operation, emerged a woman, took the name Dawn Pepita Hall, and married John-Paul Simmons, an African-American man who had been her driver, butler, and companion. At the time, interracial marriage alone was shocking, and combined with a sex-change operation, it was scandalous. Three years later, in 1971, the couple set society further atwitter when Dawn gave birth to a baby. It turned out that all along Hall had been a biological female with ambiguous genitalia, wrongly identified at birth as a male.[29]

Sexual versatility is the norm in many species. Members of some can readily change from one sex to another. In one species of coral fish, the largest and most dominant female turns into a male if the dominant male dies.[30] Even among those without genetic or congenital abnormalities the line between the sexes is blurry. Few men are totally masculine, and few women are totally feminine. Masculinity and femininity lie on an irregular continuum, with some people on either end and some in the middle, but most about at the average for one sex or the other.

This chapter has emphasized sex differences, especially as they are related to testosterone, but we should put these differences in perspective. Men and women represent distinct groups, different in many ways, but at the same time there is overlap between the two groups. Men and women have personality characteristics in common, and they share values, ambitions, hobbies, prejudices, and ways of making a living. They overlap in height, weight, strength, and other physical traits. We call traits masculine if they are associated with high levels of testosterone, but this is a shorthand way of speaking. Testosterone is present in both sexes, more in men and less in women, and it affects them similarly. The higher the testosterone level, the more it makes people, men or women, act in the way that men typically act.

Differences between the sexes are averages based on large numbers. A particular man or woman may not be like the average member of his or her sex. Some women are high in testosterone, and some men are low. Many men and women differ from other members of their sex in masculinity or femininity. Beryl Markham and Shirley Muldowney made their marks in the masculine worlds of aviation and automobile racing. Jean-Jaques Rousseau and John Dewey contributed more typically feminine communal viewpoints to philosophy and education. Some cultures allow men and women to deviate from standard sex role stereotypes, and some cultures do not. Joan of Arc was condemned and burned at the stake for her masculine behavior, but tough women among the Blackfoot Indians were "manly-hearted" and valued members of the tribe.[31] And when the forces of Geronimo, the last great Apache leader, had been reduced to seventeen warriors in their fight against the combined United States and Mexican armies, one of the warriors was a woman.[32]

3

Testosterone, Mind, and Behavior

"THIS IS NOT WHAT I HAD EXPECTED"

In 1992 a sex-change patient in Holland was in transition from female to male. He* was taking testosterone to make his body masculine, and later he was going to have surgery to complete the change. All his life he had felt that inside he was a man, and now after three months of testosterone treatments, he began to view the world differently and think differently. In an awkwardly eloquent statement, he described some of the changes he was experiencing, many of which surprised him:

> I have problems expressing myself, I stumble over my words. Your use of language becomes less broad, more direct and concise. Your use of words changes, you become more concrete ... I think less; I act faster, without thinking.
>
> The visual is so strong ... when walking in the streets I absorb the things around me. I am an artist, but this is so strong. It gives a euphoric feeling. I do miss, however, the overall picture. Now I have to do one thing at a time; I used to be able to do different things simultaneously.
>
> I can't make fine hand movements anymore; I let things fall out of my hands.

---

*Although the physical transformation from female to male was not complete, the patient was living as a man, which makes it appropriate to refer to him as "he."

41

My fantasy life has diminished strongly … unfortunately. I would have liked to keep that. I am becoming more clumsy, more blinkered. I didn't ask for this; it just happens.

I would have preferred to remain androgynous. I always considered myself to be a man, but this is not what I had expected.[1]

His testosterone doses were large, and the effect was large. He discovered in a dramatic way that testosterone influenced his mind as well as his body. These effects on his mind and nervous system, on what he saw and how he thought and reacted, are the links between testosterone and the outward manifestations of masculinity. He expected the outward changes everyone associates with masculinity, but the inner ones were surprising. He experienced firsthand the differences between women and men that researchers have only observed secondhand. The changes he described—trouble expressing himself, thinking and imagining less, acting more quickly, focusing more narrowly but more vividly, feeling euphoric, and losing fine motor skills—are all consistent with what researchers know about testosterone's role in the differences between men and women, differences that are the result of evolution and reproductive pressures on our human and prehuman ancestors.

The Dutch patient's increasing inability to express himself was consistent with what psychologists know about verbal ability and physical anthropologists know about human prehistory. Women have better verbal skills than men. Our male ancestors needed skills that made them excel at hunting and fighting, and a simple vocabulary served them nicely. Our female ancestors needed more complicated vocabularies to facilitate social interactions among the members of communal groups that nurtured and protected children. Verbal ability is part of an evolutionary package that emphasizes abstract thought and imagination.

As he began to think and imagine less, the Dutch patient began to focus more intently, feel euphoric, and act more quickly. His mental processes were becoming more masculine, more like those of his fighting and hunting male ancestors. Men who fought and hunted in dangerous primitive environments needed to focus on the task at hand and move quickly with confidence and optimism. They could not afford to worry about the bad things that might happen to them. They did not need vivid imaginations or complicated thoughts to slow them down when survival depended on speed and action.

Our primitive male ancestors needed to make and use tools and weapons, but they also needed to be strong. There is an evolutionary trade-off between brute strength and fine motor skill. In women the trade-off is toward fine motor skill and manual dexterity; in men it is toward strength. With testosterone therapy, the Dutch patient lost dexterity and began to drop things.

He also lost the "overall picture." His change in mental focus from broad to narrow mirrors the different challenges that men and women had to meet throughout human evolutionary history. While men benefited from an intensity of focus, women benefited from paying attention to many things at once. Women gathered food, carried water, fed the fire, stirred the pot, and did whatever other chores needed to be done, while at the same time keeping an eye on the children. The children's survival depended on having mothers who could keep track of the "overall picture." Anthropologist Helen Fisher calls the female style of thinking "web thinking" and the male style "step thinking."[2]

The biological basis for web thinking is complicated, but the Dutch patient's experience indicates that high levels of testosterone interfere with it. Testosterone probably has some impact on the corpus callosum, the part of the brain that unites the left and right sides. The corpus callosum is larger on average in women than in men, and its size is related to verbal intelligence.[3] While men evolved using their strength and focus, women evolved using their sizable corpora callosa.

SIMPLE THOUGHT AND ACTION

My wife, Mary, says the corpus callosum explains quite a bit. Recently I heard her talking on the telephone to our daughter-in-law, Geri. Mary said, "Just tell James one thing at a time. He can't remember a list of things. He can't help it. He's a man and he has a small corpus callosum." Mary was trying to help Geri deal with our son's evolutionary baggage.

Shakespeare's King Henry V understood the need for focus. He was worried that his men would think too much about the overwhelming number of French soldiers facing them at the battle of Agincourt. He prayed, "O God of Battles! Steal my soldiers' hearts. / Possess them not with fear. Take from them now / the sense of reckoning, if the opposed numbers / pluck their hearts from them." Just before the battle he added, "All things are ready, if our minds be so." The Earl of Westmoreland agreed, saying, "Perish the man whose mind is backward now!"[4] In King Arthur's court, Sir Lancelot objected that Queen Guinevere was teaching the young Galahad to think too much. Galahad had interrupted a fencing lesson to ask Lancelot how he would know when he was fighting on the right side. Lancelot said, "I'm sorry, Guinevere, but if you teach him such sophistry, he won't be a fit companion for decent men. Imagine some one needing his help in danger, a friend, let's say, or his father or his mother, or even a stranger, and he'll be debating which side of the quarrel is more righteous!"[5]

Sometimes our thoughts are simple because there is no extra room in our minds. Each of our minds has a limited capacity. What faces us at the moment may be so demanding that we have to ignore everything else. Tom Hanks described the captain, his character in the movie *Saving Private Ryan*, in those terms. In a 1999 television interview Hanks said that the captain, intent on completing his mission, focused on the moment, refusing to tell anyone about his life outside the army or even allow himself to think about it. The captain accomplished his mission but lost his life. Sometimes, though, the ability to focus can be lifesaving. The French pilot Antoine de Saint-Exupéry described the mind of a pilot named Sagon, who was trying to escape from a burning airplane. He said,

> The field of consciousness is tiny. It accepts only one problem at a time. Get into a fist fight, put your mind on the strategy of the fight, and you will not feel the other fellow's punches. Once, when I thought I was about to drown in a seaplane accident, the freezing water seemed to me tepid. Or, more exactly, my consciousness was not concerned with the temperature of the water. It was absorbed by other thoughts. The temperature of the water left no trace on my memory. In the same way, Sagon's consciousness was filled to the brim with the problem of getting away from the plane. His universe was limited successively to the fate of his crew, the handle that governed the sliding latch, the rip cord of the parachute.[6]

Still, a narrow focus is not always a good thing. There was a sad item in the news about a small child who drowned in the family pool near the deck where he was helping his father with a carpentry project. The father did not notice that the child was missing and had fallen into the pool until it was too late to save him. When Mary heard about the accident, she said, "If that father had known he wasn't good at doing more than one thing at a time, maybe the accident wouldn't have happened."

Some women have one-track minds, but it is more typical of men, and they can be more extreme. A one-track mind leads to persistence, and persistence can lead to stubbornness. In the novel *Lonesome Dove*, Augustus McRae and Woodrow Call crossed the line into stubbornness. They were driving cattle from south Texas to Montana. The drive was long and hard, and on the Platte River in Nebraska they stopped to visit Augustus's old friend Clara. She tried to persuade Augustus to stay. She said, "There's cheap land not three days' ride from here. You could have the whole north part of this state if you wanted it. Why go to Montana?" "Well, that's where we started for," he said. "Me and Call have always liked to get where we started for, even if it don't make a damn bit of sense."[7]

Studies show that men and animals who are high in testosterone persist at what they start, and they work longer at a task without being distracted.[8] Although the tasks studied have been simple ones that can be completed relatively quickly, we suspect that high-testosterone people also tend to persevere at tasks requiring months or years to complete. It appears likely that testosterone is a factor in stubbornness as well as persistence. Not all men like Augustus and Woodrow are fictional. There was a story in *Creative Loafing*, an Atlanta weekly newspaper, that stuck in my mind. It was about the relentless twelve-year campaign of a West Point graduate and former Army Ranger to expose corruption in local rezoning practices. At West Point he had sworn "never to lie, cheat, or steal, or tolerate anyone who does." His crusade, which he views in the context of keeping that vow, has cost him his marriage, most of his money, and his freedom during two years he spent in jail awaiting trial on forty-three counts of terroristic threats, stalking, and intimidating witnesses. He has not yet given up his fight, although the men he accuses of wrongdoing are either dead, elderly, or already punished for related crimes. Surely his background and training have a lot to do with his dedication to his cause, but testosterone probably played a role, too.[9]

Differences in intensity of focus go along with differences in cognitive style, which is easier to see in groups than in individuals. The average group of women will consider a problem longer than the average group of men, talking more about causes, complexities, and a variety of possible solutions. Members of the League of Women Voters study and discuss a problem until they reach a consensus about what action to take. A Marine platoon seizes a hill with little discussion, following the simple words from "The Charge of the Light Brigade": "...not to reason why...but to do and die." The League takes a more feminine approach, and the Marines take a more masculine approach. Detective Dave Robicheaux, the hero of the novel *The Neon Rain,* explains his high-testosterone approach to problem solving this way: "I simply had to set some things right. And sometimes you don't set things right by being reasonable. Reason is a word I always associate with bureaucrats, paper shufflers, and people who formed committees that were never intended to solve anything. I don't mean to be hard. Maybe I'm just saying that what works for other people never worked very well for me...."[10]

Men like Robicheaux think action is the best way out of a fog of confusion. Sometimes they are right, and their logic grows out of the demands of insoluble problems. They try to get rid of problems as quickly as possible, while most women try to understand problems first. Quick action works well in combat, where delay can get one killed, and it may work in a barroom fight, but it is a poor way to handle foreign policy, the continuing problems of everyday life, or sometimes even a stalemated war.

Soldiers, not inclined to let indecision paralyze them, sometimes kill arbitrarily. In Vietnam, American troops might get orders in the morning that as of noon, civilians who until then were being treated as refugees and helped in a protected area would immediately be treated as enemies to be killed in a free-fire zone. The situation was absurd, but action was demanded, and a novel solution began to appear on the back of soldiers' T-shirts: "Kill 'em all. Let God sort them out."

Simple thought and action are consistent with low verbal skill. A larger vocabulary encourages complicated thought, not speedy action.

The less time spent considering possibilities, the easier it is to keep a positive frame of mind. Perhaps consistent with the need for positive thinking, higher testosterone is associated with lower verbal ability,[11] and men in general are less skilled with words than women are. On average, women do better than men on verbal tests: women do almost twice as well at listing synonyms, and they can make longer lists of words beginning with the same letter.[12]

It is true there are more male than female names in literature, but the number of famous men may say more about limited opportunities for women than the literary superiority of men. Furthermore, some male names in literature, like George Sand, are the pen names of women. Literary men might be surprised to learn that men have less verbal ability than women, and they may not like the idea that there is a trade-off between verbal ability and masculinity. Nevertheless, it is true that both boys and men who are high in testosterone are at a disadvantage when it comes to using language well. Grade-school children who are high in testosterone are likely to have learning disabilities.[13] High-testosterone men are more likely than low-testosterone men to have blue-collar jobs. Men in white-collar jobs are on average higher in verbal ability and lower in testosterone[14] than men in blue-collar jobs.

Limited verbal ability makes it easier to accept simple solutions. President Bush showed an instinct for the simple logic of testosterone in speeches he made in his 1992 bid for reelection. He did not bore his followers with campaign speeches about the knotty points of economic and foreign policies. Instead, he used metaphors about sports and war and talked about winning and losing; like the misguided general in *The Neon Rain*, "his acetylene-blue eyes looked at you with the unflinching clarity of a man who was never inhibited by complexity or moral doubt."[15] Unfortunately for Bush, a lot of women voted in 1992, and they found Bill Clinton's complicated platform and introspective excursions more appealing than Bush's simple solutions and moral certainty. However, it is important not to overstate the difference between men and women when it comes to politics. On September 25, 1995, Atlanta radio station WGST reported a listener poll indicating that 40 percent of the listeners to talk shows geared to the tastes of "angry white men" were women.

Nevertheless, the law of averages comes into play when men get together and talk. The men are apt to sound more like President Bush than President Clinton. They may not talk about war, but their conversation centers around action and activities. At my brother Dick's farm in South Carolina, getting ready for a picnic to celebrate survival on the anniversary of Hurricane Hugo, men sat around the fire cooking barbecue through the night and into the morning, and their conversation followed the male pattern.

First, they talked about the task at hand. They talked about the right-size pig to cook (100—150 pounds), the temperature (260°— 280°F), how long to cook before turning (5—6 hours), the merits of wood and gas, the merits of oak, hickory, pecan, and other kinds of wood (white oak was best), the difficulty of managing a fire on cold ground, and how to judge temperature by the sound of dripping fat. As the night passed, the men remembered other years, other barbecues, large crowds at the hunt club, nineteen pigs cooked at once, cooking in cold weather, killing pigs, how to do it, and how nobody raises pigs anymore.

Later, they talked about hunting: small animals, large animals, birds, the reappearance of turkeys, snakes, large snakes, many snakes, a non-poisonous snake that can spread its neck like a cobra and scare you half to death, watching fights between rattlesnakes, almost stepping on snakes, deer, hunting stands for deer, the average distance at which deer are shot (50—100 yards), the curiosity of deer, the pet deer at home that drinks coffee and eats cigarettes, different kinds of rifles, taking a four-year-old son hunting two years before he is old enough to carry a gun, the loveliness of walking with one's wife in the canopied forest of the swamp, and seeing raccoons sunning themselves on branches there, before Hugo toppled the beautiful trees.

When dawn arrived some of the men took a break to go hunting, unbothered by the drizzle, keeping only their rifle scopes dry, and later they went home, cleaned up, and napped. They returned to the barbecue later in the afternoon to visit and talk. Occasionally they made brief mention of the people they knew: the hunter who could hit a deer at 500 yards with his M-1 rifle; another hunter who was too lazy to build his own deer stand and was always borrowing one of theirs; and the guy who slept through a previous barbecue, leaving all the work to them. But mostly they talked about events and action. They spent little time on feelings, anger, frustrations, or problems. They talked about the experiences and adventures of active lives. Their talk was a wandering thread that held them loosely together.

Women talk about different things. Around the barbecue fire, women would have talked more about people, relationships, and their feelings about things. When I told my sister Dorothy about the men at the barbecue, she laughed. She said she liked to listen to men talk. She said, "Men's talk is interesting, as long as you don't expect them to say anything meaningful." The way men talk is probably in part due to testosterone, but we do not know whether it is an organizing effect of testosterone on the brain long before birth, an activating effect of current adult testosterone levels, or a little of each. My students and I are beginning to explore that question. We want to see whether men begin to talk differently when they receive testosterone treatments. It would also be interesting to interview patients—women being treated for hirsutism or men being treated for prostate cancer—who are taking testosterone-suppressing drugs.

Men sometimes spend long periods of time together and talk very little. Gus Grissom and Deke Slayton were two "good old boys" among America's astronauts, and they liked doing things together. In *The Right Stuff,* Tom Wolfe said the two would go hunting on weekends, or "wrangle a T-33 from Langley Air Force Base and fly cross-country, taking turns at the controls. Sometimes they would fly all the way to California and back, and it was likely that if they exchanged a total of forty sentences, transcontinental, they would come back feeling like they'd had a hell of an animated conversation and a deep talk."[16]

Many other studies and observations show differences in the way men and women talk. At a senior citizens center in Baltimore, men and women were asked to talk into a microphone for ten minutes each. Both sexes talked about the center and the highlights of their lives, but men talked more about solitary activities and less about the people in their lives.[17] At the Old Soldiers Home in Washington, D.C., where men and women soldiers from World War II live, an interviewer asked two women whether they liked to tell old war stories. One of them said, "Nobody wants to talk ... about those stories." The other one said, "The men do that. The men—they fight the war, but we have other things to do."[18]

This does not mean that men, and high-testosterone people in general, do not think. Men and women score about the same on a measure called "Need for Cognition," which indicates how much they seek out information and think about it in making sense of the world.[19] Perhaps high-testosterone people think less about abstract things, or about subtle and complex social relationships. But we are all awake about the same number of hours, we move effectively through the world, and our minds deal with the problems that face us. I think high-testosterone people are more oriented toward a particular set of problems, ones that can be handled well with what I call simple thought and action. Maybe men, or high-testosterone men and women, are best at dealing with those problems.

Other problems call for the women's approach. With more careful analysis or a little more time, they are solved or cease to be problems. Many good solutions are compromises between acting too fast on the one hand and thinking too long on the other, and such solutions would benefit from a compromise between the male and female approach. By electing more women, voters are forcing compromise. Commissioner Jackie Scott of DeKalb County, Georgia, meets with Georgia legislators when state bills affecting counties are on the agenda, and she notices a difference in the way men and women legislators operate. Scott says the women, unlike the men, prefer reaching a consensus to rushing a vote.

Scott's observations are not peculiar to Georgia. National Public Radio's *Morning Edition,* with Wendy Kaufman reporting,[20] ran a segment on how women legislators are changing government. Washington State Representative Pat Hale suggests the difference in legislative style is historic. Women more than men have had to gain their ends "through collaboration and working through other people."

Women legislators want more information and pay more attention to how laws will affect individual citizens than their male colleagues do. According to Ray Wilkinson, chief lobbyist for the Boeing Machinists, male legislators, once they take a position on an issue, are close-minded. "But female legislators, they're more open and they listen better and they're more willing to listen to your opinion. . . ." Women are more open-minded and they want more openness in government. Rutgers University researchers report that women favor "government in public view rather than government behind closed doors." When the Senate was ready to debate whether or not President Clinton was guilty or innocent during his impeachment trial, all nine women senators voted for an open debate, but the majority of the men prevailed, and the deliberations were closed.

Different frames of mind sometimes foster suspicion and make it hard for men and women to work together. Calling the women legislators "we" and the men "they," Washington State Representative Maryann Mitchell told Wendy Kaufman, "We happened to all wear red jackets all on one day, and this place nearly went over the edge. They were sure it was some kind of a conspiracy. 'What's going to happen? What is it you're going to do? When are you going to do this thing?' ... And so, of course, we had to play it to the hilt and say, 'We'll let you know when the time is right.'"

When suspicion is aroused, there is no easy formula to assure cooperation between the sexes. Maybe experience will help. After a while, men and women legislators should get used to each other and red jackets will be like blue pin-striped suits, just a popular fashion statement. We can progress further in the direction of cooperation by understanding the nature and origins of sex differences than by resorting to stereotypes and ideology.

SPATIAL SKILLS

Like most mysteries of the universe, the nature of spatial skills has been considered in literature. In *The Crossing,* Cormac McCarthy wrote a book about two boys, Billy and Boyd, riding into Mexico in the 1930s to search for men who had murdered their parents. During their long trip they had time to think about things, including horses' orientation in space. Boyd asked his brother whether he thought horses knew where they were and knew how to get back to where they came from. Billy was dubious, but he wanted to know how they did it if they did it. He wanted to know if Boyd thought horses had pictures in their heads of where things were. That made more sense to Billy than the possibility that horses could backtrack. Boyd said he didn't think horses backtracked. He thought they just knew where things were.[21]

Boyd was wondering if horses navigate the way that men do. Men and women differ in how they orient themselves and navigate, and some of this is related to testosterone. Men have a better sense for distances and directions, sometimes compared to an internal compass or a bird's-eye view, that allows them to visualize in all directions.

Women are superior at mastering the details of specific localities, an inheritance from primitive ancestors who survived and passed on the ability to attend to multiple tasks within specific geographic boundaries. The skills that men have are particularly associated with travel. Prehistoric men hunted and traveled, and they had to be able to find their way home without getting lost. Good hunters and travelers survived to pass their spatial abilities and their testosterone on to succeeding generations. The modern descendants of prehistoric hunters and travelers go to school, and among other things, they study geography.

Young boys, who generally do less well in school than girls, can take comfort in geography. Boys today are better than girls at geography, a fact that troubles the National Geographic Society, which works to promote the equality of the sexes. Boys always win the National Geography Bee, which tests children in grades four through eight on their knowledge of places around the world. In 1993, fifty-five out of fifty-seven regional finalists were boys, as were all ten of the national finalists.[22] Among college students, males can locate almost twice as many countries on an unlabeled map of the world as females can.[23] Boys may know more about geography because they read more travel stories than girls do, but the question remains as to why boys prefer stories about travel, and girls prefer stories about people and their relationships. There is no reason to believe the preference is entirely learned.

Our prehistoric ancestors set a pattern that continued through ancient times to the present. More men than women have been explorers and travelers. No doubt some of the difference has been due to the traditional role of women in the home and the greater opportunity for men to become famous outside the home. Nevertheless, recent research indicates the difference is not entirely cultural. We know that some of this traveling behavior is directly related to testosterone, at least in animals. After testosterone injections, birds travel farther,[24] and mice are less afraid to enter new and strange places.[25]

Testosterone may do more than enhance spatial visualization. It may motivate people and animals to move around in larger spaces. Among children at a playground or monkeys in the jungle, males play less at the center and more at the edges of the group than girls do.

Researchers have observed differences in the spatial behavior of boy and girl babies. Among one-year-olds observed at play, boys on average move farther away from their mothers than the girls do, and they stay away from their mothers for longer periods of time.[26]

My students and I plan to study whether people of either sex who are higher in testosterone travel more and know more about faraway places in the world. At present, we know more about the differences in spatial abilities between men and women than about those between high- and low-testosterone people of the same sex. It makes sense, though, to hypothesize that a difference between men and women would predict a difference between high- and low-testosterone individuals.

Anyone familiar with standardized tests has seen the odd three-dimensional drawings with multiple-choice questions about how the drawings would look viewed from another direction. These drawings test the ability to visualize objects and imagine them from various angles. Mental rotation ability is related to geographical and mechanical skills. People who do well on mental rotation tests should have an advantage when it comes to throwing spears, chipping stone axes, using maps, and repairing carburetors. The psychological research on spatial ability indicates that performance on mental rotation tests is probably related to testosterone.[27]

Females who receive testosterone injections in preparation for sex-change operations show large increases in mental rotation ability.[28] Women with a disorder called Turner syndrome have only one X chromosome, and their bodies produce no testosterone. They are average or above average in verbal intelligence, but they perform far below average on mental rotation tests. Men generally do better on these tests than women, and high-testosterone men do best of all.

Target tests, which involve watching two projectiles moving across a computer screen at various speeds and judging which will reach its target first, assess a specific ability to deal with complex movement in three-dimensional space. It is not surprising that men, with their genetic legacy from prehistoric hunters, are better than women at tests of tracking and hitting targets.[29]

Three-dimensional spatial ability goes along with testosterone and the strong visual experience that made the Dutch sex-change patient feel euphoric. Visual contact with the target is one of the appeals of guns, which explains why so many men, even some who never hunt, enjoy target practice. It also partly explains why hunters use telescopic sights when shooting within the range of iron sights. Telescopic sights are popular because they are easy to use and make the target appear close and vivid. Men like to see the action. Pilots standing around talking at a small airport will always pause to watch a plane touch down; they find the sight of converging plane and ground irresistible. Similarly, a baseball soaring through the air is a sight baseball players find hard to ignore. The appeal of watching a baseball fly away after it has been hit is so strong that it is hard for batters to resist a quick peek, even though they know that looking takes away from their speed in running the bases.

Lauren Baker, a student at Georgia State University, has studied men, women, and photography. She conducted an experiment to find out if there was a difference between the kind of pictures men and women preferred.[30] She found that men liked pictures with a faraway focus that showed the horizon, while women liked close-ups with details in the foreground. Her findings were what we expected in light of what we know about men and women and their spatial skills. Where men excel at mental rotations and geographic ability, women excel at another kind of spatial ability: women notice and remember where objects are located.[31] This may be part of a more general ability women have to keep track of more than one thing at a time.

Until recently, researchers have not paid much attention to the spatial skills that are more characteristic of women than of men. Dianne Winters, one of my former students, made me aware of how useful these skills can be. She made good use of her ability to keep track of many things at once and remember landmarks. Before she came to Georgia State University, she had worked as an air traffic controller, an unusual occupation for a woman. Her particular job was to keep track of activity on the airport surface—ground control. Sitting in front of a model of the airport, she monitored where everything was and where it was going. Sometimes she monitored two runways at once, listening to radio traffic from one runway through her left earphone and from the other runway through her right earphone.

Mary and I are the stereotypical couple when it comes to finding our cars in parking lots. I find mine by remembering directions and distances; she finds hers by remembering landmarks. Men and women use their best spatial skills to keep track of their cars and to travel. When women travel, they find a place by remembering what it was near, what it looked like, or what signs were there. On trips, men remember directions and distances, and women remember landmarks along the way.[32]

Once when I was visiting my brother, Dick, on his farm in South Carolina, I told him about the research I was doing concerning the way men and women give directions. Since then, Dick had a good opportunity to take advantage of what I told him. Disney was using his place to film a movie, and there was a lot of coming and going around the farm. Dick got frequent calls from people who wanted directions about how to get from town to the farm. During the filming, I visited him again. He said, "I gave directions to the men the same way I've always done it. I tell them, 'Take 378 east about 12 miles till you hit junction 527. Turn right on 527, go half a mile, and turn right,' but I've been telling the women about landmarks. I tell them, 'Go ten miles to Black River Swamp, cross it, and then go about two miles farther on to a crossroads with a little minimart over to the left. Then you take a right and go down about a half mile to where the first paved road comes in on your left. Then you turn right on the dirt road.' Women have been telling me, 'You know how to give good directions. Most men don't.'"

Dick is able to tell women about landmarks because he is in an area he knows well. If he were not so familiar with a place, he would have to rely on directions and distances. Like most men, he pays little attention to landmarks when he travels. Again, this bears on skills used in hunting. Hunters follow indirect and wandering paths in searching for game, and they do not remember detailed landmarks or return home by the same route. Instead, they keep track of the directions and distances they travel, and when the hunt is over they return home directly across country.

Some women are better than men at dealing with all sorts of space. I once saw a little girl who convinced me that little girls can have the spatial sense of astronauts. I saw her on a Saturday morning when I was making my way through the maze of aisles at our local farmers' market, a huge warehouselike building piled high with produce and crowded with shoppers. She was about seven years old, and she was helping her father shop. He was pushing a buggy, and she was riding on the front. She was standing on the outside of the buggy with her feet over the front two wheels, holding on and swinging backward while she talked. As they came to an intersection, she glanced to one side. Something caught her eye, and in an instant she looked back at her father, flung out her right arm, and said, "Quick, Daddy! Turn that way! My right, your left!" I had never seen anyone give directions so quickly. I wondered how she got that way. Was it just learning, or had she been exposed to extra testosterone *in utero*? If testosterone was behind her navigational skill, was it behind anything else, such as her decision to joyride backward on the outside of a buggy?

I wondered if she would grow up to like mechanical things, maybe even enjoying the twenty-first-century equivalent of fixing carburetors. People who are good at fixing carburetors are skillful at visualizing and manipulating objects in various configurations. They have a particular kind of mechanical ability, which is, along with geographical ability, included in the set of spatial skills that evolved with testosterone. Modern mechanics, plumbers, and electricians need mechanical skill to work with wires, gears, and pipes, just as their Stone Age ancestors needed it to work with rocks, sticks, and animal hides. Studies indicate that mechanical work goes with masculinity, and the average man does better than the average woman on most, but not all, tests of mechanical skill.

Fifty years ago, anthropologists like George Murdock studied the details of what people did for a living. Murdock listed occupations of men and women in 224 tribes from all parts of the world.[33] He found only one occupation that was exclusively male, and that was metalworking. Metalworking and mechanical work have a lot in common. More men than women are mechanics and engineers, which makes me wonder whether testosterone affects a person's decision to choose an occupation requiring mechanical skills. Even television character Murphy Brown's feminist humor acknowledged the handyman. She suggested women get rid of all men in the world except two, one for plumbing and one for electrical work.

Some of the mechanical-skill difference between men and women is due to learning, but more than learning is involved. Psychologist Melissa Hines has studied girls born with adrenal hyperplasia, an adrenal gland disorder that produces high testosterone levels. When given a choice, these high-testosterone girls prefer boys' toys, which are more mechanical than girls' toys.[34] They like transportation and construction toys, including helicopters, cars, fire engines, blocks, and Lincoln Logs, better than dolls, kitchen supplies, toy telephones, and crayons and paper. Hines jokes that it is almost as if there were a gene for liking toy trucks.

The research on adrenal hyperplasia points to personality and cognitive differences between women at the high and low ends of the normal range of testosterone. Not all women have the same interests, abilities, or testosterone levels. There are women who do jobs traditionally held by men and do them well. As more jobs open up, more women will work with heavy equipment and machines. A woman employee, a member of the maintenance crew at a Nucor steel factory, wanted one of those jobs. She was a grandmother, she wore a hard hat, and she wanted to handle the real stuff, the molten steel. She said,

> We all have a dream, right?... I want to be a ladle-crane operator. I want to carry steel from the furnace to the casting machine. I don't know if they'll give me that job. They only want the most experienced people to carry ladles of steel. I'll probably end up on a scrap crane. But to carry a ladle to the caster, that's the dream. That's the dream.[35]

More women will realize such dreams as cultural changes help equalize the work of men and women. Nevertheless, to the extent that testosterone is a factor, men will probably continue to outnumber women in some traditionally male jobs, regardless of cultural changes.

Men appear to like mechanical work more than women do, although women have an advantage over men when it comes to some kinds of mechanical aptitude.[36] Women do especially well at tasks that call for a combination of mechanical aptitude, fine motor skill, and computational ability. Women have better fine motor skill and computational ability than men.[37] An interesting report concerning the effect of hormones on computational skill came from a male-to-female transsexual who was taking estrogen in preparation for a sex-change operation. After she started taking estrogen, her computational skills improved to the point that she no longer needed a calculator to keep track of prices in her shop.[38]

At the atomic weapons center in Los Alamos in 1945, a job came up that called for a combination of mechanical aptitude, fine motor skill, and computational ability. A group of women, many of them wives of atomic scientists, were selected for the job. They sat in a room full of mechanical desktop calculators, working together to solve thousands of equations to predict what would happen during each millisecond of the explosion of an atomic bomb. They were the world's first super-computer. The women were more accurate and faster than men would have been.[39]

Although men have a handicap when it comes to fine hand movements and computational skills, they have the physical strength and frame of mind that makes heavy-duty mechanical work especially attractive. Evidence from research on animals and diverse human populations, ranging from children to adult transsexuals, indicates that testosterone contributes to this frame of mind.

The cognitive style and spatial abilities associated with the masculine frame of mind evolved along with a compatible set of psychological, physical, and behavioral traits that aided our prehistoric hunting and fighting ancestors in their struggle for survival. Those who survived and passed along their genes were strong, dominant, and full of libido.

STRENGTH, DOMINANCE, AND SEX

With all the recent scandals about athletes who enhance strength training with illegal doses of testosteronelike anabolic steroids, it should come as no surprise to anyone that testosterone builds muscle.[40] Track fans also know that testosterone is more helpful to sprinters than to marathon runners. That is because testosterone has its largest effect on the fast-twitch muscle fibers needed for rapid movement and peak performance.

Along with strength and energy, testosterone promotes an interest in sex. While men still sometimes fight over women, many of our evolutionary forebears, whose genes we carry, made a habit of it. Those who evolved with the optimal amount of testosterone had an advantage over other primitive men. They had the focus, motivation, and muscle they needed to win fights and mates. The optimal amount of testosterone is not necessarily the largest amount. Men with too narrow a focus, too much motivation toward fighting, or too much muscle might not notice danger or be agile enough to run from it if need be. While evolution has resulted in increased testosterone levels in males, it has also exerted a moderating effect that holds down extreme levels. The moderating effect may be more important than ever for contemporary men who must compete in a job market that increasingly values education and verbal skill over brute strength.

The optimal level of testosterone helps balance focus with vigilance, motivation with prudence, and muscle with agility. Thoughts trigger glands to release testosterone, which further activates the brain and triggers new thoughts. The mind gives form to the behavioral effects of testosterone on the brain. In *Genes, Mind, and Culture,* the sociobiologist Edward Wilson describes the mind as a link between biology and culture.[41] Biology gives a background of vitality to our decisions, but it cannot determine exactly why we act as we do or why we have developed the culture in which we live. Testosterone is part of the link between biological origins and social behavior, but it is our minds that filter our experience and allow us to control our behavior, keeping the peace between biological needs and daily experience.

Theoretical physicist Michio Kaku said, "Our brains are identical to the ones which emerged from Africa 100,000 years ago. You take a cave man, shave him, give him a 3-piece suit, and put him on Wall St., and he looks like all the other barbarians on Wall St. Our brains haven't changed at all in the last 100,000 years. The only difference is that these cave men now have nuclear weapons."[42] What Kaku said is close enough to the literal truth to warn us that the mind, as Wilson defines it, must be nurtured in order to meet the challenge of adapting the caveman brain to civilization. If the mind prevails, then even in an age of technology and overpopulation it should be possible to channel the energy and focus that comes with testosterone in useful ways.

Fortunately, high-testosterone individuals are influenced by good parenting, education, and the social restraints of civilization. Suzanne Womack, a student of mine who has thought at length about high-testosterone men, might say that for them channeling the energy and focus of testosterone minus its aggression will take some doing on the part of civilizing institutions. She believes high-testosterone men see fighting as "the natural order of things." Many of them enjoy fighting. Fighting is a game for them, but it is also more than a game—it is a way of becoming dominant over others.

"Dominance" is the theme that brings together the masculine qualities associated with testosterone; it is a kind of personal power. Dominant people can influence others because the others admire them or fear them. Dominance includes the way a person stands, walks, and talks; it includes skills, personality, and frame of mind; it includes brute force, violence, and fighting. All these elements are related to testosterone, tending to make higher-testosterone individuals more dominant. Perhaps the most straightforward way of becoming dominant is by fighting.

Fighting is a natural part of life to Mike Roseberry, the construction superintendent who agreed to help with my research. He and I met in a bar to talk about hormones and violence. Fighting comes easily to him, and he thinks about it often. He gets irritated when he remembers hitting someone he should not have hit, or, even worse, not hitting someone he should have. I told Mike I wanted to know how a person's testosterone level would change during a fight. He quickly said, "I'll start a fight for you." I was taken by surprise and said to him, "Oh, no, thanks. I don't want you to have to fight." He said, "I won't fight. I'll make somebody else do it." That sounded remarkable to me, and I asked how he would do it. He said, "It'll be easy. One day when it's raining and we're all off work at a bar, I'll go up to some guy I know having a drink. I'll put my hand on his shoulder and point across the room to someone else and say, 'I heard him say your old lady's a slut.' Then he'll go beat the other guy up." Mike thought it would be easy and fun.

Mike was telling an old story, one extending beyond what construction workers do on a rainy afternoon. He was talking about sex, violence, masculinity, and dominance. Men fight for the same reasons other animals fight, but their fights are also symbolic. Songs and stories, like the movie Casablanca's "fight for love or glory," are full of romantic references to fighting, and men live by those images in war and in barroom brawls.

Not long after that, Mike and a GSU student friend of his went to a party for Carl Sagan. It was 1991, and people at the party were talking about the Persian Gulf war. After the party, Mike told his friend, "Sagan and them was talking like there was something wrong with the war. People been fighting for centuries. Hell, fighting's a lot more natural than being a damn scientist." Mike's simple macho view brings to mind lines from Kipling: "These four greater than all things are, Women and horses and power and war."

The drive toward dominance is so much second nature to high-testosterone men that they, like Mike, are often quite casual about it. Mike would find it easy to start a fight in a bar because there would be plenty of men looking for a fight, men like the workers at the Nucor Steel Company. One such worker, delayed long after midnight in starting a new cast of molten steel, was cheerful when he told his coworkers, "Look at it this way. By the time we get a cast, it'll be morning, and the bars will be open again. So after we cast we can get a drink, and then maybe we can get into a fight." He would like to win, but just having a fight sounded like a good idea.[43]

A construction worker or a steelworker who ignores an insult to his "old lady" seems less of a man to his friends, and maybe to his "old lady," too. Some women, maybe themselves high in testosterone, push men who are slow to take offense. The writer Katherine Dunn knows the appeal of dating bad men and the power that comes from controlling them. She wrote, "When he starts falling down on his badness, you have to test him, goad him. Maybe you have to lean back on the bar and thrust out your Wonderbra and say, 'You gonna let him talk to me like that?' Then you can glow as the hot beast fights for you and proves that his badness is yours to command."[44] With no joy or enthusiasm, and no desire to encourage men to fight, a Cormac McCarthy character voices sad agreement with Dunn's bottom line. Three times a war widow, a grandmother in *The Crossing* advises her granddaughter about men. She says it is unfortunate that women find rash men so appealing, but they do, and it is because women know in their secret hearts that men who won't kill for them are useless.[45] Lady Elaine, who lived in King Arthur's day, opposed men's fighting. She knew many women encouraged men to fight, but she thought it was a bad idea. She said, "Most women want their men to go out and fight for glory. When the men are brought in killed or wounded, the same women feel that life is very hard, and some of them complain it's hardest on women. Silly, I say."[46]

One good reason for women to discourage fighting is to protect themselves. Men mostly attack each other, but they sometimes attack women. Men are most likely to attack women they think have belittled or insulted them, as happens with women who leave them or threaten to leave. The high-testosterone drive for domination can translate into the desire to control a wife or girlfriend, with the result that when a woman leaves a man, she not only insults him, she makes him feel as though he has lost control.

I heard about a young plumber who was upset when his wife filed for divorce. He used a strategy of mixed messages to win her back. Each Friday he sent roses and a love note. Each Sunday, disappointed by her continued rejection, he called up to browbeat and bully her. If he saw her on Sunday, he was likely to be physically abusive. Some men in similar situations resort to killing. An Australian study found that men who killed their mates more often did so when their mates tried to leave them.[47] Even when a high-testosterone man is not violent, his need to dominate can cause problems in a close relationship.

Men who want to control things show up everywhere. An airline flight attendant told me she finds competition among men always close to the surface. She said the airlines do not like to have men sitting together near an emergency exit, because in a crisis they may fight over who is in charge, rather than behaving in an orderly fashion to get out of the airplane. She was speaking of men in general, and I am sure the risk is even greater among high-testosterone men.

Most scientists do not think children have enough testosterone to affect their behavior, but I disagree, and my students and I have studied testosterone and dominance in children.* The drive for dominance, and its link to testosterone, asserts itself early. Before children reach the age of three, groups of boys play differently than groups of girls: boys dominate each other, while girls show give and take.[48] Girls don't like to play with boys, because the boys try to beat them up. Boys don't like to play with girls, because they think girls are "wimps" who won't fight. Girls argue more reasonably than boys; they make their points and listen to each other and say, "Yes, you're right, but let's . . . ," while boys steamroller each other with "No you're not!" "Yes I am!" "No you're not!" "Yes

---

*This work is described in more detail in Chapter 4.

I am!" The boys' words are about as rational as the heated exchanges between Judge Clarence Thomas and members of the Senate judiciary committee during Thomas's Supreme Court confirmation hearings. Boys argue from the principle of sufficient obstinacy, which fills their little heads.

Aggressive behavior is evident in little boys and persists into adulthood, but it is nevertheless subject to cultural influence. In a cross-cultural study of preference for violent versus nonviolent ways of resolving conflicts, Dane Archer and Patricia McDaniel discovered the sex difference in violence to be relative rather than absolute. They found that within each society, young men were more inclined toward violence than young women, but young women in some societies were more violent than young men in others.[49]

Cross-cultural studies and observations of everyday life make it clear that violence is not the invariable outcome of high testosterone levels. More typically, testosterone makes people want to be in charge: drive the car, pick the topic, run the war. Men compete in work and play, using recreational activities to establish dominance. A study of four couples sailing the north coast of Scotland showed high testosterone among men jockeying for dominance. The men were physicians on vacation, and every day they collected blood samples from themselves for later testosterone assay. Unknown to them, the women on the boat were rating them on dominance, on whether they were assertive, aggressive, bossy, and insisted on doing "important" things, like holding the wheel and steering the boat. The results showed more signs of dominance in the high-testosterone men.[50]

Like the doctors on vacation, one of my former student assistants, who is high in testosterone, takes time off from work but not from competition. On weekends, he and his friends travel for miles to find windy hillsides where they can compete with stunt kites. The kites are so big it takes two hands to hold one, and it can drag its owner along with his heels dug into the ground. The men have turned a child's game into a macho sport.

Another macho sport is hunting. While some men still hunt for the same reasons our ancestors did—to provide food for their families—many modern hunters hunt just for sport, a tribute to the legacy of the hunters in their evolutionary family tree. Hunting is consistent with a predatory frame of mind, which includes the will to dominate, single-mindedness, and an ability to disregard discomfort; the spatial skills needed to stalk, chase, kill, and find the way home are its ancient components. As hunters became more civilized, hunting often took on a social patina, with special clothing, fancy equipment, and various rituals with connotations of social status and character, as well as dominance. In England upper-class men and women engage in foxhunting, a sport with an aristocratic lineage, a strict dress code, and lots of protocol.

There are fewer wild animals to hunt today and fewer hunters, but the genes men inherited from their hunter ancestors still affect the way they think. Modern men, even many who never hunt, watch television shows about wild animals. The National Geographic Society has found that its nature films are most popular among young men, and the shows young men like most are those in which a predator chases, catches, and kills its prey. Some men, and now some women, approach business, politics, and sports much as they approach hunting or war. People with predatory instincts compete for glory in these quasi-civilized activities, playing games that produce winners and losers.

This idea that men are predators is a metaphor, but it may help us understand evolutionary pressures that produced one very odd difference between men and women. That difference is a larger brain size in men than in women. Testosterone appears to have given men big heads, literally and figuratively. Men have larger brains in part because they have larger bodies, but even after adjusting for body size, men have larger brains than one would expect.[51] The difference is not great; it amounts to about a hundred grams, or three teaspoons full. Scientists don't know what, if any, difference in intellectual functioning is associated with the difference in brain size.[52] Researchers who studied Einstein's brain reported, "Einstein's brain weight was not different from that of controls, clearly indicating that a large (heavy) brain is not a necessary condition for exceptional intellect."[53] Maybe the geographic and mechanical abilities needed for tracking victims and predicting their movement take up a lot of space.[54] Maybe outwitting a victim takes more brainpower.[55]

Scientists are not even sure that men's larger brains contain more brain cells than women's. Research indicates that cells are more densely packed in women's brains, especially in areas responsible for understanding language.[56] Einstein's brain seems to indicate that being smart might be a matter of the number of cells and not one of total brain size. His brain was of average weight, but had wider parietal lobes, reduced or missing fissures, and an underdeveloped operculum. It contained more glial cells, which stimulate neurons, and more neurons in the cortex.[57] As yet, there have been no studies showing whether or not there is a difference in brain size between high- and low-testosterone men.

Fighting is at the competitive core of dominance, and other features surround this core. Beyond simple thoughts and action, geographic and mechanical skills, and willingness to fight, one thing more is needed. Dominant people need to look and sound dominant. They need panache.

PANACHE: LOOKING THE PART

"Panache" is a word that summarizes qualities of appearance and manner that contribute to getting the attention and respect of others. A person with panache scores points by looking dominant. Bluffing often works just as well as fighting when it comes to getting attention and respect. Male animals bristle, puff, strut, preen, spread their tail feathers, control space, intimidate their opponents, and show off to get their way and impress the opposite sex. Male orangutans use their jaws to threaten more than to bite,[58] and large deer use their antlers to intimidate small deer. In 1576, Turbervile wrote in a hunting book that stags who encounter receptive females

> . . . will rayse their nose up into the ayre, and looke aloft, as though they gave thankes to nature which gave them so great delight. And if it be a great Hart, he will turne his heade, and will looke if there be none other neare to anoy or interrupt him. Then the young deare being not able to abyde them, and seing them make such countenances, will withdraw them selves from them and runne away.[59]

Threat, bluff, and flamboyance are far less costly than fighting. Acting powerful is an easy route to success for people as well as animals. People in primitive societies use body paint, tattoos, scars, headdresses, and ritual postures and dances to signal their importance. Political leaders use oratory and charisma to rally their followers. Testosterone seems to be positively related to putting on a good show. Actors, along with football players, have higher testosterone levels than the other professional groups we have studied so far, as will be described in more detail in Chapter 6.[60]

Sometimes male bluster is hardwired into the brain by early testosterone. Once the pattern is set, it may even survive castration. An acquaintance who raises horses told me about a gelding named Buffet, who was neutered late in life, after testosterone had determined his development. He cannot mate, but he raises his tail, tosses his head, snorts, and paws the ground. He acts so much like the horse in charge that the young colts run away and the mares present themselves to him for mating.

Like Buffet, Cyrano de Bergerac presented an image that is manly and, following Hemingway's definition of courage as "grace under pressure," courageous. Cyrano dueled with panache, with verve and a saber and feathers in his hat, reciting poetry. Men want to look the part, and sometimes their last thoughts on earth are about their appearance. Sekou Sundiata, an African-American poet, tells about his great-great-grandfather Papa John, who was a slave in South Carolina. Papa John had lived on many different plantations because he was so unmanageable that no one wanted to keep him. He was finally lynched, and when asked for any last words he said, "Hand me my mirror, so I can see my hair."[61]

Vanity goes along with high levels of testosterone. I thought of Papa John on a pleasant fall afternoon recently. I was out driving, and I had stopped at a red light behind a couple in a shiny red convertible. The driver, a balding man on the young side of middle age, was lean, muscular, and physically fit. He looked at himself in his rearview mirror and ran his hand back through his thinning hair. When he was satisfied with the way it looked, he turned to the attractive woman beside him and started talking. He had expansive gestures, moving his arms and pointing at things as he talked. When we got to the next stoplight, once again he leaned over to check his hair in the mirror. Showing off is a part of everyday life that I have noticed more and more since I have been studying testosterone.

Men do not have fancy tail feathers, but they are peacocks just the same. My overall impression from the research we have done is that men who are high in testosterone think well of themselves. They see themselves as people of consequence. They don't make little jokes about themselves or put themselves down. They know that being dominant includes thinking, looking, and acting dominant, and their manner displays a sense of confidence, power, and superiority. Tattoos, gold chains, and convertibles are among the accoutrements of looking dominant.

Audie Murphy understood the psychology of dominance. He was the most decorated American soldier in World War II. He later became a professional actor, but he had always been a man with a keen appreciation of the importance of style. He believed in the shock value of behavior. He said,

> If I discovered one valuable thing during my early combat days, it was audacity, which is often mistaken for courage or foolishness. It is neither. Audacity is a tactical weapon. Nine times out of ten it will throw the enemy off-balance and confuse him.[62]

Audie Murphy used audacious physical threats, but audacity can work in the absence of threat. Sometimes unexpected one-upmanship is audacious enough. A friend who once worked for Greenpeace was involved in the 1995 protest over French nuclear testing. He delighted his mother with a story about a female volunteer who bested the French authorities with a grand gesture. They boarded a Greenpeace ship and demanded the keys. She showed the men the keys and then, right under their noses, pitched the keys overboard. All flamboyant behavior carries a kind of audacity. Women can be as flamboyant as men in dress, hairstyle, personal manner, even body art and tattoos. In a high-testosterone delinquent group we studied in Atlanta, both men and women had tattoos, dramatic dress, and a lifestyle that included car wrecks, fights, and trouble with the police.[63]

Panache can be audacious and flamboyant, or it can be more subtle. People can stand out because they have "presence," a quality that suggests physical, moral, or intellectual power. People who have presence convey the force of their personalities immediately and effectively. John Wayne epitomized presence. Cultural critic Garry Wills said, "His body spoke a highly specific language of 'manliness,' of self-reliant authority ... It was a body impervious to outside force, expressing a mind narrow but focused, fixed on the task, impatient with complexity."[64] Recently, students Rebecca Campo, Rebecca Strong, and Rhonda Milun, psychologist Frank Bernieri, and I have studied presence in high- and low-testosterone men and women. We measured testosterone levels in 358 subjects and videotaped them as they participated in a series of experiments. In the experiments, we asked each subject to walk into a room and speak to a person or to a camera. We scored their speed of movement, patterns of gaze, and general demeanor. We found that high-testosterone subjects entered the room less hesitantly, looked around less, and focused more directly on the task before them than low-testosterone subjects did. Overall, high-testosterone subjects seemed more purposeful and confident. They seemed to have more presence.[65]

Panache and presence can turn up almost anywhere. Marian Hargrove, who collected saliva samples from female prison inmates in a study that will be described in Chapter 4, found a striking example in one of the prisoners. Diana (I've used a different name to protect her privacy) was a tall, attractive woman with an alert, confident manner. She stood up straight and looked people directly in the eye. Hargrove said that Diana wasn't overtly aggressive or physically threatening, nor was she "scary looking" like some of the other prisoners. Nevertheless, Diana seemed to get away with ignoring minor prison rules. Hargrove gave Diana a stick of chewing gum to facilitate saliva flow for the experiment. Chewing gum was forbidden in the cell blocks, and Diana knew she was supposed to spit the gum out after she donated her saliva, but she kept it in her mouth. She was quiet about the gum until she left the research room. Then she flaunted it and chewed it in front of the guards. Instead of telling her to spit it out, two guards called the sergeant with whom Hargrove was working. They reported, "Diana's chewing gum." After another similar call, Hargrove asked the sergeant, "Why don't they just ask her to spit it out?" The sergeant replied, "Diana has unseen powers." When the saliva samples were assayed, Diana turned out to be high in testosterone, just as Hargrove had expected.

In or out of jail, strong people—through physical prowess, political skill, ability to inspire, or talent for projecting "unseen powers"—exert strong influence over others. Among people and animals, presence has an element of fearlessness, which contributes to that influence. Animals injected with testosterone show striking changes in behavior.

Mice, as mentioned earlier in this chapter, are less fearful of strange places after they get testosterone injections.[66] Cows injected with testosterone become dominant in their herds. They seem fearless in strange situations and do not hesitate when they enter new pastures, and they show indifference when attacked by other cows.[67]

John Wayne's archetypical American hero persona conveyed fearlessness without audacity or flamboyance. The strong, silent type played so well by Wayne presents an image of dominance in some cultures but not in others. Psychologist Harry Triandis, in his book *Culture and Social Behavior*, explained how opposite masculine styles resulted in a cross-cultural misunderstanding that contributed to the Persian Gulf War.[68] In 1990 Secretary of State James Baker was calm, cool, and blandly unexpressive when he told the Iraqis that the United States would attack Iraq if they did not get out of Kuwait. The Iraqis, who go for exaggeration rather than understatement in masculine displays, did not take Baker seriously. They assumed that if he had meant business, he would have shouted threats, pounded the table, and maybe thrown something.

The strong, silent John Wayne strategy may not work in Iraq, but it comes naturally for many men. There is some indication that high levels of testosterone are associated with blunted feelings, and to the extent this is true, showing no feeling may not always be an act. On the average, men smile less than women, perhaps because men feel less pleasure than women or because they don't want others to think they are trying to be nice. Men underscore their lack of expressiveness with beards, which obscure their smiles.*

Smiling is not just a sign of good feeling. It is polite, disarming, and nonthreatening. It is a strategy that people with less power use more often than people with greater power. The sex difference is part of an ancient pattern in which women maintain community by smiling and men maintain dominance by not smiling. The pattern holds today, in business meetings and social settings. Men not only smile less, but as anyone who watches talk shows on television knows, they are less expressive about their own feelings and less concerned with the feelings of others. Women's unhappiness with silent and unresponsive mates

---

*In Chapter 7, I will describe studies showing that high-testosterone men smile least of all.

has become a cliché of the talk show circuit and was an inspiration for a brief study by a student of mine. She wore a large bandage on one of her fingers for several weeks and kept a record of how people reacted. Women who saw the bandage were sympathetic. Men just wanted to know what had happened.

Men gain credit in each other's eyes for their fearless behavior. Athletes try to intimidate and "psych out" their opponents; it would be interesting to know whether male athletes use this strategy more than females do. Stephen Potter wrote a book, *The Complete Upmanship*, on how to win by making your opponent nervous. His starting axiom was "the first muscle stiffened is the first point gained."[69] Men try to look as if they have everything under control, even when they do not, hoping to solve the problem before anyone learns they are bluffing. They keep driving when lost, refusing to stop and ask directions, looking unperturbed, not straining forward to search for missing street signs, pretending nothing is wrong. One of my students found a good spot to study the behavior of people who were lost. She worked in a building that had an express elevator, which she rode regularly. People unfamiliar with the building would enter the elevator and discover they didn't know how to get to their floor. When this happened to women, they asked her for help. Men seldom asked for help, preferring to go to the wrong place rather than admit they did not know what they were doing. Being lost does not convey toughness and authority.

In the minds of most people, toughness, leadership, and authority have a particular look and sound. Joseph Kennedy understood that. He told his children that it mattered less what they were like than what people thought they were like.[70] Movies and television have intensified the role of dress, voice, and physical appearance in conveying the impression of strength and dominance. In contrast to some of the eccentric-looking and -sounding old-timers in the television news business and the Friday night gangs who get together on PBS, Dan Rather is a good example of the trend. Rather did not become an anchorman just because he knew about current events. His craggy features, authoritative voice, and knowledge of when to wear a red scarf, a trench coat, or a safari shirt helped, too. Although there are exceptions, leaders, like anchormen, need to look the part, and they need to sound right for the part, too.

Low-pitched voices add to the authority of men, women, and other animals. Perhaps a low voice makes a person sound big and strong, because throughout the animal world, deeper vocal sounds are associated with greater size and strength.[71] The pitch of the voice appears to be correlated with testosterone levels. Researchers know that testosterone lowers the voices of developing adolescent males, and we suspect that it lowers the voices of adult men and women according to how much is present. Preliminary findings indicate that surgeons, who have the reputation for being the most macho group among doctors, have lower-pitched voices than internists.[72] There have been studies showing higher testosterone related to lower voice pitch among male opera singers.[73] At Georgia State University, we have studied how testosterone levels are related to differences in voice pitch in both men and women. So far, we have found a correlation between high testosterone and low voice pitch in men, but not in women.[74] We think that further research might reveal conditions under which the correlation would hold for women, too. Endocrinologists have told me that treating female patients with testosterone, especially in larger doses, can result in a temporary drop in voice pitch.

In Pat Conroy's *The Great Santini*, the colonel tells an officer under his command to forget about ever being a real leader, because his voice is too high-pitched.[75] With generally higher-pitched voices than men, women, on average, have to work harder to convey authority with their voices. I know an Army general who was unhappy when a woman became head of the cadets at West Point, because she did not have the "stentorian voice" that would carry on the parade ground.

Like voices, faces convey strength or weakness. Some researchers have suggested that testosterone shapes the faces of men and women differently, and there is a report that men who are higher in testosterone have larger jaws.[76] In another study, researchers asked a group of students to look at pictures from an old West Point yearbook and rate the young men pictured according to how dominant they looked. The ruggedly handsome men, those with strong features and square jaws, were rated high in dominance. They were also more likely to have been cadet leaders and to have achieved higher rank by the time they retired from active duty.[77] Handsomeness helps men in the business world, too, and it helps men more than beauty helps women, because many people believe that attractive women lack intellectual ability.[78] Hollywood's portrayal of "dumb blondes," made famous by Judy Holiday and Marilyn Monroe, reinforced the idea that feminine beauty and brains don't go together. The weathered, craggy look of hard experience does not diminish masculine attractiveness or perceptions of masculine ability. Like a German dueling club member's *Schmiss*, scars can enhance a manly image. I read about an engineer whose face had been disfigured when he was trying to identify a peculiar noise in a piece of heavy machinery. His ear was pressed against it when it exploded. His coworkers viewed his scar as the badge of a hero who has been through it all, survived, and learned the dangers of the world. He became a legend in his company, and the other engineers treated him with great respect. They sought his opinions and his approval.[79]

Being tough, ignoring broken bones and other kinds of pain and discomfort, is a masculine characteristic that spans time and culture. Tom Wolfe described fighter pilots with the "right stuff." They risked their lives routinely and never expressed fear or mentioned danger. One of these, Chuck Yeager, was the first pilot to break the sound barrier, and he did it with two broken ribs. He'd had a horseback riding accident two nights before, and not wanting to be grounded, he kept his injuries secret from his superiors. British colonialists in East Africa admired the Masai, who could walk for miles on a broken leg and show no pain. Some military assignments require routine stoicism, a fact appreciated by General Charles Anderson, former head of the Tennessee National Guard. He manned the tanks of his star military unit with country boys who were used to discomfort. The dirt, grease, and 120-degree heat inside the tanks did not bother them.

While bravery in the face of discomfort and danger is generally associated with masculinity, many women are braver than most men. Women served as nurses on the battlefields of the Crimean War, crossed the North American continent with pushcarts in mid–nineteenth century migrations, and faced armed and violent Alabama state troopers during the civil rights movement of the 1960s. The traits discussed in this chapter are statistically linked to testosterone and to men, but they can be present in individual women. It is important to keep in mind that masculinity and femininity are on a continuum, with more men at the masculine end and more women at the feminine end, but with a great deal of overlap in between.

Part Two
SOCIAL LIFE

4

Ruthless Creatures

HYENAS

Spotted hyenas, who look like unkempt, malevolent dogs, live and hunt on the plains of Africa. They have short hind legs, powerful necks and shoulders, and jaws strong enough to crush the thighbones of zebras. Adults weigh between 147 and 165 pounds, and they are tough enough to compete with lions for food.[1] Male hyenas are dangerous, and females even more so. Female hyenas have higher levels of the adrenal hormone androstenedione than males. (Androstenedione is the hormone St. Louis Cardinal Mark McGwire made famous during the 1998 baseball season.) Adult female hyenas have high levels of testosterone, too, but unless they are pregnant, not so high as adult males. During pregnancy female hyenas have a shortage of the enzyme aromatase, which converts androstenedione into estrogen. Without aromatase, androstenedione is converted into testosterone, and the result is that pregnant females have more testosterone than males.[2]

Female hyenas are exposed to high enough levels of testosterone *in utero* to masculinize them. Females, who are larger than males, have masculinized external genitalia, including penislike clitorides and empty scrotal pouches. The pseudopenis contains the urethra as well as the birth canal, and it becomes erect with excitement when the female hyena greets friends or threatens strangers. In ancient times people thought hyenas were hermaphrodites, having the sexual organs of both male and female, an idea that was later promoted by the writer Ernest Hemingway but is incorrect. Despite their high testosterone levels and masculinity, female hyenas are true females: they have ovaries and no testes, whereas male hyenas have testes and no ovaries.

Hyenas live in groups led by the alpha female—the adult female with the most testosterone. She dominates the other females and shows little respect for males, who are allowed to eat only after she has finished eating. One of her daughters usually grows up to be the next alpha female. Hyena pups are born with open eyes, sharp teeth, and nasty tempers, and in the first few days of life it is common for the dominant pups to kill their same-sex littermates. Frequently one female and one male survive, with the female usually emerging as the dominant member of the pair. Researchers have found that pups were most murderous when competing for a limited supply of milk, usually from an undernourished, low-ranking mother.[3] This high-testosterone version of sibling rivalry kills an estimated 25 percent of all baby hyenas before they are a month old,[4] reducing the number of offspring, holding down the population, giving a surviving female a better chance to be the leader of the pack, and giving a surviving male a greater chance to mate. The first chore of a baby hyena is to do its part for the "survival of the fittest."

VIOLENT MEN AND WOMEN

Although the ratio of testosterone between the sexes is different in people and hyenas, both species have the same kind of testosterone, and it works the same way in both. Testosterone is related to unruly and violent behavior in people as it is in hyenas. Human violence that attracts our attention is often extreme, emerging in war, terrorism, fights with fists and weapons, spouse and child abuse, rape, and murder. These acts are defined as immoral, illegal, justified, or sometimes even heroic, according to where they take place. In one country, spanking a child is a crime, while in another country, terroristic killing is a patriotic act.

The big difference between people and hyenas is not the animal quality of testosterone, but the concepts of crime and morality, which are human inventions. Hyenas do not try to be civilized, but people do. Violent people and hyenas harm others, but violent people are often punished. They may be ostracized by their friends and families or locked up in prison. The result is that most people are fairly well-behaved, following the rules of their particular societies, as long as there is no extended period of social chaos. In times of war, famine, and economic collapse, however, people are not so well-behaved, and when things get bad enough, as they did in Bosnia and Kosovo in the late 1990s, it is hard to find a moral difference between the combatants and the hyenas. While there is no direct tie between testosterone and human criminality, there is an indirect tie: testosterone leads toward violence, and violence is often criminal. There are more than a million men and women in prison in the United States. They have committed crimes ranging from forgery to mass murder, and they vary in intelligence, personality, background, and testosterone level. To understand how testosterone is related to criminal behavior, my students and I have spent years studying differences among prison inmates.

In doing this, we first went to a maximum-security prison that held about fifteen hundred men, eighteen to twenty-two years old. With the blessing of the Department of Corrections and the prison warden, and some uneasiness on our part, we went in and met the inmates. We visited them in dormitories and day rooms. We visited them in individual cells, where we stood on the landing outside and talked through the bars. We told them we wanted to understand what they were like and how testosterone might affect their behavior. We explained that we could measure testosterone in a saliva sample. Most inmates we talked with agreed to participate. For them, the study was a break in a boring daily routine. For us, it was a chance to meet people we would not otherwise meet. Each inmate chewed a stick of gum and spit a teaspoonful of saliva into a plastic vial. In some cases, we had guards and other inmates rate the behavior of inmates. We took the samples back to the laboratory and froze them for later assay. Over a period of six years, we tested more than seven hundred male inmates.[5]

After we had their testosterone scores, we searched prison computer records to see what crimes the inmates had committed and what prison rules they had broken. The inmates had spoken to us nicely enough when we visited, but their records were hair-raising. They had been convicted of crimes ranging from theft to assault, murder, and rape. My students were often surprised to find that a polite and friendly inmate had committed an especially cruel or bloody crime.

We classified each crime as violent or nonviolent. Violent crimes are what the FBI calls personal crimes, where someone is threatened, hurt, or killed. Nonviolent crimes are what the FBI calls property crimes, where something is taken but there are no threats or personal violence. The main violent crimes among our inmates were rape, child molestation, homicide, assault, and robbery. The main nonviolent crimes were burglary, theft, and drug offenses.

We found that testosterone was related to an inmate's crime and to his behavior in prison. Figure 4.1 shows mean testosterone levels among inmates who behaved in different ways. The mark at the top of each column is an error bar, showing the statistical limits within which the results should fall if we repeated the study. We found that inmates who committed violent crimes were higher in testosterone than those who committed nonviolent crimes, and inmates who violated prison rules were higher in testosterone than those who did not violate rules. We also found that the kind of rules violated by high-testosterone inmates involved disruptive and combative behavior, and that these inmates were noticed by others around them. Guards and other inmates called high-testosterone inmates "bo-hogs," a country term meaning tough, and they called low-testosterone inmates "scrubs." It is common for men's prisons to have a pecking order, in which a few inmates at the top control the others,

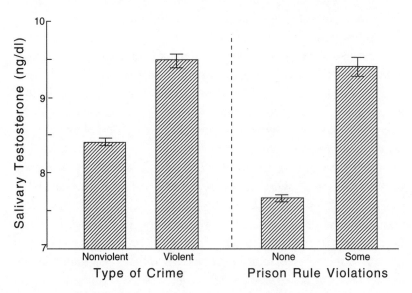

Figure 4.1. Relation of testosterone to crime and to behavior in prison.

and those at the top of the pecking order were higher in testosterone.[6]

Kant said that with men, the normal state of nature is not peace but war,[7] which leaves us wondering what the normal state is with women. Not all men are violent, and not all women are peaceful. One out of twenty prison inmates is a woman, and many women commit violent crimes. Sometimes women who commit violent crimes are provoked and act in self-defense, and sometimes their violence is unprovoked. Testosterone is an equal-opportunity hormone, affecting women the same way it affects men. As mentioned earlier, women have less testosterone, but they are more sensitive to small amounts. My students and I studied 171 women in two prisons.[8] As with the men, we visited the prisons and asked inmates to spit, measured their testosterone, and related it to their crimes and prison behavior.

Working with women was different from working with men. There are no "bo-hogs" in a women's prison. Unlike men, women do not have a pecking order in which a few of the tough ones dominate the rest. They organize into pairs and small groups, where they support each other. Fighting often breaks out because somebody has wronged a friend. Women bring to prison some of the more polite behavior that goes with being female in our society, and that includes not spitting in public. Getting women inmates to spit into a vial took some encouragement on our part.

As with men, testosterone in women was related to misbehavior. Women who committed violent crimes were higher in testosterone than women who committed nonviolent crimes. Women who were more aggressive and dominant in prison, as rated by staff members, were also high in testosterone. The inmates we studied ranged in age from seventeen to sixty years, a wider range than in our male sample. Older women were lower in testosterone than younger women, had committed fewer violent crimes, and were less aggressive and dominant in prison. As women get older, their behavior changes partly because of the lowered testosterone that comes with age and partly because of other psychological and physical effects of aging. Figure 4.2 shows a statistical model of these findings. The striking relation in the figure is that age lowers testosterone, thereby decreasing the biological support for both violence and dominance.

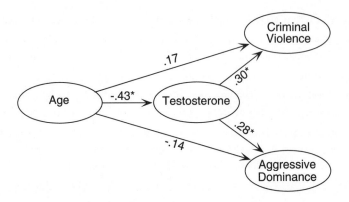

Figure 4.2. Age, testosterone, and behavior in women prison inmates. Age lowers testosterone levels, and in so doing it decreases criminal violence and aggressive dominance associated with testosterone. The direct effects of age that are not mediated by testosterone are negligible. The numbers indicate how much of the standard deviation of the variable following an arrow can be accounted for by the variable preceding the arrow. Minus signs mean that an increase in the first variable leads to a decrease in the second variable. Asterisks indicate statistically significant relationships.

Women sometimes kill men who have abused them, and it is a popular view that women kill mostly in self-defense. If women themselves are victims who kill in self-defense, we might expect their circumstances to be more important than their testosterone levels. However, as we studied women in prison, we found that women murderers were higher in testosterone than other inmates, just as we had found with men. Testosterone alone did not make the women kill, but it apparently helped to mobilize them into action. We have not studied as many women as men, and much remains to be learned about how their testosterone is related to violence.

Classifying a crime as "violent" or "nonviolent" leaves a lot unsaid. The same crime can be committed in more or less violent ways. It may be that how much testosterone people have affects the way they commit the same crime. Marian Hargrove, a student of mine who was once an assistant to the Alabama attorney general, knows quite a bit about murder and mayhem. When she read detailed descriptions of crimes committed by our inmates, she said, "I think when a high-testosterone man kills you, you are *very* dead." High-testosterone killers seemed to do more than necessary to kill their victims, like stabbing them twenty-eight times, or shooting them twice in the front and five times in the back, or killing the victim and then burning the body. Their behavior seemed especially calculated and ruthless.

We have begun to examine parole board records to see whether testosterone is related to the way in which a crime is committed. So far, we have found that higher-testosterone murderers more often know their victims and plan to kill them ahead of time. Looking at the details surrounding various crimes and examining background factors related to those crimes will help us understand more about the relationship between testosterone and crime.

RAMBUNCTIOUS PEOPLE

It is easy to get caught up in the drama and evil of crime. Violent crime attracts our attention. But the fact is, much of the trouble in the world is caused by behavior that is not violent and people who are not criminals. The people to look out for are ordinary people, behaving in legal ways, but unruly and thoughtless in their treatment of others. Not only strangers, but our relatives, neighbors, and associates can injure us, cause us economic hardship, and disrupt our lives in numerous ways. Everybody knows about reckless drivers, careless smokers, and negligent baby-sitters and the problems they cause for themselves and other people. As with criminals, some of the misbehavior of these people is related to testosterone.

I think "rambunctious" is a word that describes nonviolent trouble-makers well. Rambunctious means boisterous and disorderly. It has generally humorous connotations, but the *American Heritage Dictionary* includes a serious meaning, as in the sentence "Jackson's subordinates did not need whiskey to become rambunctious."[9] Many high-testosterone people I have studied are like Jackson's subordinates. Whiskey, of course, would make them worse.

The largest rambunctious group we studied came from the military. Twenty years after the Vietnam war, the Veterans Administration decided to reexamine the Vietnam military experience. It wanted to find out how the war affected soldiers and whether the chemical Agent Orange, which had been used to clear the jungle for fighting, had damaged their health. There were 4,462 men in the study, some who had served in Vietnam and some who had served elsewhere. The men underwent medical examinations, which included testosterone measures, and they answered questions about their military experience, background, family, and work. After the study was completed, the Veterans Administration made the data available to people like me, who wanted to explore other questions. Psychologist Robin Morris and I used this set of data to examine relationships between testosterone and behavior.[10]

We did a "risk ratio" analysis among the veterans, first by dividing the men into two groups. One group included the 10 percent who were highest in testosterone, which we called the high-testosterone group. The other group included everyone else, and we called this the normal-testosterone group. We then computed the likelihood of members of each group engaging in particular activities. We found that high-testosterone men had been more likely to misbehave in school as children, get into trouble with the law as adults, use drugs and alcohol, go AWOL in the Army, and report having ten or more sex partners in one year. Table 4.1 shows what we found. On the right side of the table are risk ratios, which show the relative risk of various behaviors among high- versus normal- testosterone men. For example, a risk ratio of 1.5 would mean that the behavior was one and a half times as likely in high-testosterone men as in normal-testosterone men. The average risk ratio for all of these activities was 2.0.

Table 4.1.

Men's delinquency. Numbers show percent of normal- and high-testosterone men engaging in the different misbehaviors.

| | TESTOSTERONE | | |
	Normal	High	Risk Ratio
Childhood delinquency	12	18	1.5
Adult delinquency	10	23	2.3
Hard drug use	10	25	2.5
Marijuana use	22	48	2.2
Alcohol abuse	12	16	1.3
Military AWOL	6	13	2.2
Many sex partners	23	32	1.8

Soldiers are not the only people who engage in "combat." At any street corner or community gathering there are likely to be a few rough characters, and some of these people belong to what we call the counterculture. They reject the mainstream values of society, and they stand out in dress, manner, hairstyle, body decoration, and behavior. They are different enough to make others feel threatened and uncomfortable.

Terry Banks was an undergraduate honors student who had friends and acquaintances in the counterculture. She wanted to know whether testosterone might explain some of their behavior. We compared twenty-nine delinquent acquaintances of hers (sixteen men and thirteen women) with thirty-six college students of similar age. All the delinquents used drugs and listened to grunge music, and some were former skinheads; several of the men were musicians, and several of the women were strippers. Everyone in the group had a strong dislike for authority, which made them likely to encounter problems with the police. Nineteen of the twenty-nine had body art, tattoos, or piercings other than for earrings. Twenty-four had used a weapon on someone, twenty-five had been in fights in the last year, twelve had been arrested, and four had served prison time. Two had killed someone, and a third had shot someone and thought he might have killed him, but had not stayed around long enough to see whether the person had died. We analyzed spit samples from these people and found that the delinquent group, including both men and women, was higher in testosterone than the college student group. Banks took photographs of all her subjects. Their expressions were friendly—after all, she was their friend—but along with their smiles came skull, snake, and dagger tattoos, striking hairstyles, and flamboyant attire, including Ted Bundy T-shirts.[11]

Trying to find people who were a little tamer than Banks's friends, but still rambunctious, we examined college fraternities.[12] A popular image of fraternities includes young men partying, drinking, smoking, and chasing women. Usually the image does not include young men studying, but fraternities are a mixed bunch and a good place to get testosterone scores from groups that show a wide range of behavior. Two of my student assistants, Marian Hargrove and Colleen Heusel, collected saliva samples from twelve fraternities on two southeastern university campuses. Hargrove collected samples at one university, and Heusel collected at the other. One or the other visited each fraternity just before noon, when members were gathering for lunch. The researcher waved a handful of cash, asked to see someone in charge, and explained that she would pay $75 for saliva samples from a group of twenty members. When the members heard this, volunteers gathered quickly. A leader in one fraternity listened to what my assistant had to say and then shouted out, "Hey, guys, want to spit for a keg?!" We measured testosterone in the saliva samples and related it to other characteristics of the fraternities.

Fraternities with lower mean testosterone levels had a calm and polite atmosphere, responded quickly to the visitor, made her feel at home, and considered the legitimacy of her request. The president of one asked the researcher for a telephone number he could call for official verification of what she had told him. On the other hand, the fraternities with higher average testosterone levels were rambunctious. They had more chaotic surroundings, were less gracious toward the visitor, left her standing alone, and were interested in getting the money, not in discussing the experiment. One high-testosterone fraternity had wrecked furniture in the living room, and the housemother volunteered that "the house is only standing because it's made of concrete and steel." Members at another "animal house" were crude, rude, and half dressed, and after her visit there, the researcher wrote, "I felt like I was being thrown to the lions." Not all the high-testosterone fraternities were so extreme, but there were consistent differences in manners and friendliness between the high and low groups at both universities. When we examined yearbook and chapter room photographs of the members, we found twice as many smiling in the lowest- as in the highest-testosterone fraternities. At one of the universities, the higher-testosterone fraternities had more parties, worse grades, and fewer community service activities.

Results from the fraternities suggest that testosterone does not work quite the same way in groups as it does in individuals. In the fraternities, small differences in testosterone seemed to produce large differences in behavior, and there may be something special about how the testosterone adds up among members of a group. The total group effect of testosterone may be more than the sum of the effects in all the individuals separately. This could happen as individual members talk with each other, reinforce each other's ideas, and bring out behavior from each other that would not appear under other conditions. A high-testosterone fraternity man could be more rambunctious when he is with a high-testosterone friend than when he is visiting his grandparents.

The "fraternity" effect may hold true for other young male animals. Animal-behavior experts suspect that rambunctious elephant fraternities resulted from a South African wildlife management program. Culling operations in Kruger National Park made orphans of many young elephants. Beginning in 1978, game wardens moved about fifteen hundred of these orphans, including six hundred males, to parks and private reserves to establish elephant populations. Elephants in the wild live in tight-knit mixed-age groups, but these relocated young elephants had to live without guidance from responsible adults. In natural herds, older elephants teach younger ones how they are supposed to behave, and older bulls have the particular responsibility for keeping young males under control during musth, when their testosterone levels peak. Some of the relocated young males began to go into musth at age twenty, instead of the normal age thirty, and they stayed in musth for as long as three months, instead of the normal few days. Without adult supervision, they started getting into trouble. One of the things they did was kill white rhinos, apparently for sport. Further endangering an already endangered species was not what the wildlife managers wanted, and they quickly made plans to bring some adult elephants, including a few forty-year-old bulls, into the new herds. Kruger Park has quit culling older elephants and now relocates elephants in family groups.[13]

Young animals, including young human animals, tend to be more rambunctious than old ones. In general, the young have higher levels of testosterone than their elders, and testosterone may also affect younger people more because they have had fewer years to become civilized and to learn self-control. Many of the inmates in our prison studies were in their teens, and one of the most violent rapists was only fourteen years old. Fortunately, his was an exceptional case. Many juvenile delinquents are convicted of status offenses, such as running away from home, skipping school, smoking cigarettes, getting drunk, or having sex.[14] These are called status offenses because they are offenses only when committed by minors, who do not yet have adult status. In children and adolescents, testosterone is related particularly to status offenses and to aggressive reactions to provocation and restriction.[15]

Even small children can be rambunctious and badly behaved, sometimes without any apparent provocation. Everyone who has been around children knows that some children are harder to handle than others, and that a few are almost impossible to manage. People who have not spent much time with children sometimes blame parents entirely for their children's misbehavior. It is true that not all parents are good parents, but it is also true that some good parents have to work a whole lot harder than other good parents. Research indicates that hormones probably play a part in making it easy or difficult to raise a particular child. If hormones are related to adults' behavior, it should not be surprising to find that they are also related to children's behavior.

Children do not have much testosterone, but they have enough to measure. Studies of grade-school children show that those with higher levels of testosterone have more learning disabilities and behavior problems.[16] The effect may appear even earlier. In an exploratory study, I found that the highest-testosterone child in a day care center was a little girl whom her teachers described as likely to "hit for no reason." We are continuing to examine testosterone levels of young children in day care centers and also of children in the same family. Two of our early subjects, aged two and four, were the sons of one of my students, who told me that the younger one behaved much worse than the older one. We assayed saliva samples and found that the younger one was, as his father had suspected, higher in testosterone.

In two other studies concerning testosterone and behavior in children, we found similar patterns. One study compared five- to eleven-year-olds from a psychiatric group of boys having disruptive behavior disorders with a control group of boys,[17] and the other study focused on normal boys and girls ranging in age from three to twelve.[18] The first study suggested that testosterone may be a useful biological marker for children at risk for disruptive behavior disorders. Among older boys, testosterone levels were higher in the psychiatric group than in the normal group. Testosterone was associated with withdrawal and aggression, especially among older boys, and low social involvement in activities, especially among younger boys. We found it interesting that the more intelligent boys seemed less adversely affected by high testosterone levels than the less intelligent ones. The second study indicated that high testosterone is associated with moodiness and low levels of attachment in normal boys and girls. It also indicated that testosterone is related to independent and unsociable behavior in very young children, and that this relation is reduced by the approach and onset of adolescence.

Every person has his or her own natural average level of testosterone. Some people increase their levels by taking testosterone or steroids, which include testosterone, to make themselves stronger, more athletic, or better looking. Testosterone is a Class III controlled substance in the United States, illegal to get without a prescription. Women may wonder why the government has not declared men, who are loaded up with natural testosterone, controlled substances, too. Nevertheless, the only people whose hormones get much public attention are athletes and bodybuilders who use steroids. The behavior of most of these people does not change much, as indicated by a number of studies.[19] However, steroid users sometimes do experience uncontrollable rage, which the press calls "'roid rage." One of my students, who was naturally high in testosterone and took additional steroids to increase his strength, said it was hard for him to control his anger when someone cut him off in traffic. He had an inherent tendency to react impulsively, and steroids magnified the tendency. I heard a similar story from an older woman whose hormone-replacement therapy included a small dose of testosterone. She said, "I felt really good unless someone tried to give me a hard time about something. Then I could feel my face getting hot and my vocal cords would tighten up so that I couldn't yell. That would make me even madder. After a couple of times, I wondered if the problem was my hormones. I cut the dose in half and everything was fine. Now I understand men a little better."

WINNING AND LOSING

What I know about testosterone and violence and rambunctious behavior leads me to believe that the testosterone comes first, and rambunctious behavior follows. The situation is less clear-cut with winning and losing. When I tell people about my work, often the first thing they say is, "Isn't it like the chicken and the egg? How do you know which comes first? Does testosterone make you fight, or does fighting make you have more testosterone?" The short answer is that testosterone comes first. We inherit our testosterone level, just as we inherit our height, body build, eye color, cholesterol level, and other characteristics. Testosterone is part of the body, the physical background out of which we think and act.

But there is also a longer answer, which is that the effect goes both ways. Each of us has an average testosterone level, which remains about the same over the long term, but like our blood pressure, it is subject to short-term fluctuations that follow our physical and emotional ups and downs. Testosterone appears to be most sensitive to success and failure in dealing with other people, which is consistent with the fact that it evolved out of struggles for dominance among our ancestors.

Researchers have learned a great deal about testosterone changes in people in recent years, although animal studies began around 1960. In early experiments with rats and mice, scientists found that male aggression was related to testosterone and could be reduced by castration. This work was extended to monkeys, where it was found that testosterone led to success in fighting, and that success in fighting led to increases in testosterone. As I learned from psychologist Irwin Bernstein at the Yerkes field station, when two male monkeys fight, testosterone rises in the winner and drops in the loser.[20] It is not clear why this happens, but it probably helps get the animal into the frame of mind to pick the right opponent for his next fight. When he has won, he should know he is in a good position to fight someone as strong or even stronger next time. When he has lost, he should lower his expectations and fight a weaker monkey next time. Testosterone in some female animals is also related to fighting,[21] but there has been no research on testosterone changes associated with winning and losing in females.

Strong competition, where much is at stake, can change the body, and in many animals the change is dramatic. Among cichlid fish in Lake Tanganyika in Africa, males who defeat their competitors produce a bright coat, more brain cells, and more testosterone and sperm. Males who are defeated become submissive. Their coat becomes drab, their brain shrinks, their testicles wither, and they swim away into ignominy.[22] When male snakes fight, the outcome affects them greatly. Male rattlesnakes fight by rearing up, entwining their necks, and forcing their opponents to the ground, in a kind of disembodied arm wrestling.[23] The loser avoids further fighting, slinks away, and hesitates to approach females and mate. The snake's cortisol level rises sharply after he loses, which probably reduces the testosterone level, though too few people study testosterone in snakes for us to know for certain what happens.

Winning and losing also affects human testosterone levels. Going to prison is one kind of losing. In one of our prison studies, we took saliva samples from thirty young inmates who were serving three-month sentences in a program modeled on military boot camp. We measured their testosterone when they entered prison and at the end of each month.[24] Their testosterone dropped to a low after one month and gradually increased back to the initial level. The drop may have occurred the first day, when inmates' heads were shaved, their clothes were taken away from them, and the guards shouted into their faces and called them scum. The experience is in ways more humiliating than losing a fight, and inmates often break down and cry. Similar changes in testosterone occurs among the young lieutenants in the Army's basic officer training course.[25] Strictly speaking, basic training is not prison, but it has much in common with the prison boot camp program, and it has similar effects on testosterone.

I think testosterone probably increases when inmates are released from prison, though I have been unwilling to approach newly released criminals on the street and ask them to spit. I found some relevant data, however, without taking any personal risks. When the American hostages were released in 1980 after spending a year and a half as prisoners in Iran, testosterone measures were part of medical examinations for the men. Their measures during the first three days of freedom dropped from high to medium, suggesting that their testosterone levels had peaked around the time of their release and were returning to more normal levels.[26]

Human sports contests are like animal fights, in that one person wins and the other loses. The feelings around these contests are strong—the victory is sweet and the loss is bitter—and testosterone may be behind these feelings. Tennis players increase in testosterone when they win a tournament and drop when they lose; they also increase in testosterone just before a match, as if in preparation.[27] Even in an intellectual game like chess, testosterone levels drop when players lose.[28] On the other hand, the psychological boost of winning at chess can raise testosterone levels. The chess findings make it clear that mental as well as physical aspects of winning and losing influence hormonal changes. There is a great deal more to be learned about the effects of victory and defeat on testosterone. I would like to have data on boxing, which may be the modern sporting equivalent to the age-old one-on-one battle for dominance.

The pattern of changing testosterone, rising with anger and dropping with defeat, leads to questions about how testosterone helps people when they fight. Testosterone is related not only to strength and energy but also to concentration and confidence, both important psychological factors when it comes to winning fights. Someone going into a fight should have body, mind, and emotions working together and be confident, as were Henry V before the battle of Agincourt and Patton before his North Africa tank battles in World War II. Confidence has the double effect of rallying supporters and rattling opponents. When Steven Potter said, "The first muscle tensed is the first point gained," he was talking about making an opponent feel nervous and off balance. Men who abuse their wives often show a decline in heart rate when an argument starts, a sign they are absorbing information and calculating what to do next.[29] Testosterone may help wife abusers, just as it helps heroic soldiers, concentrate on the goal at hand. By thinking only about what he wants and not about what his wife wants, the abuser avoids the trap of "playing the other person's ball game."

Just watching a contest is often enough to affect one's testosterone level. Fans in the audience get excited, and when their team wins they bask in reflected glory and say, "We won, we're great!" When a team loses, the fans get angry and depressed and say, "They lost. They made us look bad, the bums!" If fans identify with the players, their testosterone should change just as it changes in the players. We tested this idea by collecting saliva samples from fans before and after sports events.[30] We found that at basketball games testosterone levels did change in fans from before to after the game, especially when fans identified strongly with the players.

The biggest effect we saw of this kind was around the final game of the World Cup soccer tournament in 1994. Brazil and Italy were tied. Two of my students, Candice Lutter and Julie Fielden, went to sports bars in Atlanta where soccer fans gathered. Lutter went to a bar frequented by Italians and Fielden went to a bar frequented by Brazilians. They recruited twelve Brazilian men and nine Italian men to provide saliva samples before and after the game. Brazil won the game with a penalty kick at the last possible moment. The Brazilian fans were ecstatic, and the newspaper the next day showed pictures of them being arrested for rioting on Peachtree Street, Atlanta's "Main Street." The Italian fans were devastated. One of them had injured his throat cheering, and there was blood in his saliva sample. He said to Lutter, in his Italian accent, "Saliva Girl, it is my heart that is bleeding." Although only men were in the study, there were a few Brazilian women at the Italian bar, and after the game, they were quite rowdy. They found Lutter's group of Italian men and taunted them with insults. When we assayed the samples, we found that eleven of the twelve Brazilian men had increased testosterone levels after the game, and all nine Italian men had decreased levels. These changes are shown in Figure 4.3.

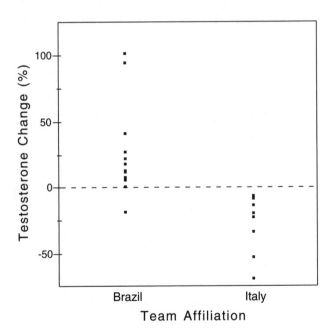

Figure 4.3. Changes in testosterone levels among Brazilian and Italian fans around the final match of the 1994 World Cup of soccer. The Brazilian team defeated the Italian team, and within minutes testosterone levels had increased among Brazilian fans and decreased among Italian fans.

The results of the study did not surprise our son, Alan, at all. Alan's work, which involves calculating the economic benefits of environmental conservation, takes him to South America frequently, and in 1994, he was living in Rio de Janeiro. He got a close-up look at World Cup fever, so much so that on the day Brazil played the United States, he and an American friend left their neighborhood and watched the game in a bar where nobody knew them. When another customer asked where they were from, they said, "Canada." Despite the dangerous edge of the high emotions surrounding the games, Alan was optimistic about the effect that winning would have on Brazil's economy.

At the time of the World Cup, Brazil was in the midst of currency reform. Inflation was so bad that people spent their money on payday, because just a few days later it would buy only half as much. The buzz around Rio was that if Brazil won the World Cup, the new currency would be successful. Sure enough, Brazil won and the new currency virtually eliminated inflation. Of course, the World Cup victory alone did not cure Brazil's economic woes, but it did spark a nationwide can-do spirit. Good political and economic leadership worked together with post–World Cup optimism to turn the economy around.

Testosterone changes may have other effects on fans. Wife abuse has been reported to increase in the Washington, D.C., area after the Redskins win their football games.[31] If testosterone increases in the male fans, and they have arguments with their mates, the increased testosterone could lead to increased violence. While we would expect fans of a winning team to be in good spirits and be easy to get along with, that isn't always the case. Good spirits plus testosterone can equal rambunctiousness and sometimes violence.

Winning and losing in small ways is a part of everyday life. In writing this book, I had spent about a month working on one of the chapters. I thought it was pretty good, and I asked Mary for her opinion. She read the chapter carefully, fidgeted a bit, and said it needed more work. She was polite about it, but I could tell she thought I should wad the chapter up and make it into a ball for our dog, Bogart. Mary had been right in her judgment before, so I could not just dismiss what she said. She made her comments in the evening, and by the next morning I still had not quite recovered. I was depressed. I went to work and collected a saliva sample from myself. By the second day things looked better. I was more optimistic, and I felt I might succeed after all. I went to work and collected another saliva sample. We assayed the two samples and found my testosterone level to be about 30 percent higher on the second day than on the first. My testosterone was lower when I was depressed and higher when I was optimistic.

Sometimes we lose in big ways, defeated not in a game but in real life. People can be kidnapped, drafted into military service, thrown into jail, or captured by a foreign power. Disaster is not always so dramatic. It can strike at home or at work. A physician acquaintance told me that when large numbers of men lost their jobs in the Northwest during aircraft industry layoffs, there were widespread reports of increased cases of impotence. This was likely related to lowered testosterone levels. It would be interesting to know if the reverse was true when the Saturn automotive plant opened in Spring Hill, Tennessee, making many new jobs available. It is possible that major events, like the German invasion of France at the beginning of World War II or the Allied liberation at the end of the war, might affect the testosterone levels of whole nations.

Suicide is the ultimate defeat. People committing suicide may be trying to take charge of their lives, seizing control of their fate and ending an unhappy state, but they have also failed at finding a satisfactory way to live. Would their testosterone increase because they have finally taken charge, or would it decrease because they have failed at living? We measured testosterone in a small sample of patients hospitalized after having made suicide attempts, and we compared them with patients admitted for other reasons. We found that those who had attempted suicide were low in testosterone. We do not know whether the suicide attempters had been low in testosterone for a long time, or how they might be different from people who were successful in committing suicide. These findings suggest, however, that suicide is in some way related to testosterone, and thus presumably to dominance, success, and failure.

HYENA VALUES AND HUMAN VALUES

We began this chapter with hyenas. Hyenas are not civilized. They have simple values, closely tied to life, survival, and hormones. Their values of the day are what their hormones "want." Human values are different.

Human values are guided by human history and experience. They come from our parents, friends, schools, clubs, and religious organizations, and experiences of everyday life. They develop and change from generation to generation. Testosterone is well suited to helping one person become dominant over others, using fighting and violence when necessary. But because of other values, the violence that testosterone would produce in a hyena or other animal is restrained in a person. Human values exist separately from hormones, and they temper the effects of hormones. With good manners and nonviolent moral values, people can control testosterone, though testosterone is always there to be reckoned with.

5

Love and Sex

LOVE, MAGIC, AND MOLECULES

After reading about violence in Chapter 4, it may be hard to believe that testosterone has anything to do with love, but it does. This chapter is about testosterone and other molecular conjurers that dally with the magic of love and sex.

Cindy* understands the molecules and appreciates the magic. She is a lover, and although she has recently settled down to a monogamous relationship, she is what my mother-in-law would have called "a man's woman." That means that Cindy is comfortable with men and enjoys their company, and they enjoy hers.

Cindy was a student at Georgia State University several years ago and was involved in some of the research reported in this book. Like most of the students who work in our lab, she had a sample of her own saliva assayed. Her testosterone turned out to be so high that I asked her to provide saliva we could use as our high female control, which we include in all assays. Cindy is no longer at GSU, but her saliva is.

Cindy came from a rambunctious family. Her mother's father was a Los Angeles policeman, and her father's mother was an armed robber who wore boots and a cowboy hat, drove a hot pink Chevy truck, and served three sentences in Texas prisons. With cops and robbers in her family tree, it is not surprising that Cindy is a high-testosterone woman. What might surprise a lot of people is that she is attractive in a feminine way.

---

*Cindy is a real woman, but Cindy is not her real name.

Growing up, Cindy was a tomboy, and as a young adult she liked to hang out with guys staying up late, shooting pool, listening to old favorites from the Grateful Dead, and drinking tequila. She amazed all her friends with how much tequila she could drink and remain standing. She amazed her women friends because so many of the guys she hung out with fell in love with her.

Not everybody is as comfortable as Cindy with the symbiotic relationship that chemical molecules have with magic. Most people believe in the magic of love, but many of them don't want to talk about the molecules, preferring to think of love in more romantic terms. Some people are offended by any scientific prodding into the psychology or biology of love. Senator William Proxmire once denounced two of my colleagues for looking at love scientifically, saying that love was a mystery, not a science, and he wanted it to stay that way. My colleagues agreed that love was a mystery, but they thought the senator should welcome all the help he could get in solving the mystery, given his own problems with divorce.

Oberon, the king of the fairies in Shakespeare's *A Midsummer Night's Dream,* had a view of love different from Senator Proxmire's. Oberon thought that love was fair game for scientific experimentation and practical jokes. Once, after a spat with Titania, the queen of the fairies, he used her as an experimental subject and the butt of a practical joke in a project that wouldn't get past a human-subjects ethics committee today. While Titania was sleeping, Oberon squeezed the juice of a cupid's flower, nowadays more often called a Johnny-jump-up, onto her eyelids, and said to her, "What thou seest when thou dost wake, Do it for thy true-love take...." What she saw when she woke up was Bottom, a man with a donkey's head, and until the spell wore off she was madly in love with him. Shakespeare didn't mention the cupid's flower's active ingredient, but I suspect it might have been something like the phytotestosterone found in cotton.

Even though Titania thought Bottom was a beautiful donkey, he was a man, albeit of a different species from herself. In that respect, their love affair was oddly like one that took place on our farm when I was a child. We had a steer who fell in love with the mule named Belle. Belle would stand patiently while the steer tried to mate with her. This was doubly remarkable because a steer is a castrated bull, who should have no interest in sex, and a mule is the sterile offspring of a donkey and a mare. Oberon might have had something to do with their love affair, but more likely it was Mother Nature's doing. She has many devices, including erotic memories and the time-delayed effects of prenatal testosterone, to keep her creatures from losing interest in love and sex, which are too important to entrust entirely to hormones of the moment.

The world conspires to make us fall in love. Attractive partners, sweet memories, and tender feelings are part of the conspiracy, as are romantic settings. When it comes to romance and men between the ages of eighteen and forty, it appears that the setting is most effective if it goes beyond meandering streams and wildflowers to include something scary. Researchers went to Vancouver, Canada, to study love and fear on the Capilano Suspension Bridge.[1] This is a long pedestrian bridge that swings gently high above a deep canyon in a spectacular natural setting. Mary and I walked across it in 1992, and we can attest to the fact that the scenery, height, and uncertain footing make the experience both exhilarating and unnerving.

In the Capilano study, an attractive female graduate student stood in the middle of the bridge and asked men who were walking alone to help her with a research project concerning creativity in beautiful places. If they agreed to participate, she asked them to write brief stories about pictures she showed them. She also gave each man a slip of paper with what he thought was her first name and telephone number on it and told him to call her if he had questions about the research project. She did the same thing on a low, sturdy bridge nearby in a scenic wooded area. The men on the swinging bridge put more romance in their stories than the men on the low bridge did, and of the twenty men she interviewed on the swinging bridge, eighteen called the number she gave them. Only two out of twenty from the other bridge called. Another graduate student took all the calls and answered questions. The swinging bridge men's interest in the interviewer, along with the romantic content of their stories, indicated that being on the Capilano Suspension Bridge put them "in the mood for love."

People involved in dangerous or challenging activities are likely to experience psychological and physical arousal, which may be related to a temporary testosterone increase,* along with other chemical changes that prepare the body for action. Generalized arousal produces a state of emotional readiness to feel a variety of emotions, including love. Psychologists say the emotions people feel when they are primed by arousal are a product of "excitation transfer."[2] Our son, Alan, gave us a good example of excitation transfer. He told us about a couple he knows who married soon after falling in love at first sight atop Mt. Kilimanjaro. All the factors at work on the Capilano Suspension Bridge would have been at work there, but more so, and there would be the giddiness that comes with breathing thin air. It's likely a little extra testosterone would be part of the mix. If mountain climbers react to success as other athletes do, Alan's friends would have summited Kilimanjaro with victory testosterone in their blood.

Along with excitation transfer, the magic of love includes imagination, memory, thoughts of the future, and biological sleight of hand. Biology can be potent magic. Like testosterone, oxytocin, vasopressin, and other hormones we don't know so much about appear at unexpected moments to cast spells on lovers, using fakery and delight to transport them to another world. Lovers don't notice the hormones, just their effects. This magic works even on the smallest animals. A shot of the hormone oxytocin is as good as cupid's-flower eye drops to the mouse-like female prairie vole. She is immediately attracted to any little male vole she is looking at when she gets her injection. The oxytocin focuses her attention on him and sends her a message that he is the most masculine of voles. There is a similar love potion for male prairie voles; for them it is the hormone vasopressin.[3]

It's hard to tell if prairie voles have tender feelings when they mate, but in the case of people, love and sex usually go together, though not always. Prostitutes and their patrons have sex without love, and medieval knights in fourteenth-century France gloried in romantic love without sex. Puppy love is another kind of love without sex. We usually treat the romantic feelings that children have about girlfriends and

---

*Temporary testosterone increases among chess players and athletes have been discussed in Chapter 4, and temporary testosterone increases among firemen will be discussed in Chapter 8.

boyfriends lightly, but puppy love can be intense. When psychologist Elaine Hatfield asked a little girl about a boy she might like to marry, the girl burst into tears and cried, "I will never see Todd again."[4] She was only five years old, and she had known Todd at the preschool she once attended. He was gone now, and her parents had no idea of the depth of her feeling. Love can reach anyone at any age, but testosterone reaches its highest levels in late adolescence and early adulthood. That is when people are especially preoccupied with sex and likely to fall in love, and that is when we encourage people to fall in love and marry.

BETTER THAN MONKEY GLANDS

Joseph Mitchell wrote a *New Yorker* story about sexual potency attributed to eating terrapin, which was said to be "better than monkey glands."[5] People have long tried to gain animal powers by eating or injecting animal parts. In the 1920s, before doctors learned about tissue rejection, men had surgical implants of testicles or parts of testicles from executed prisoners, monkeys, goats, or other animals.[6] The operations remained in vogue until the apparent efficacy of the implants was revealed to be a powerful placebo effect. The Irish poet William Butler Yeats, famous for such lines as "O that I were young again," had an operation in 1934, designed to increase blood flow to his testicles, and he wrote of "lust and rage" surrounding him in his last years.[7] Some men think eating rhinoceros horn will make them potent. Eating rhinoceros testicle would seem to be a better bet, but no one recommends that. Many men would sacrifice the last rhinoceros on earth on the outside possibility that it might help. Others, who believe more in modern technology than folklore, provide a ready market for potency aids that are easier on endangered species.

However they try to do it, with powdered animal parts, Viagra, or high-tech pumps and splints, many men think that prolonging the sexual energy of youth into old age is important enough to warrant extreme measures. The libido that comes with puberty is very much related to testosterone, and testosterone injections can reduce the normal drop in libido that comes with age.[8] There is some risk associated with using injections to raise testosterone to above-average levels; for instance, prostate cancer is common among older men and is related to high levels of testosterone. Fortunately, high levels are not necessary for men to enjoy love and sex.

Doctors sometimes prescribe testosterone to increase energy and sexual activity. The effect is clear, though we do not know exactly how much effect there is for a given dose of testosterone. One patient told me about how he felt before and after he started taking testosterone. He was married, and before testosterone therapy he had sex about once a year. He was miserable, and his wife was too. After taking testosterone he had sex every week or two and was very happy. Marriage is more than sex, but a lack of sex usually brings home its importance. The man I spoke with started off low in testosterone, and an increase in testosterone might not have the same effect in a person whose level is average or high.

The testosterone levels of both members of a couple are important. A couple's decision about sex is not made by one person alone; it involves both people, and the likelihood of sex depends on both. We know more about testosterone in men partly because studying testosterone in women is more complicated than studying it in men. Women's testosterone levels change during their menstrual cycles, peaking around ovulation, which makes controlling for the time of month desirable when comparing testosterone levels among women.[9] Another reason we know more about testosterone in men is that it is called a male hormone and researchers are more likely to think of it when they are studying men. Nevertheless, women's testosterone is just as important— and sometimes more so. One study found that the sexual activity of a married couple could be predicted from the testosterone level of the female in the couple. In the study, forty-three couples charted their sexual activity over a three-month period, and researchers measured the wives' midcycle serum testosterone levels. The researchers found a strong statistical relationship (a correlation of $r = 0.62$) between the testosterone measures taken the day before ovulation and the frequency of intercourse over the three-month period. While higher-testosterone women did initiate sexual activity somewhat more often than did lower-testosterone women, researchers attributed most of the difference in frequency to the high-testosterone women's receptivity to their husband's advances.[10]

Testosterone is related to sexual activity, but the relationship is not a perfect straight line. Men within the normal range of testosterone, including those with low-normal levels, usually have satisfactory sex lives, as do many men whose testosterone levels fall below the normal range.[11] Nevertheless, above-average levels of testosterone are generally correlated with above-average levels of sexual activity. I found that among the military veterans described in Chapter 4, those high in testosterone more often answered "Yes" to the question "Have you ever had more than ten sex partners in one year?" The relationship holds true for women as well as men. High-testosterone women have sex more often than do low-testosterone women, and they have sex with more different people.[12] This finding comes from a group of college students, and we think it applies to other women as well. For men and women who are high in testosterone, immoderation and variety are the spice of life. Low-testosterone people have sex less often, and with fewer different partners.

There have been proposals to use Depo-Provera, a synthetic form of the female hormone progesterone, to take away the testosterone of rapists, in what is called "chemical castration." European studies have shown that castration reduces crime, but these studies involved criminals who volunteered to be castrated, which makes them quite unusual.[13] Ordinary prisoners might not show the same effect, but the topic is occasionally debated in state legislatures. When chemical castration works, it may do so by decreasing the general violence of an inmate more than by decreasing his interest in sex. In general, psychologists believe that rape has more to do with violence than with sex, although this view has come into question recently.[14]

People find creative ways to use the finding that lowering testosterone will lower sexual activity. An endocrinologist told me about a gay male couple in which both partners wanted their testosterone lowered so they would be less tempted to have sex with other men. Their request appeared to be within the limits of ethical medical practice, and their endocrinologist prescribed Depo-Provera. The men are now happy and content in their monogamous gay relationship.

What works with men also works with women; testosterone increases libido in both sexes. Testosterone as well as estrogen decreases in women after menopause, and a number of studies show that when a little testosterone is included in hormone replacement therapy, it increases positive mood and frequency of intercourse in postmeno-pausal women.[15] A little is enough because women's bodies are sensitive to low doses of testosterone. I know women who take testosterone pills every day and swear by them.

These findings make it sound as if the effect goes only one way, with more testosterone producing more sex. Things are more complicated than that: Testosterone increases sex, and sex increases testosterone. Studies with male mice, rats, rabbits, and a bull named Jambo show that even the anticipation of sex increases testosterone. In a study of mice, the presence of a strange female caused the greatest increase in testos-terone. In one famous study, a man who lived and worked alone in a lighthouse on an island shaved twice every day with an electric razor and weighed the trimmings from his beard.[16] Every Friday he left the lighthouse and spent the weekend with his girlfriend. The trimmings from his razor showed that his beard grew more on Fridays, suggesting that his testosterone level was higher then. Anticipating romantic moments with his girlfriend affected his body, increased his testos-terone, and put him in the mood for love.

Suzanne Bell and I studied the "lighthouse" effect further.[17] She asked four couples to collect saliva samples after dinner and again around midnight every day for a week, and she asked the couples to indi-cate whether or not they had sex each evening. We found that salivary testosterone levels increased across the evening hours when there was sexual activity and decreased when there was no sexual activity. The results were similar for male and female subjects. Testosterone levels were not higher in the evening measures before sexual activity, suggest-ing no effect of anticipation. The subjects were established couples, however, for whom sex with each other had become a familiar pleasure. Because they had not spent a lonely week apart from each other, they might not have looked forward to sex with the same degree of anticipa-tion as the man in the lighthouse did. Couples not so well acquainted with each other may be more aroused by anticipation and conse-quently more likely to have a testosterone increase. Suzanne and I con-sidered a study in which we would measure testosterone in newly acquainted pairs, who, depending on how things go, may or may not be starting long-term relationships. However, we couldn't figure out the logistics of that kind of study. We didn't know where to find such couples or how to approach them about spitting for science. Another problem is that spitting in a vial might spoil the magic of a new romance.

Several years after we published our study, I had a call from a professor of pharmacology. He was trying to make sense of an unusual testosterone score. He had been talking with an Olympic-class athlete who failed a drug test, which indicated that the athlete had been taking testosterone. The athlete also called me and explained to me, as he had explained to the pharmacologist, that he had flunked the drug test right after returning from his honeymoon. He thought he had enjoyed sex on his honeymoon so frequently that his testosterone level had increased. I doubt that even a honeymooner's joyous excess could account for so big an increase, but the topic is worth another study.

Little is known about how testosterone affects sexual activity in very young or very old people. We do know that criminals often have early sexual activity in their backgrounds.[18] When he was six years old, one future criminal told a shopkeeper he needed to a borrow a dollar for his parents. He took the dollar, and he and his five-year-old girlfriend disappeared. The parents became alarmed when they missed the children, and they found them two hours later. The boy had used his ill-gotten money to take his little girlfriend to a movie. Still, romantic impulses in children are not always a sign of high testosterone levels. An eight-year-old child in one of our studies made a pass at my student assistant, who was four times his age. At the end of their interview, he planted a most unchildlike long kiss on her cheek and asked her to be his girlfriend. That child turned out to be average in testosterone. Maybe aggressive behavior is a more reliable sign of high testosterone than are romantic gestures. Another child in the study, one who had kicked the teeth out of a six-year-old schoolmate, was high in testosterone.

THE SEASONS OF LOVE

Testosterone varies with the seasons, and interest in love and sex varies more or less predictably along with it. Tennyson said, "In the spring, a young man's fancy lightly turns to thoughts of love."[19] The large number of June weddings support his view, but there's more to the story. According to research data, testosterone levels are lowest in late spring and early summer.[20] (There will be more about June and low testosterone later in this chapter.) According to the data, a young man's fancy should turn to thoughts of sex in late fall and early winter. That's when testosterone levels and sperm counts are highest.[21] The peak time for human births in the Northern Hemisphere is around August or September, nine months after the high testosterone levels of the preceding fall. There is another, usually smaller, peak in the birthrate around March. March comes nine months after June, the traditional time for finishing school, getting married, and starting families. Many animals are seasonal breeders, but people are not. Nevertheless, there are some fairly regular trends in human birth statistics that become apparent when they are charted on graphs.[22] The human birthrate is influenced by poetry, social customs, testosterone, and probably magic.

Most birds breed in the spring, and that's when they have high levels of testosterone. For birds, it makes evolutionary sense to find mates, build nests, and start families in the spring. When it's warm and when bugs, worms, and berries are plentiful, baby birds have the best chance for survival. Some animals, including rhesus monkeys, mate in the fall. That's when their testosterone is highest. Rhesus monkeys begin breeding every year in mid-October, come rain, shine, snow, or sleet, and their offspring are born in the spring. Many other animals have seasonal testosterone changes that correspond to changes in sexual activity. High testosterone and sexual activity go together in most snake species. There are two times a year when Arizona copperheads are high in testosterone and likely to mate—once in late winter when they come out of hibernation and once again in the spring. Snakes may mate only once a year, so they have to make the most of every sexual encounter. Each male has two penises, and each penis has a testis and a large duct in which to store semen. Almost as surprising, according to researchers who studied males in three species of rattlesnakes, male snakes have high levels of $17\text{-}\beta$ estradiol, a form of estrogen.[23] Perhaps it was his elaborate sexual apparatus and his complicated mixture of male and female sex hormones that qualified the snake to bring sexual knowledge to Adam and Eve.

Seasonal hormonal variations were probably not as profound for Adam and Eve as for the snake and the other animals in the Garden of Eden, but people, too, are affected by the seasons. Research into seasonal affective disorder (SAD) shows that light has an effect on how our brains work.[24] People who suffer from winter depression feel fine during the spring and summer. Sunshine, long days, and even bright artificial light are antidepressants for SAD victims. Other seasonal differences can affect us, too. A friend from Hawaii who spent a winter in New England said people were so bundled up there that they looked like Michelin tire advertisements. He lost interest in sex in New England, but when he returned to Hawaii, surrounded by flowering shrubs, sunshine, ocean breezes, and lightweight clothing, his interest in sex returned. I suspect his testosterone increased.

Many things influence human sexual behavior. One staple of the news business is how specific events, natural or technological, precipitate a rise or a fall in the birthrate exactly nine months later. There may be some truth to some of those stories, but when statistics are compiled on the basis of hindsight, who knows? It is not easy to predict when there will be a population surge in testosterone sufficient to raise the birthrate nine months later, or even when a particular person's testosterone level will rise. Every person has an average testosterone level, which is subject to small changes around that average. Greater or lesser interest in love and sex often parallels increases or decreases in testosterone.

Seasonal changes are one of the more or less predictable patterns in testosterone production. There are others. Testosterone is higher in the morning than in the evening, higher in youth than in old age, and higher in winning than in losing. In women, it is highest around the middle of the menstrual cycle. It is easy to understand menstrual cycle changes. Women ovulate at midcycle, when their testosterone levels are highest, making them most interested in sexual activity when they are fertile.[25] During human evolution, women with this pattern of sexual activity would be more likely to conceive, have offspring, and pass the pattern on to future generations. It is harder to understand why there might be changes in testosterone across the day. Testosterone is highest in the morning for men and women, but sexual activity is more likely at night. Probably testosterone levels are high in the morning for the same reason that other hormone levels are high. When our ancestors woke up in the morning and went out to face a dangerous world, their systems needed to be on go, ready for action. When evening came it was time to rest, and testosterone dropped accordingly. These ancient patterns influence how we live today. Husbands and wives go to work in the morning when their testosterone levels are high, and then, when their work for the day is done, they have time for love.

Continual changes in testosterone level make the whole system flexible. Different levels support different actions, and all animals change with time. The deer in spring is not like the deer in fall, and people at twenty are not like people at sixty. Testosterone levels are higher when it is time to be dominant and lower when it is time to avoid fights. High testosterone in the breeding season is linked to both sex and fighting. Men are high in testosterone when they are competing for mates as adolescents and young adults. Women are high when they ovulate. Animals decline in testosterone outside the breeding season, females decline when they are not ovulating, and we all decline as we grow old. It would be risky for testosterone levels to stay high indefinitely. As discussed in Chapter 2, testosterone increases the chance of success in one-on-one encounters, but it also increases the risk of dying young. Testosterone is costly to the individual, and economy in its use is needed to minimize wear and tear on the body. When people and other animals are high in testosterone, they focus on sex and dominance and tend to ignore everything else. They neglect their health, eat too little, and misjudge such dangers as loaded guns, charging elk, or oncoming automobiles.

TESTOSTERONE AND MARRIAGE, LIKE A RHINO (OR A PEACOCK) AND A CARRIAGE

Let us consider how the sexual energy of testosterone might affect marriage and mate relationships, using rhinocerous and peacock analogies. Rhinos have one kind of machismo, and peacocks have another.

The rhinoceros is a hoofed animal with an odd number of toes, a member of the family that includes horse, donkey, wild Abyssinian ass, and extinct giant North American tapir. His territoriality, ferocity, and slow growth rate made him an unsuitable candidate for domestication. Scholars say that if it had been possible for Africans to domesticate the rhino as Eurasians had domesticated the horse, the history of the world might have been different.[26] Rhinoceros-riding Africans might have invaded Europe, set up colonies there, and then gone on to colonize the New World. Then the song from the Broadway musical *Oklahoma!*, which presents the happy image of love and marriage going together like a horse and carriage, might have been about a rhinoceros and a carriage instead. When it comes to rhinos, it is easy to anthropomorphize and say they are like macho men. With their thick heads and hides, they would seem equally likely to pull a carriage down the road or into a ditch, oblivious to the needs of passengers.

Peacocks have another set of characteristics typical of macho men. Peacocks appear to have plenty of male ego, and we often say men are peacocks when they show off. I was lucky enough to be visiting the zoo with my family one morning when a peacock was courting. He knew how to show off. He spread his beautiful tail feathers, held his head proudly, turned around slowly so that the little brown peahen could see him from every impressive angle, and from time to time he would stand still and raise a clamor with his special rattling tail feathers. Although he surely wanted admiration from the peahen he was courting, he didn't appear to be looking at her. Courtship was clearly his show. It is hard not to make assumptions about peacock psychology and think they view peahens as "sex objects" only.

Don Juan was a great lover who was not a rhino or a peacock. I read that women loved him not because he was handsome and clever but because he listened to them. While other men chased women and showed off for them, Don Juan paid attention to women and listened to what they had to say. They were so amazed and grateful to find a man who thought what they said was important that they bestowed their deepest affections on him. Don Juan's attentiveness could have helped him succeed in doing business with women, too. The TV show *48 Hours* reported on a woman who was amazed at how helpful salesmen were when she entered a men's clothing store disguised as a man.[27] They listened to her, and they tried to understand what she wanted. When she entered dressed as a woman, they spent less time listening and more time telling her what they thought she needed. Because women are ignored so much, they appreciate men who listen to them. It is not surprising that women compare men to rhinos and peacocks.

Not all male behavior is explained by testosterone. What men learn as boys explains much of what they do as men. I know a man whose mother always shined his shoes when he was a boy. When he married, he thought his wife would shine his shoes, as part of her job as woman of the house. She told him he was wrong, and he learned to shine his own shoes. We usually continue to do things the way we first learned to do them, unless we have good reason to do otherwise. While men may have rhinolike and peacocklike tendencies, those tendencies can be moderated by education and social expectations.

Nevertheless, I think men with high levels of testosterone might act like rhinos or peacocks more often than do other men. A student of mine had two boyfriends, and she was fond of them both. The one she knew first was a sportswriter who liked to spend a lot of time alone or with other men. When she went to parties with him, he would often ignore her for a good part of the evening. He liked to go outside to smoke and think his own thoughts. He became a more enthusiastic suitor when the second boyfriend appeared on the scene. The second boyfriend was a sociable and attentive ex-Marine. We assayed the testosterone levels of both men. Both were within the normal range, but the sportswriter was nearer the high end of normal. She married the ex-Marine, the one with lower testosterone, and she has no regrets.

A study of female vervet monkeys indicates they also prefer males who are not too high in testosterone. As discussed earlier, female vervet monkeys have a say in which male will become leader of the group. They pick males who are not especially aggressive or high in testosterone and who have high levels of serotonin, a brain chemical that makes animals more mellow, as if they were taking Prozac.[28] There are some indications, including the "gender gap" that political analysts talk about, that women, like female vervet monkeys, often prefer leaders who do not have traits associated with high levels of testosterone. Iroquois women were exemplars of the feminine influence in politics at the height of Iroquois civilization in the eighteenth century, when the Iroquois were forging peaceful alliances with neighboring tribes. Iroquois women held property and were politically active; the women of each clan selected a clan mother, and the clan mothers selected the men who would serve as chiefs representing the clans at the Grand Council. The clan mothers selected chiefs on the basis of "wisdom, integrity, vision, fairness, oratorical ability, and other statesmanlike qualities."[29] These are qualities that would be consistent with moderate levels of testosterone and high levels of serotonin.

It is not surprising that many women are less like the women who leave their telephone numbers at construction sites and more like the Iroquois women, who prefer men who are not too macho, because less macho men make better husbands. A general restlessness and dissatisfaction with marriage goes along with high testosterone, as was found in a study of three dozen professional married men.[30] Each man had been married about eighteen years, most were in their first marriage, and none of the men were physically abusive. Overall satisfaction with marriage was less among those who were higher in testosterone. They were likely to say that they did not get along well with their wives and children, that they rated the quality of their marriages low, that they were not happy in their marriages, and that they preferred activities and relationships outside their marriages. This undoubtedly affected their health, because other studies show that satisfaction with marriage and children is related to men's health and well-being at mid-life.[31] The men who were lower in testosterone enjoyed their marriages more.

Another large study, which included married and divorced men, also showed testosterone to be very important. In this study Alan Booth and I analyzed marital relationships among 4,462 military veterans in their thirties and early forties.[32] The most striking finding was that high-testosterone men were less likely to marry, and if they did marry they were more likely to get a divorce. Figure 5.1 shows that the lowest-testosterone men were those who had married and stayed married. Next were those who were married and had been married at least once before. Above these were single men who had never married, and highest of all were men who had been married but were currently single.

Another way of looking at this is to examine differences in the marital behavior of low- and high-testosterone men. Individuals in the top 2 percent of the testosterone distribution were twice as likely to have extramarital affairs than men in the bottom 2 percent. Examining other kinds of marital disorganization and misbehavior, the overall picture of the macho extreme is bad. The top 2 percent were twice as likely to be physically abusive, hitting or throwing things at their wives. High-testosterone men are also psychologically remote from their wives. When asked, "Whom have you felt closest to in past years?" higher-

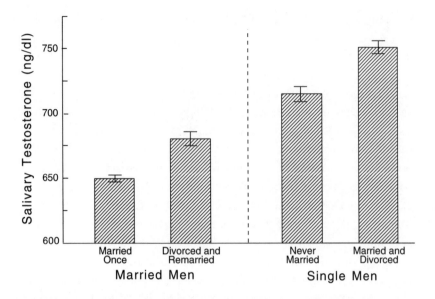

Figure 5.1. Testosterone and men's marriages. Testosterone is lowest among men who are married and have never been divorced. It is highest among men who divorced and are now single.

testosterone men were more likely to name someone other than their wives.

A study of the ability of men and women to identify facial expressions reveals an ability difference that may underlie masculine remoteness and insensitivity. The study reported that although women were equally good at identifying unhappy facial expressions in people of both sexes, men were poor at recognizing unhappiness in women.[33] Ruben Gur, who helped do the study, believes that sex hormones play a role in the difference. It seems probable to me that high-testosterone men are less likely than average men to notice when their wives looked unhappy. Perhaps egocentrism, along with insensitivity, leads men, particularly high-testosterone men, to brush aside their wives' complaints as trivial. They may not see problems with their marriages until their wives threaten them with divorce; then the men often feel they have lost control of the relationship and tend to respond with anger. Men are most likely to become violent when they feel belittled or insulted, as happens when women leave them or threaten to leave. Men who feel rejected or abandoned sometimes become violent toward their mates. In such a situation, the husband is likely to be thinking, "She double-crossed me," while the wife is thinking, "He ignored me for years. Why should he get so mad when I want to leave?" The problems that high-testosterone men have with marriage are likely to include drinking, drug taking, infidelity, an unwillingness to spend time with the children, and so forth. Nevertheless, I suspect a major reason for divorce among high-testosterone men is that there is more peacock in men than there is peahen in women. To some men, a good relationship allows them to strut while their wives admire them. Many women want more than this from a relationship.

There are differences in what bothers men and women about their marriages. Men are more jealous over sexual infidelity, and women are more jealous over emotional infidelity.[34] Men are prone to violence toward women who leave them; women seldom are violent toward men who leave. There are more male than female stalkers, people who pursue others relentlessly and cannot believe that their "prey" do not want them around.

Rhinolike behavior, in courtship and marriage, comes more from men than women, but we should not ignore the behavior of women. Women have testosterone, and some women are pretty tough. When Geraldo interviewed Animal's girlfriend Michelle, the camera zoomed in on her smile. One of her front teeth was missing. Geraldo thought maybe Animal had attacked her. She said no, it was not his fault. She explained:

> "Ah ... Jack Daniel's one night. I decided to grow balls, and I hit him and I made him bleed. I cut his nose open, and so he, in reaction, hit me in the face, knocked my tooth out."

Michelle was tough. Animal was tough, too, and she did not hurt him badly, but suppose a more peaceful man ended up with her as a mate? Given the way we think about men and women, it may sound like a joke to hear that a wife has beaten her husband. People laugh when they hear it, and the victim is ashamed to go to the police. Few women beat their husbands, but it can happen, and when it does happen the pain of the male victim is great. I would like to discover whether testosterone in women explains some of these rare cases of reverse abuse. I have been unable to find any information about the testosterone levels of women who abuse men, and I assume that no research on that subject has been done. I would also like to find out whether high-testosterone women, like high-testosterone men, tend to have trouble with close relationships. I suspect they do, because testosterone generally affects men and women in similar ways.

The conclusion of all this is that high-testosterone men are built for dominance, and dominance is a risk factor in marriage. Marriage to a high-testosterone man may work out, but there are many ways it can go wrong. Good fighters do not usually make good husbands. We know this from the veterans studies, where high-testosterone men were preferred by wartime field commanders[35] but tended to treat their wives badly. When high-testosterone men are intent on dominating their wives, they put their marriages at risk. John Gottman, a University of Washington psychologist who has studied marriage for twenty years, says that in most successful marriages, the husbands and wives share power.[36] Sharing power may be as hard for a rhinoceros as pulling a carriage.

WHY DO GOOD WOMEN MARRY RASCALS?

To be fair, we'll also consider why good men sometimes marry rambunctious women, but first we'll consider the question people ask more often. "Why do good women marry rascals?" is among the big questions of life, questions such as "Why do bad things happen to good people?" and "Why is there evil in the world?" It's common knowledge that some women want rhinos for their carriages when horses would do better, but why? Maybe it's the appeal of strength and energy. We admire strong characters, whether they are sports heroes, politicians, businessmen, professional people, or film stars. We gain reflected glory from their presence, and we would like to have them among our acquaintances, but if tabloid headlines are to be believed, we should think twice about marrying many of them. Construction workers, though rarely famous, are strong and energetic, and they have a reputation for being ardent but not so faithful lovers. Animal, from the *Geraldo* show, had plenty of girlfriends. Michelle explained how she met him:

"He was working on the main street, and I would drive by and watch him working with no shirt on, and I'd say 'Hi,' and I'd bring him his little sugar treats when he'd need them in the afternoon. And two weeks from that he finally asked me out."

Mike Roseberry knows many women who, like Michelle, find construction workers attractive. Women who are offended by wolf whistles find it hard to understand why so many women stop by Mike's construction sites and leave their telephone numbers, but they may admire macho men less blatantly. I have a woman friend who would have never considered leaving her phone number at a construction site, but as a teenager, if she had found herself near a movie set where Charlton Heston was working, she might have given at least a fleeting thought to leaving it there. Not too long ago, when she had been happily married for more than thirty years, she waited in a long line for a glimpse of that charismatic screen idol of her youth. Actors as well as fighters, on screen or in real life, tend to have testosterone levels that make them poor marriage risks, but they have no trouble getting attention from admiring women. Women often find men with intensity and passion thrilling, but when it comes to marriage, sensible women know those qualities have to be put on the scale and balanced against reliability and sensitivity.

When women are concerned about how much stability is needed to balance the characteristics associated with high testosterone, they can blame their cavewomen's genes, which date back to the time when the mates and offspring of good hunters and fighters had the best chances for survival. To be successful, cavewomen had to have resources and protection for their young, and so in courtship and mating, they favored dominant and powerful suitors who were likely to provide what was needed. "Cavewoman" values persist today. Maturity is associated with dominance, and modern women generally prefer men a year or two older than themselves. Money is associated with power, and a study of ten thousand people in thirty-seven countries showed that women want men with "good financial prospects."[37] Although financial success is not positively correlated with testosterone, cavewomen genes do not necessarily distinguish between animal vigor and financial potential. Nevertheless, the energy that goes along with testosterone does contribute to gumption and initiative, useful assets appreciated by modern men and women as well as by their ancestors. Research shows that men with moderate levels of testosterone have plenty of gumption and initiative, and, when it comes to pursuing both mates and careers, they do well in contemporary society.

In Shakespeare's play, the beautiful Desdemona fell in love with Othello, a great warrior who was old and not very handsome. His enemies said he had bewitched her, but he said she was won by the battles he had fought. He said, "She lov'd me for the dangers I had pass'd . . . this is the only witchcraft I have used."[38] Men try to impress women and other men. Traditional courtship lets men display their strength and skill, and it gives women a chance to decide whether they like this strength and skill. Both sexes play the game, with men showing off and women cheering them on.[39]

Sometimes the roles are reversed. A few years ago Mary and I paid several visits to a recently divorced man who was living with his mother on an isolated farm. Visiting him gave us an opportunity to watch women show off like courting peacocks. Some of the women had traveled long distances to visit, and while they were visiting, they demonstrated various skills. One woman helped him with a carpentry project that involved using his radial arm saw. All the women brought things they had made themselves, not only the usual pies and cookies, but hand-crafted leather goods, including a wallet and a belt. The belt came with a hand-made silver buckle. One woman brought salt-free banana bread for his mother, who had a heart condition. Mary said, "They're auditioning. He's twenty-nine, heterosexual, and single. News like that travels fast, even in the boondocks." He did not stay single long. He married the woman who baked the salt-free banana bread, which turned out to be ironic because she couldn't get along with her new mother-in-law, and the marriage didn't last.

Among birds, as with people, the usual pattern of males courting females is occasionally reversed. This happens in the red-necked phalarope, a small wader that nests on the ground in the Arctic tundra. In this species, males build the nests and incubate the eggs, and females make no contribution beyond laying eggs. In this species females have bright plumage and males have dull plumage, and females fight each other for the opportunity to have males mate with them. This behavior follows the rule that whichever sex within a species contributes the most scarce and valuable reproductive resources—here building the nest and caring for the eggs—will be courted by the other sex.[40]

The women of the Samburu tribe in East Africa think men should do the courting. Women take advantage of the traditional Samburu belief that God gave them all the cows in the world. In recent history they felt they had the right to take cows from others, and cattle raids were a respected activity. Cattle raids are less common today, but tradition is strong, and girls are attracted to boys who have stolen at least one cow. At tribal dances, the custom has been for girls to make fun of boys who have never stolen a cow, and then the boys take up the challenge. A Samburu man described how he felt watching a beautiful girl sing about the cattle thefts of another man:

> "You are standing there at the dance, and a girl starts to sing. She raises her chin high and you see her throat. And then you want to go and steal some cattle for yourself. You start to shiver [a Samburu sign of manliness]. You leave the dance and stride into the night, afraid of nothing and only conscious of the fact that you are going to steal a cow."[41]

Like the Brazilian women mentioned in Chapter 4, who mocked the Italian men for their losing soccer team, the Samburu girls expect men to be manly and win. Life in prehistoric times was rough, and it still is rough in many places in the world where physical danger is close. In those places, it is important to women to have mates who will protect them from danger. In rough places, tough men do well. In places that are not so rough, tough men and the women come together in, among other places, honky-tonks, where men and sometimes women get into bar fights. Mike Roseberry told me an easy way to get a guy to fight in a bar is to insult his wife or girlfriend. The woman being defended may know that she provides a ready excuse for a fight, but that knowledge is balanced by the hope that her guy will protect her if she falls into real danger. Women want to be more than sex objects for men to fight over, but they also want men who will protect them. When fighting and winning a face-to-face confrontation is needed, a high-testosterone mate is most likely to do what needs to be done.

Some cultures develop a romance of violence. The women of the Yanomamo tribe in the Amazon, who are often injured by their mates, romanticize violence and believe it shows passion. They say that women without scars have weak or inattentive mates, and the women proudly show off their scars to each other. The Yanomamo do not distinguish between passion and violence, and the women accept violence as a normal part of passion. Perhaps the women are also trying to justify in their own minds an unhappy life, but their attraction to the men is very deep. A Yanomamo woman who married an anthropologist and moved to Boston finally left her husband and returned to her tribe in the Amazon. She tried to take her daughter back to the jungle with her, so the daughter could find and marry a proper man there.

The question "Why do good women marry rascals?" is partly answered by the fact that rascals are likely to have positive traits, at least when viewed from an evolutionary perspective. The energy of testosterone is attractive, despite its less civilized side. The question is also partly answered by the saying that birds of a feather flock together, and some women who marry rascals are rascals themselves. A long line of research shows that similar people are attracted to each other. They can be similar in age, race, background, religion, politics, height, personality, or almost any other characteristic.[42] Sociologist Richard Udry, of the Carolina Population Center, found a low but statistically significant correlation between the testosterone levels of husbands and wives.[43] Both Animal and Michelle on the *Geraldo* show acted like high-testosterone individuals. They were at ease with violence, and they often fought. Michelle said, "We get into it. We go out drinking, and I start drinking a Jack Daniel's or tequila, or whatever, and we get stupid, end up going at each other." They try not to fight in front of the children, and the fights are brief. Michelle said, "We usually do it outside the bar, or outside our house." When a violent woman and a violent man decide they like each other, one can hardly expect a peaceful relationship.

COURTSHIP, OR THE ONLY WHEEL IN TOWN

A man traveling in the Old West arrived at the train station in a small town. He stepped out and spoke to another man standing nearby, who looked like a gambler:

"Any action around?"

"Roulette."

"You play?"

"Yes."

"Is the wheel straight?"

"No."

"Why do you play?"

"It's the only wheel in town."[44]

Given the uncertainty of love and the uneasy lives of men and women together, one might wonder why anyone gets married. According to a 1994 poll, a significant number of girls were wondering the same thing. Fewer girls than boys were planning to marry. While some single women elect to have babies, widely publicized statistics concerning the drawbacks of single parenthood discourage that. Why not be single and celibate? Why gamble? Why not do something else? Women are taking these questions to heart. Ann Lee and her Shaker disciples asked those questions, too. They decided to do something else and won converts to their point of view. In the 1840s there were six thousand members of the Shaker religious sect, which practiced celibacy and engaged in furniture-making as a livelihood. Today Shaker chairs are valuable antiques, but there are no Shakers to sit in them. Other people's children sit in them, and there are plenty of other people's children. When it comes to survival of the species, courtship is the only wheel in town.

In 1874, when they began to run out of converts, the Shakers solicited membership in ads that emphasized comfortable accommodations.[45] The ads didn't work. Hormones and the desire for genetic immortality stack the odds against celibacy. The great majority of men and women want to have children, and many of those who can't are willing to endure prolonged and expensive discomfort pursuing fertility.

We doubt that animals think about whether or not they should mate, but it does appear that animals use one of two broad mating strategies. One strategy is pair bonding, in which male and female come together and form a mutual tie. In pair bonding, animals go two-by-two, as they boarded Noah's Ark, to ride out the flood and face the future together. Usually they appear to like each other, but they don't have to. Gibbons, small arboreal apes, sometimes remain together like cranky old human couples, because neither partner has any other choice. The male chases away other males, and the female chases away other females, and the two are stuck with each other, for better or for worse. They are like many people, for whom habit counts more than love in holding a relationship together.[46]

Pair bonding is also the style of the hornbill, but reliability and trust, not crankiness, keep hornbills together. The female moves into a hollow tree, where she pulls out her feathers and uses them to line the nest in which she lays her eggs. She and her mate build a wall that seals her up in the tree, leaving only a small opening through which he can feed her small frogs and lizards. After the eggs have hatched, the male and female break down the wall together, and she comes out. If he is a lazy hunter, or gets into trouble, or runs away with another hornbill, she will stay sealed up and die. She needs to know that he will be reliable. During the courtship, before she lets herself be walled up, the male has to prove his reliability and gain her trust. Whereas the Samburu warrior wins a mate by stealing cows, the male hornbill wins a mate by bringing her many gifts of small frogs and lizards. The hornbills bond to ensure their future, and they invest equally in the same offspring.

The other mating strategy is that of a tournament, in which each male competes with all other males and the winner takes all. One male gets many females and the other males get no females. In pair bonding, a male needs enough testosterone to win one female, and the pair is then held together by something other than testosterone. In the tournament strategy, the dominant male depends more on testosterone. He needs enough to fight males and pursue females on a larger scale. With so much fighting and pursuing to do, his quality time with any particular female is limited to the courtship ritual and mating.

Elephant seals favor the tournament style of mating. A successful male elephant seal prevails over many other competing males and in the process accumulates a large harem. Females stay with him because he is their only choice, the only wheel in town. He breeds with the females and produces many offspring, but he provides no resources for the females or the offspring. Male and female elephant seals are ensuring their futures in different ways. The female invests a year of her life in one offspring, giving it her full attention and the richest milk produced by any mammal. The male fights to gain access to the females, invests sperm and a few moments for breeding, and completely ignores the offspring.

Neither strategy is "better" in an evolutionary sense. If it were, that strategy would have become the standard way of doing things. Viewed across all of nature, animals invest no more than necessary in their offspring. Among species where the young require care but not more than one parent can provide, one leaves and lets the other do the nurturing. This happens with many mammals—offspring stay with their mothers. Among species where offspring are so helpless that they need care from both parents to survive, both parents will contribute. This is usually, but not always, the case with birds, where male and female cooperate to build a nest, incubate the eggs, and feed the babies together.

Human beings are flexible creatures, and they use both strategies. Which they will choose depends upon circumstances, personal preferences, and established practices of their culture. Some men make it clear that they are faithfully pair bonded. They tell their associates they are married, wear wedding bands, and center their lives around their homes and families. Other men chase women as though they were competing in a tournament. These men include pimps, philanderers, and bachelors who "play the field." They direct their energy outside of marriage and, if they have mates, they are not emotionally close to them, except occasionally and briefly. They say, "When I'm not near the one I love, I love the one I'm near."

We think of this tournament behavior as characteristic of men, but there is a women's version of it. A girl can have many boyfriends, and wives can be as unfaithful as husbands. Sometimes this is surprisingly useful. A woman with many men friends is likely to find support and a place to stay wherever she goes, and each man will be protective toward babies who might be his—it is to the woman's advantage to let each man think he is the father. A study of the Ache women in eastern Paraguay found that 17 women had 66 children by a reported 140 fathers, or 2.1 fathers per child![47] Some female birds use a similar strategy. The English hedge sparrow female forms a lasting pair relationship with one male, but then she sneaks away and mates with another male. When she lays eggs and hatches them, each male seems to think that he may be the father, and both work to bring food to the chicks.[48] A tournament strategy is hard for a female to keep up, however. She can win the affection and support of many men, and thereby gather many resources for her offspring, but biology limits the number of children she can bear and thus limits her success with the tournament strategy. On the other hand, males are limited less by the number of children they can father than by the number of fights they can win, a number that can be very large indeed. Theorists are now beginning to examine shifts between these strategies and conditions under which human males and females show changing preferences between bonding with a single mate and seeking many mates.[49]

The pair-bonding and tournament strategies seem to call for different testosterone levels. Testosterone helps a male compete with others, and testosterone remains high as long as competition remains important. In tournaments, males have to compete with many others, and their testosterone levels stay high. Male birds that have many mates are high in testosterone throughout the breeding season. In pair bonding, testosterone is high long enough to compete for one mate, and then it drops. Male birds that, like the Lapland longspur, settle down with one mate are high only at the beginning of the breeding season—high in testosterone when courting and mating, and low when taking care of their young.[50] This pattern can be disrupted by experimentally extending the period in which testosterone levels are high. Researchers injected Lapland longspur males with subcutaneous testosterone implants and compared their behavior to a that of a control group without testosterone implants. The high-testosterone males visited their nests less and fed their young less often than did the controls. Fortunately, the baby birds had hard-working mothers who made up for their temporarily macho fathers' neglect.[51]

Male plainfin midshipman fish do not form pair bonds, but they take care of their young. Their testosterone patterns support a period of tournament breeding followed by a period of responsible parenthood. The plainfin midshipman fish fertilizes the eggs of as many females as possible and then guards multiple clutches at various stages of development. As long as the nests contain only eggs, the males remain high in testosterone and ready to fertilize new clutches, but when embryos begin to develop, their testosterone levels drop and they lose interest in sexual conquests. They devote themselves to their families.[52]

Testosterone levels are also important in the kind of sexual strategy that humans use. People who have high levels of testosterone seek many sexual partners, as reported among male military veterans and female college students.[53] Perhaps like birds, some people have chronic high levels of testosterone, and others have high levels only when they are pursuing mates. We know little about this possibility, although there is evidence from a study of Air Force officers that men's testosterone levels fall around the time they marry and settle down, and rise around the time they divorce and start looking for new mates.[54] Over shorter periods of time, testosterone has been observed to fall in men in the days immediately after their wives give birth.[55] Perhaps their bodies are preparing for helping their mates rather than competing with other men; or perhaps they are just tired. Changes in testosterone are associated with changes in size of certain areas of the brain. Psychologist Marc Breedlove has been studying the amygdala, which is known to be important in mating. His research with laboratory animals has shown that a part of the medial amygdala increases and decreases in size as testosterone levels increase and decrease.[56]

While it is clear that testosterone plays a role in love, sex, and reproduction, it is less clear what role it plays in sexual orientation. There is no difference in testosterone level between lesbians and heterosexual women, although among lesbians, those who identify themselves as "butch" tend to have higher levels than those who identify themselves as "femme."[57] One researcher, using hirsutism as an indirect measure of dihydrotestosterone, has reported preliminary findings that dihydrotestosterone levels are higher in gay men than in heterosexual men.[58]

Biologist Simon LeVay has found that sexually dimorphic regions of the hypothalamus, a part of the brain known to be important in regulating male-typical sexual behavior, are two to three times as large in heterosexual men as in gay men or heterosexual women. LeVay suggests there may be a genetic difference in the way the developing brains of gay and heterosexual men respond to androgens *in utero.*[59] It seems unlikely that adult testosterone levels influence sexual orientation, although they do influence sexual activity.

AN EVOLUTIONARY MODEL

I began this chapter with love and testosterone and continued it with different kinds of relationship and mating strategies. At this point I want to present an overall model showing the links between testosterone and reproductive success. The model includes ideas about evolution and qualities associated with testosterone. It shows how people's biology leads them along conflicting directions, toward pair bonding and fidelity on the one hand, and tournaments and philandery on the other.

The model assumes that the underlying function of sex is to carry life into future generations. Feelings of love and happiness are wonderful, and we seek and enjoy them, but they are a side show. Reproduction is the main event. People who have offspring pass along their genes to the next generation, and the genes of people who have no offspring die out. Evolution selects genes and traits that produce children who in turn produce grandchildren and great-grandchildren, continuing indefinitely. Thriving offspring are the obvious key to survival across the generations.

This model, shown in Figure 5.2, focuses on the role of testosterone in men. The arrows show testosterone leading to activities and behaviors that in turn lead to reproductive success. Testosterone contributes directly to sexual activity and the qualities in Chapter 3 that define a macho kind of dominance—simple thought and action, spatial skill, strength, sexual activity, panache, and roguery.

Dominance is central to the model, and it has two broad effects. First, it increases the likelihood of having children. Dominance makes it easier for a man to find a mate, because it makes him more competitive, more attractive to females, and better able to influence women through either charm or coercion. Dominant men are also more likely to have resources that make life easier and safer for their families, increasing the families' chances for survival. At the same time, however, dominance brings rambunctiousness, independence, and a tendency to wander off to compete with other men and pursue other women, leaving the original family at risk and decreasing its chances of survival. Pair bonding and tournament strategies differ in their relative emphasis on bringing resources and wandering. A pair-bonding man invests everything in one mate and her children, and he stays close to home. A tournament man invests a little in a mate and her children, then wanders off in pursuits that will lead to other mates, in each of whom he also invests only a little. With higher testosterone levels, males are inclined more toward wandering and less toward being faithful providers. Following the discussion of the previous few paragraphs, high-testosterone men display more tournament activity and less pair-bonding activity and support, which makes it more likely that they will have children but less likely that these children will survive to produce grandchildren. Testosterone levels in the population as a whole are held to a generally medium level across the generations by the competing benefits of having offspring and supporting them.

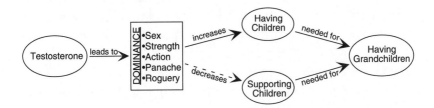

Figure 5.2. Testosterone and reproductive success. The model shows testosterone contributing to and interfering with reproductive success. Testosterone leads toward being dominant and having children and grandchildren, but it also leads toward restlessness that interferes with responsible parenthood. Evolutionary success requires that men attract women, father children, and give the children enough support for them to grow up and have children of their own. Too little testosterone interferes with having children, and too much interferes with giving support.

The model shows that testosterone is a mixed blessing in raising a family. It also suggests that there is room for different kinds of behavior. Every population has pair-bonding men and tournament men, and both types of men are successful in reproducing. The strategy a man uses will depend partly on his testosterone level. There is a point in the population where men teeter between pair bonding and wandering off to a tournament. If too many men bring resources, women become less aware of the unreliability of wandering males, and wandering males gain an advantage. If too many men wander, women begin to demand commitments, and pair-bonding males gain an advantage. The end result is a balance that keeps testosterone from rising too high or falling too low. Richard Dawkins describes processes like this in his book *The Selfish Gene*.[60]

"But," you might say, "where's the love? Even if love is a side show,

doesn't it count? I think the model is too mechanical, too cold and calculating. It has no romance. There must be something else." The answer
is, yes, of course, there is something else. There is love, and there are
many other things, all of which are important. In the real life of individuals, more is involved than just the lines and arrows of the model.
One thing or another may be more important for different people in different settings. Airline pilots and traveling salesmen, by the nature
of their work, wander more than farmers. Resources matter more in
harsh northern climates, where offspring will die without those extra
resources to protect them from the cold.[61] Wandering is more common
in societies where other people can take care of children one leaves
behind. Testosterone, and the kind of dominance that comes with it,
is not much needed by men who have the power of money or social
position.

Variations in how well a model fits occur in all sciences, whether the
model deals with human behavior or atomic forces. A model is good not
because it contains everything, but because it provides a useful and sim-
plified view. Unlike art, which deals with more reality than we are accustomed to in everyday life, science deals with less reality than we are
accustomed to.[62] Art makes real life epic, as *Gone with the Wind* sets
Scarlett, Rhett, Melanie, Ashley, and all their complicated passions to
music and adds Technicolor. Science would put these characters on a
chart and compare them to a control group. Science is good at abstract-
ing things, tearing them down and reducing them to their bare essen-
tials. In doing this, it loses the richness of individual cases, but it gains the
vision to see underlying relations more clearly. The model in Figure 5.2
points to aspects of the human social world where testosterone, mate
relations, and reproductive success come together. The model outlines
some of the ordinary processes behind the apparent magic of love and
some of the tricks and illusions that make us keep doing what our ancestors did—finding mates, establishing relationships, and having offspring
who survive and repeat the pattern in the next generation.

6
Earning a Living

AT THE BAR

Colleen Heusel worked for me as a student assistant. She was called for jury duty, where she met Bruce Harvey, a well-known Atlanta lawyer. Colleen didn't know that he'd been a subject in a Georgia State University study written up in a *New York Times* column on lawyers and testosterone.[1] I knew him from that study, and before that I knew his wife, Paige, who was a heroine in my neighborhood. She was a volunteer tree climber for Roadbusters, a group that helped stop the Georgia Department of Transportation from building a freeway through a park designed by Frederick Law Olmsted, Sr. Before the courts stopped the project, DOT tree cutters came to the park, and Paige was among the protesters in the trees. Mary and I, who were among the Roadbuster ground troops, watched the men cut down a large dogwood tree as Paige bravely hung on to its upper branches.

Later, a GSU student recruited Bruce to participate in our lawyer study. Knowing he was Paige's husband predisposed me to think he was a good person, but it took Colleen a while to see his positive qualities. She wrote about her jury duty experience as follows:

> The day before I reported for jury duty, my boyfriend and I were talking about a lawyer we'd seen a lot on the news. We didn't know his name. We called him "that sleazy lawyer with the braid who's on TV all the time." His long hair and contrived look were very unappealing. We saw him as a megalomaniac

who took on sensational cases to satisfy his ego. It seemed his clients were consistently the dregs of society.

When I reported to court, the clerk assigned me to the pool for a child molestation case. The accused was fat, had greasy hair, a mustache, and looked very nervous and guilty. As soon as I saw him and heard the charges, I made up my mind he was guilty. Then his lawyers walked in, and there he was, the TV lawyer guy with the braid.

His name was Bruce Harvey. He was tall, slim, and muscular, and his braid was long and grey. His hands were tattooed, and he was wearing a lavender cotton suit, a flashy-but-tasteful tie, and an earring. The associate lawyer was shorter and more subdued, but he also had a ponytail and an earring. "Just perfect," I thought smugly. "This will be entertaining and I'll be out quickly." I planned to tell the judge I had a busy week at school and didn't have time for jury duty.

Much to my dismay, the judge thought my civic duty was more important than school, and I was stuck until they picked a jury. I hoped I wouldn't be on it.

When it was Harvey's turn to ask questions, he began by asking for a show of hands.

"How many of you have a problem with lawyers? With defense lawyers?"

Most people raised their hands in response to both of these.

"People with motorcycles?"

"... because I drive a motorcycle."

"Tattoos?"

"... because I have tattoos." He held out his hands so we could see his tattoos.

"Men with earrings?" He showed us his earring.

"Me?"

We all smirked or laughed. I still thought he was a bit of an idiot, but I admired him for being so open and straightforward. I was also starting to notice he was actually quite attractive.

He went on to say it was important to recognize any biases we had, not because they were wrong, but because it would be unfair to hold his lifestyle and appearance against his client. He was relaxed, but sharp and confident. He was very much in control of the court room but still showed proper respect to the judge. I thought, "This guy is really putting on a good show. He's quite an actor."

The prosecution made less of an impression. The two lawyers were polite but seemed to care less about establishing rapport. They looked like "conservative professionals" from central casting. They each had neat short brown hair, dark blue suits, and red, white, and blue ties. One of them wore American flag cuff-links.

When it was time for Mr. Harvey to ask us questions individually, he began by smiling, looking directly at each person, and saying "Hello." He spoke to each person by name, and when he finished he said, "Thank you for coming and answering these questions." The questions went on for hours, and he seemed concerned about our comfort.

By the time he got to me, I really wanted to be on the jury. I had started to think I could be fair and perhaps his client was really innocent. I was trying to think of what I could say to make myself sound "progressive."

He smiled and said, "Hello," and called me "Colleen." He asked about my major and what classes I was taking. I smiled back at him and said, "abnormal psychology," which, because of the nature of the case, got a laugh from him and everyone else. He wanted to know whether I believed children always told the truth, whether I thought psychologists had any special insight into human behavior, and if I would be inclined to believe a psychologist's testimony. He closed by asking about my hobbies.

I was very impressed by his broad base of knowledge. He could speak to every potential juror on his or her level and make an intelligent comment on each one's line of work.

I was disappointed to learn that I had not been selected for the jury. Mr. Harvey had completely turned me around. I had gone from thinking he was a buffoon to being just about smitten with him. I really wanted to be on his jury.[2]

Colleen's story was particularly interesting because we knew that Bruce Harvey was one of a group of lawyers who had higher-than-average levels of testosterone. We figured he would put on a good show before a jury. We were pleased to learn that in spite of his toughness as a trial lawyer, he had perfected a warm and friendly smile.

TRIAL BY COMBAT

Lawyers are a good starting point for thinking about how testosterone is related to occupations. Lawyers have to do many things, and they must be geared always to the possibility of combat. They have to be considerate of the jury, but they use bluff, threat, and aggression against their opponents. The illustration with the *New York Times* article about our lawyer study showed a lawyer-rooster strutting down the courthouse steps, wearing a three-piece suit with his tail feathers sticking out, smoking a cigar and carrying a briefcase.[3] Lawyers differ among themselves, of course, and some are more like roosters than others. In our research, we began with the premise that trial lawyers have more in common with roosters than nontrial lawyers, and we divided the lawyers in our study into those two groups.

Trial lawyers work with a jury in the courtroom, and nontrial lawyers work with papers and documents outside the courtroom. Trial lawyers are gladiators, hired to win in a war of words. They are tenacious, like pit bull dogs. They threaten with letters, phone calls, and face-to-face meetings. Gerry Spence is a lawyer who is a master of the body language of threat and intimidation. Spence is a large man, 220 pounds and six feet two inches tall, plus two inches of heel on his cowboy boots.

Spence uses what he calls a "subconscious knowledge between animals including human animals, as to who is superior and who can win" to convince the other lawyer that if it were knives or knuckles, instead of a courtroom contest, Spence could take him apart.[4] "If I can physically subdue my opponent, I will probably win in the courtroom," says Spence, who, when called to the bench with the opposing lawyer, will "stand close—shoulder to shoulder—so he feels my physical presence in the courtroom, feels my whole being." After that, the other lawyer's "subconscious knowledge" works to Spence's advantage.

Nontrial lawyers are less combative. They draw up wills and contracts, figure taxes, and check real estate transactions. They specialize in paperwork, not head-on confrontation, and they try to avoid going before a jury. They deal with rules and regulations. Aggression and drama are of limited use in winning their cases.

I had been trying to study lawyers for several years, with little success. They would say they were interested but then not follow through. It took Elizabeth Carriere to show me how to do it. Elizabeth was a student who came from a family of lawyers, and she understood their habits. She knew where to find them, and she was brazen enough to go right into their offices and ask them to spit. Good looks and charm were on her side, too. With her in charge, we soon had saliva samples from eighty-one male Atlanta lawyers, including Bruce Harvey.

When Elizabeth began to meet the lawyers, she quickly noticed a difference between the trial and nontrial groups. Trial lawyers were talkative, inquired about school, spit in the vial in her presence, wanted to know the results, asked her out to dinner, and called friends on the phone to help: "Hey, Joe, I've got a young lady down here studying hormonal lawyers. You're a hormonal lawyer. Get on down here and help her out!" Nontrial lawyers were quiet and reserved. They went off alone to spit, did not ask her out, did not want to know the results, and did not send her on to others who might participate.

When we analyzed the saliva samples, we found trial lawyers had higher testosterone levels than did nontrial lawyers. This was especially true among the younger ones. Testosterone seems more important in the early years of a trial lawyer's career. By middle age testosterone levels have declined in all lawyers, and careers are maintained more by experience and seniority than hormones. Mary has a cousin, a successful small-town trial lawyer, who exemplifies the pattern. When he was young, he loved to go up against "silk-stocking lawyers from the city," and he took great joy in totally demolishing them. When he reached his fifties, he continued to enjoy winning, but he said he'd lost his enthusiasm for overkill.

We wondered if testosterone followed a similar pattern in women lawyers, and Elizabeth began collecting saliva samples from them. Later Julie Fielden collected more samples, and we were able to include women trial and nontrial lawyers in our study. What we found with the women was similar to what we had found with the men: trial lawyers, on average, had higher testosterone levels than nontrial lawyers. The woman trial lawyer who had the highest testosterone level among the women subjects acted very much like the men trial lawyers. She said, "You need to call Sally. She's a real bitch." Then she hesitated, sensing a competitor and a problem, and said, "No, wait a minute. What if she's higher than I am?"

The data that Elizabeth and Julie collected supported our belief that there is a difference between trial and nontrial lawyers. We suspect further research will show there are differences between subgroups of trial lawyers. Some trial lawyers are better suited to courtroom work than others. The difference between types of trial lawyers reflects what is needed on the two opposing sides of a case. Here there is an important difference between civil and criminal law.

In civil law, a plaintiff brings suit against a defendant, and each hires a lawyer. An automobile accident can lead to a contest between the plaintiff's attorney, the "car wreck lawyer," and the defense attorney, the "insurance company lawyer." The car wreck lawyer is paid if he wins, and he is eager to get to court. The insurance company lawyer works by the hour, and he delays, makes motions, and tries to settle out of court. We suspect the average car wreck lawyer has more testosterone than the average insurance company lawyer. Until he was convicted in 1994 of federal racketeering charges, which included arranging his wife's murder, Frederick Tokars's television ads made him the Frank Perdue of Atlanta car wreck lawyers. Few lawyers resort to murder, even when their wives know too much and are getting ready to file for divorce. Nevertheless, that is what the jury said Tokars did, and it makes us wonder whether the drive and energy that helps a person become a successful plaintiff's attorney may under some circumstances also help him or her become a criminal.

In criminal law, the prosecution lawyer pursues a defendant, whom the defense lawyer tries to protect. The two lawyers differ in their attitudes toward authority. The defense lawyer is a hired gun. He usually works alone or in a small law firm and spends his time fighting the establishment. The prosecutor works for the state and tries to put people away who break the law. The two sides usually do not like each other. Sometimes prosecutors call defense lawyers sleazy, and defense lawyers call prosecutors "persecutors." I know that high-testosterone delinquents are rebellious toward authority, and I suspect high-testosterone defense lawyers also have tendencies in that direction. I suspect criminal defense lawyers have more testosterone than prosecutors, though we have not yet compared the two groups.

People sometimes wonder whether high testosterone makes a person a trial lawyer, or whether being a trial lawyer raises a person's testosterone level. I believe the high testosterone comes first and leads a person toward trial or nontrial work. One way to study this would be to measure testosterone in people before they become lawyers, and then see what kind of law they go into. We are currently collecting saliva samples from incoming Georgia State University law students, and we plan to keep track of them to see what courses they do best in and what kind of law they go into after they graduate.

"A HARD AND SHIFTY FELLOW"

While we don't have testosterone data on every occupation, our research suggests we will find high-testosterone individuals in occupations where a person excels by being strong and dominant in face-to-face confrontations. For example, real-life private detectives, who help lawyers dig out the facts for their cases, and their fictional counterparts display these characteristics. The classic private detective was Sam Spade, in *The Maltese Falcon*. He was "a hard and shifty fellow, able to take care of himself in any situation, able to get the best of anybody he comes in contact with, whether criminal, innocent by-stander or client."[5] Testosterone oozed from his every pore. He had a soldier's frame of mind, as did the Sioux warrior Crazy Horse, who was willing to kill or be killed. Sometimes before going into battle, according to lore about him, Crazy Horse would say, "Today is a good day to die."

A soldier's job is "to grapple with the enemy and seize his vitals,"[6] and testosterone helps get that done. According to a study of Vietnam veterans by sociologists Cynthia Gimbel and Alan Booth, there is a link between testosterone and combat.[7] High testosterone interferes in performing support roles in the army, where rationality, reliability, and technical skill are needed, but it helps in combat, where force overwhelms reason. Booth and Gimbel looked at the Vietnam data to see which men were drafted, which men went to Vietnam, and which men served in combat. Booth and Gimbel found that when men entered the Army, those with lower testosterone levels often got administrative and support jobs, perhaps because they had slightly more education. For the soldiers who went to Vietnam and served in the field, the situation was different, because many of the qualities associated with testosterone are desirable in combat. In the study, each soldier answered "never," "rarely," "sometimes," "often," or "very often" to each of twelve questions about the extent of his combat experience. Included were questions about receiving enemy fire, encountering mines or booby traps, being ambushed, firing at the enemy, seeing Americans or Vietnamese killed, and killing Vietnamese.

Responses to the twelve items were averaged to give an overall combat exposure score. Figure 6.1 shows the number of men who on average either answered "never" or gave answers in the range from "never to rarely," "rarely to sometimes," "sometimes to often," or "often to very often." The results indicate higher scores among high-testosterone soldiers. These data were collected twenty years after the men served in Vietnam, so it is unlikely that the war experience caused the testosterone differences. Booth and Gimbel concluded that high-testosterone men tended to have more combat exposure than their low-testosterone comrades because their commanders sensed that they would be good fighters and assigned them to combat positions.

Findings from the Vietnam veterans data show that testosterone levels are positively correlated with violent behavior and sexual activity. High-testosterone soldiers were better in combat,[8] and as mentioned in Chapter 4, they had more sexual partners than did other soldiers. Lt. Col. John Paul Vann, a Korean War hero, although not a subject in the Vietnam study, exemplified its findings. Vann was a soldier's soldier,[9] and he embodied the characteristics associated with high testosterone levels. He was a small, strong, fearless, persistent, and inexhaustible maverick who had an aptitude for heroism and sexual excess.

In 1950, the North Koreans had the American 35th Infantry Regiment under heavy attack, surrounded and cut off from reinforcements and supplies. The men were trapped in an area too small for conventional airdrops. The twenty-six-year-old, 125-pound Lieutenant Vann convinced the general to assign him a few slow, low-flying L-5 observation planes to drop supplies to the surrounded men, a mission so dan-

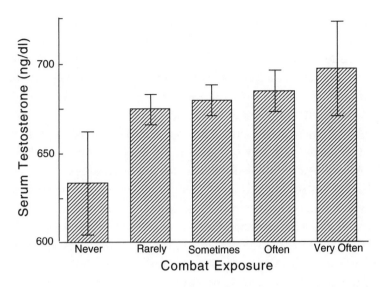

Figure 6.1. Testosterone among American veterans who faced different amounts of combat in Vietnam. Higher-testosterone soldiers saw more combat. Testosterone in this study was measured from serum rather than saliva, which is why the values are higher than those in graphs in earlier chapters.

gerous that the pilots were asked to make only one run each. Vann, however, flew every mission. He wrestled two-hundred-pound boxes of ammunition into the back of the plane, held a third in his lap, and took off with the pilot. He also carried a bag of hand grenades. The plane flew twenty or thirty feet off the ground, over bare terrain with no cover except for the smoke and dust from the mortar and artillery shells exploding all around. When they passed over the surrounded Americans, in isolated pockets about a hundred feet across, Vann would throw out a box of ammunition. As the pilot pulled away from the drop, Vann threw hand grenades at the North Koreans for good measure. The planes were not hit by enemy fire, in part because of luck and in part because infantry soldiers, unless carefully trained, will misjudge the speed of a plane flying close to them and miss when they shoot at it. Vann made twenty-seven flights across the battlefield the first day and forty-two more over the next three days, until the surviving Americans were finally rescued.

Fifteen years later, Vann was a civilian adviser in the Vietnam war, where he pursued women as tirelessly as he pursued the enemy. He had two mistresses and many girlfriends in Saigon. His friends noted that he often made love to two or three different young women a day, an activity that would have exhausted most men but seemed to invigorate him. After his last sexual liaison in the evening, he would settle down to reading reports and writing memos late into the night.

After I studied the Vietnam veterans data, I read a book about mercenary soldiers, and they sounded to me like a pretty rough bunch. These men (and occasionally women) attack with weapons, strength, and skill. They risk their lives and they are callous toward their enemies. They like stories of fighting and war, and they read *Soldier of Fortune* magazine and *Shotgun News*. They are competitive among themselves, and the toughest ones look down on the others and call them "wannabes." It is difficult to study their testosterone levels, because they are hard to find. They are usually not listed in the phone book, although a few years ago, I did find one former soldier of fortune who lives in Florida and has a 1-800 telephone number. I asked him if he could put me in touch with some of his former colleagues, because I wanted to ask them to participate in a testosterone study. He told me that would be nearly impossible, because American soldiers of fortune at that time were mostly in Bosnia, the Ukraine, and Rwanda. We talked for a while, and what he told me indicated that mercenary soldiers have characteristics that go along with high testosterone. They fight, live on short rations, make camp under harsh conditions, and leave their families for long stretches of time.

Unlike soldiers, scientists lead quiet lives, and, on average, they have testosterone levels lower than those of combat veterans. Nevertheless, based on what we know about testosterone and occupational choice, there is reason to think high-testosterone behavior has a niche in the usually quiet world of science. Scientists spend a long time in school, and people who stay in school longer are usually lower in testosterone.[10] Sitting in school year after year requires too much patience and submissiveness for many high-testosterone people. However, some high-testosterone people manage to complete advanced academic training and even achieve eminence as scientists. Roger Guillemin and Andrew Schally were a pair of macho physiologists who were bitter rivals until they won a Nobel prize together for discoveries about hormones in the brain. They raced each other for seven years to reach the prize,[11] with each seemingly as interested in beating the other as in discovering the secrets of the brain.

Many physicists are introverted, stable, and cautious, but some of the most creative and productive ones have been described as having "impatient masculinity," being brutal, insensitive, and predatory.[12] As with trial lawyers, physicists are a varied bunch. There are two types of high-energy-particle physicists, experimentalists and theoreticians, who are as different from each other as if they came from two different tribes.[13] Theoreticians work with abstract ideas. Experimentalists work with equipment, and they compete with each other for access to the high-energy beams in the atom-splitting particle accelerators they need for their experiments. The usual best way to succeed in science is to pick the right problem and pursue it diligently, but for some scientists the search for knowledge is almost like combat.

As with physics, other occupations have specialties that would seem to appeal to high-testosterone individuals. In the world of business, repo men steal back cars from owners who fail to make their payments, overenthusiastic IRS agents threaten citizens with punitive action, and businessmen cross over the line to engage in organized crime. In opposing the larger society, terrorists commit violent acts, revolutionaries work for changes in the political system, and extremists work to preserve or destroy the environment. It seems reasonable to speculate that testosterone should help wherever there are harsh personal relationships and a premium on toughness. For example, good bail bondsmen have to chase down their clients who skip bail, and like private detectives, they work without the support that police and other law officers have. Hector Cora, a young bail bondsman who was a friend of my student Denise de La Rue, would go into crack houses to bring back clients who had run away. Hector now has a law degree, and not surprisingly, he specializes in criminal defense. Some men hunt other men for a living. Howard Safir, of the U.S. Marshal service, headed a team of men who hunted down armed fugitives and brought them back to justice. He said, "There is no hunting like the hunting of armed men, and those who have hunted armed men long enough and like it never wish to do anything else thereafter."[14]

Some people make professions out of other people's recreational activities. They succeed by putting strength, energy, and intensity of focus into tasks they enjoy. We found NFL players high in testosterone, and the same should hold for professional players in tennis, soccer, and basketball. I suspect testosterone is highest in people concerned with defeating or dominating other individuals, teams, or dangerous animals. My son, Alan, told me about animal trainers. He worked for a while in the education department at Zoo Atlanta and got to know some of the men and women who worked as trainers. They told him stories about how badly things can go wrong when a trainer makes just a small mistake.

Many animals may turn on their trainers, but elephants are the most deadly. Elephant training, when it is going well, is a fairly nonviolent but constant struggle for dominance. The trainer must understand the elephant's rules for dominance and let the elephant know that it is the trainer who is in charge. The trainer must always keep in mind the old cliché, "If you give an elephant an inch, he will take a mile, and some of it might be over your dead body." One of Alan's friends at the zoo was a small woman who trained elephants. One day she was leading an elephant, who was usually handled by another trainer, through his elephant show paces. The elephant had been trained to suck up one trunkful of water from a trough and blow it toward the audience. He did it twice, which the trainer recognized as the opening gambit in what could become a dangerous threat to her authority and maybe to the audience. She tapped him with her training baton, and the elephant knocked the baton out of her hand. A woman in the audience, who did not realize the elephant was considering a rampage, started yelling accusations about cruelty to animals. The trainer managed to retrieve her baton, conceal her uneasiness, and stay in control.

Alan was impressed by her bravery. He said he thought large animal trainers, elephant trainers in particular, would be a high-testosterone group. I agreed with him. Alan and his friend collected saliva samples for me from a small group of trainers, a group too small for a proper scientific project, but which nevertheless revealed higher-than-average levels of testosterone.

Like trainers at the zoo, successful rodeo riders have to dominate large and dangerous animals. At the rodeo, the job is more physical than psychological, although psychology cannot be ignored. Rodeo cowboys do not have to maintain their intensity of focus for as long as animal trainers do, but once cowboys are in the ring, they are engaged in double competition: they are in competition with the animals for dominance and with the other cowboys for points. The owner of the Bruce Ford Rodeo School described the natural competitiveness of his most promising students. He said, "There's one boy, you know, that's from Arkansas, that you can see the look in his eyes that he dreams of being a world champion. It's almost a scary look."[15] My students and I are familiar with that look. We've seen it in the photographs of high-testosterone subjects who participated in our study of testosterone and facial expressions.

Several years ago, a student told me he was interested in studying testosterone in "pathological liars." He knew a group of these people, and he described them as amateur confidence men. He said they "would rather tell lies than tell the truth" and enjoyed taking advantage of other people. He wanted to begin by collecting saliva samples from them, and if they proved to be high in testosterone, he wanted to do a bigger study. They turned out to be well above average. Although the student left GSU without going beyond the pilot project, his findings prompted me to do some library research on confidence men. I learned that they have distinguishing characteristics that are consistent with high levels of testosterone.

Like animal trainers and rodeo cowboys, confidence men understand the psychology of dominance. They use it with subtlety and charm to deceive and manipulate their marks into parting with their money. They rarely resort to violence or even appear aggressive. D. W. Maurer, in *The American Confidence Man*, describes a typical con man as "always traveling somewhere and seeing and doing new things. If he is in California, he looks forward to going to Florida, from there to the Caribbean, and so on. Then, too, he is always with young people. He acts and dresses like a young man, even when he is seventy. His talk and manners are up to date. I never saw an old pappy con man. Besides, con men never loaf around much. They are always actively rooting out a mark. Much of their time is spent in the open air. Nowadays you'll find the old-timers on any golf links where they can get by."[16]

Con men are as ruthless as Sam Spade, but Spade's hard-boiled approach isn't their style. They conceal their ruthlessness and use friendliness and feigned sincerity to win their marks' trust. A con man has to be a smooth liar and a convincing actor. Acting is a profession we have found to be related to high testosterone levels. There will be more about actors later in this chapter.

Recently, few women have been successful players in big-time confidence games. Maurer found only one full-fledged con woman, Lilly the Roper, who was recognized by her male colleagues as a competent professional. There are women in the smaller con games, but the big cons have been run mostly by men. One old-timer said there once were many women in the business, and there are still "plenty of women today who would make good, too, but they haven't the chance because they don't know any good grifters."[17] To be successful, even in the underworld, beginners need mentors.

TOUGH WOMEN AND TOUGH WORK

Like Lilly the Roper and Britain's "Iron Lady," Prime Minister Margaret Thatcher, a few women do well in occupations, legal and illegal, that are dominated by men. Blackfoot Indian men admired "manly-hearted women" because they were tough, hardworking, and sexy. Manly-hearted women wouldn't put up with abuse, though, and the men didn't like that.[18] Like the Blackfoot men, most men are at least a little ambivalent about tough women. That means that being tough helps women get jobs usually held by men, but sometimes being tough is not enough. Even allowing for the fact that there are not as many high-testosterone women as men, there are fewer women in such occupations than would be predicted by testosterone scores alone. The shortage exists partly because men want to keep the jobs for themselves. Sometimes a woman has to be really tough.

Automobile racing, with its speed, action, grease, and carburetors, has been almost entirely a male domain, but a few really tough women have become successful racers. The "Queen of Drag Racing," Shirley Muldowney, told journalist Sam Moses, "I think the difference between me and the other guys is that a lot of them don't have, truly don't have, that *kick-ass* attitude."[19] Muldowney's "kick-ass attitude" survived a 250 mph crash that almost killed her in 1984. After five surgeries and eigh-

teen months of arduous rehabilitation, the fearless and fiercely competitive Muldowney was eager to get back to racing, where she continued
to do well.[20] The petite, attractive, and aggressive Muldowney is proof
that dominance can look feminine.

Opportunities in some previously all-male occupations have been
improving recently for women. Several years ago, I talked to two women
who worked as petroleum engineers in the offshore oil drilling business
in the North Sea, where most of their coworkers were men. Each of the
women had a level gaze and a straightforward manner, suggesting complete self-confidence. Both were fashionably dressed, and one wore a diamond in her nose. They enjoyed high pay, long days on duty, and weeks of
time off, which they used to travel and see the world. I measured their
testosterone and found it higher than average for women.

Another mostly male profession is horse training, and women who
do well in the business have to be rugged. I suspect they, like animal
trainers at the zoo, have high testosterone levels. I talked with a woman
horse owner about what trainers are like. She knew a woman trainer
who handled a group of Arabian horses that were so difficult they had
apparently caused a male trainer to collapse with a heart attack. The
horse owner described the woman trainer as a forceful person with
many boyfriends. The writer Beryl Markham was a horse trainer, too,
training horses in Kenya in the 1920s. Markham succeeded in two masculine endeavors, horse training and aviation. She was the first person to
fly the Atlantic solo from east to west, and that was in 1936. Only
recently has the Navy begun to train women as carrier-based fighter
pilots. Sexual discrimination is still stopping other tough women in
other occupations, like Pam Postema, coauthor of *You've Got to Have
Balls to Make It in This League: My Life As an Umpire*. She almost, but
not quite, made it to the major leagues.[21]

Like some of the men described earlier in this chapter, women can
intermix toughness and gentleness. One such woman was a brave
American soldier killed in the Persian Gulf war. Her grieving husband
made a poignant statement at her funeral. He said, "I prayed that guidance be given to her so that she could command the company, so she
could lead her troops in battle. And I prayed to the Lord to take care of
my sweet little wife."[22]

WHEN SHOULD TESTOSTERONE
REALLY MAKE A DIFFERENCE?

Among animals, there is a species of desert tree lizard, *Urosaurus orna-tus*, that includes two different types of males.[23] The two types differ in their dewlaps, the extensible throat fans they use to show off and com-municate with others. One type has a solid orange or yellow dewlap, and the other type has a dewlap that is blue surrounded by orange or yellow. The blue lizards compete and fight to control territory. The others avoid fights and look for unclaimed real estate. Both types succeed well enough—they survive, find mates, and reproduce—but they go about things differently. High- and low-testosterone men, or women, are not as clearly divided into two groups as the lizards, but when all the character-istics that go with testosterone are taken into account, it may not be too far-fetched to think of high- and low-testosterone individuals as two spe-cialized variations on the basic human model. From this viewpoint, it isn't surprising that they tend to seek out different kinds of work.

So far, we have looked at several occupations and thought about what would make them attractive to high- or low-testosterone individ-uals. Trial lawyers, New York taxi drivers, explorers, Masai Mara game poachers, travelers, professional football players, and sex industry oper-ators have interests and abilities different from those of corporate lawyers, accountants, computer programmers, health care profession-als, ministers, and managers. Testosterone brings energy, strength, sex-ual activity, certain spatial and mechanical skills, one-track mental focus, and panache. These traits make better competitors and predators than faithful and supportive partners. They are traits that should be useful to those in rough-and-tumble occupations, occupations that are often associated with low social status. The opposite traits, including steadi-ness, reliability, empathy, friendliness, sincerity, and deliberativeness, are associated with low testosterone and with success in many high-status jobs in the modern world.

Now we will describe studies that systematically examine testos-terone differences among people in a wide range of occupations. The way that high levels of testosterone affect performance in various jobs is complicated, and when my students and I first started relating testos-terone to occupations, we were sometimes surprised. We learned early on that white-collar workers as a group differ from blue-collar workers in many ways, including their testosterone levels. Not every occupation, however, fits neatly into one of these groups. Oil-field engineers, who are rugged outdoor workers with college degrees, have both white- and blue-collar skills. Oil-field engineers were a group that surprised us when we looked at them more closely.

We knew the two women who worked on oil platforms in the North Sea were high in testosterone, and we expected that men doing similar work would also be high. One oil-field engineering service company selects applicants in a testing session that survivors call a "weekend from hell." Applicants visit an oil platform in the Gulf of Mexico and work for three days with little sleep. Those who make the cut are a tough group.

We studied nine of these tough new engineers who were working in field conditions. We found that nine months after they started, the four who were lowest in testosterone all liked their jobs and were doing well. Among the five who were highest in testosterone, one had been fired, two had quit, and one was actively looking for another job. Oil-field work is dangerous, and the service company is very safety-conscious. Men who are high in testosterone are attracted to the dangerous work, but on the job they feel restricted by the rules, supervision, and monitoring made necessary by safety concerns.

To understand the role testosterone plays in job selection, we accumulated testosterone scores from men and women in several diverse occupations. There were lawyers. There were people like Flame, a professional wrestler from Lovejoy, Georgia, who met us wearing a ski mask with flames painted up the sides of his face. There were the two women engineers from the offshore oil company in the North Sea and the nine men engineers from the oil-field service company. There were housewives, lobbyists, politicians, and a very successful door-to-door newspaper salesman. As we expanded our research from individuals to groups of people representing different occupations, we widened our scope and felt more confident about our findings.

ACTORS AND OTHER MEN

In one of our early studies, we looked at eighty-six men in seven occupations.[24] They were physicians, firemen, football players, salesmen, professors, ministers, and actors. The physicians were neurologists and neurosurgeons at a large hospital, the firemen worked for city and county fire departments,* the football players were professional players on an NFL team, the salesmen sold heavy earth-moving equipment, the college professors were in arts and sciences, the ministers were Presbyterian clergymen, and the actors were full-time working stage actors. These occupations varied in ways that we thought would be related to testosterone, seeming likely to reflect differences in physical strength, assertiveness, aggression, benevolence, sensation seeking, social status, and economic status. For comparison, we added a group of unemployed men from a street corner labor pool. We expected they would be low because they would be depressed about being unemployed. Like the oil-field service company engineers, the unemployed men surprised us.

Most of the working men collected their saliva samples early in the morning at home and gave them to us later. The unemployed men were different. Two students, Denise de La Rue and Charles Cummins, set up shop on a street corner one morning and offered the men there five dollars each to participate. Word quickly spread about the spit-for-pay scheme, and a large and unruly crowd gathered. Some of the men tried to spit twice for double pay, and some tried to "audition" by showing how well they could spit. The students ran out of money and the men became angry and rowdy, but the students escaped with the spit. In spite of our efforts on the street corner, we ended up not including these men in the study, because their scores were a bit high, and we thought this might be because their samples were collected too late in the morning to be compared with samples from the other groups. Later, when we had more experience collecting saliva samples, we realized that if we had taken samples from the unemployed men earlier, their scores would have been even higher. Depressed or not, unemployed men, at least the ones who gather on street corners, seem to have higher testosterone levels than men who have jobs.

Ministers were lowest in testosterone, actors highest, and the other groups in between. Actors and football players were close together, and the only statistically significant difference was between actors and foot-

---

*We didn't learn much about firemen in this early study, but later Noel Fannin collected more data on firemen, and her work is described in Chapter 8.

ball players on the high end and ministers on the low end. We would expect football players to be high in testosterone, because they are strong and their playing is violent, but the actors surprised us. We did two more studies on actors and ministers to make sure our finding was not just chance. In both these studies, ministers were low and actors high in testosterone.

Some ministers are also actors. Jim Bakker, Jimmy Swaggert, and Billy Graham are television evangelists, saving souls before enormous crowds in staged electronic productions. Their showmanship and charisma set them apart from other ministers who are, as a group, quite different from actors. Actors seldom have steady work; they go from job to job, and their reputation is only as good as their last job. With every new job they have to convince a director they are the best available, and with every performance they have to win the approval of the audience. Ministers have steady work in stable organizations, and a few bad sermons will not hurt them. The groups differ in how they view themselves; actors take credit for their performances, while ministers give credit to God. Actors create a reality of their own, and ministers present the reality of God as defined by their religious doctrines. Actors want to be stars, while ministers want to help.

It is perhaps worth noting that acting and fighting are both routes to dominance, and it is not unusual to see the two together. Audie Murphy, the World War II hero described in Chapter 3, became an actor after the war. Douglas MacArthur was a great general, one who always put on a good show and liked to dress for the part. In the 1930s, when he was serving in the Philippines as President Quezon's military adviser, MacArthur made himself the only American "field marshal" and designed his own uniform, an elaborately filigreed white tunic with black trousers. Eisenhower, who served under MacArthur in the Philippines, later said, "I studied dramatics under him for seven years."[25] Even George Washington had a flair for showmanship. He stitched together a uniform to make himself look impressive, hoping the Continental Congress would put him in command of the colonial army.

A *60 Minutes* segment in which Meredith Vieira interviewed Charles Dutton, a knife-fight killer turned actor, strikingly illustrated that fighting and acting can be important parts of one person's life. Dutton was a seventeen-year-old grade-school dropout when he was con-

victed of manslaughter. He later went back to prison for a parole viola-
tion. While there, he got an additional eight years for assaulting a guard.
He was in solitary confinement at the Maryland State Penitentiary reading a play, *Day of Absence*, when he decided to turn his life around. The
play affected him so profoundly that he had an epiphany; he knew that
he had been born to be an actor. After almost eight years in prison, he
went back to school, worked in local theater for two years, applied to
the Yale Drama School, became one of sixteen out of seven hundred
applicants accepted, and went from Yale to Broadway.[26] Frank Rich, a
New York Times theater critic, reviewed Dutton's performance in *The
Piano Lesson*, and said, "He's a force of nature on stage, a human
cyclone."

It is clear there is a relationship between high testosterone and acting, which leads to questions about other people in the entertainment
industry, including those who work behind the scenes. When the
moviemakers mentioned in Chapter 3 were filming at my brother's
farm, I sent Jasmin Riad and Rebecca Strong in a rented LeBaron convertible to visit the film crew in South Carolina and collect saliva samples from them. We wanted to find out if they, like actors, had high
testosterone levels. Before we went, my son, James, suggested that I talk
with his friend, Rick Nelson, who is a gaffer, an electrical and lighting
technician.

Nelson explained to me how film crews, like the one we would be
studying, functioned. Crew members are freelancers employed by a
production company incorporated to put together one movie. The
production company works under contract with a large corporation
like Disney or Tri-Star. When the movie is completed, the production
company dissolves itself, and the members of the crew are unemployed
until they sign on with a new company for a new project. People who
work on film crews move around the country from one job to another,
living in motels and associating with other crew members, some of
whom they will know only for the duration of the project. These free-
lance moviemakers, like actors, have little job security in a highly competitive field, and as the saying goes, "they are only as good as their last
job." Producers and directors work under time and money pressure,
knowing that factors beyond their control, such as bad weather, can put
them behind schedule and over budget. Crew members are aware of

their responsibility not to waste time or money. In addition to that, their work often involves long hours, heavy lifting, and physical discomfort. We predicted that the energy and single-minded focus that goes along with high testosterone would often be an asset to filmmakers. Our study provided mild support for our prediction.

When we visited the set, the filming was almost complete and everyone was tired. That was particularly true about my brother and sister-in-law. They were exasperated with people treating their home "like a movie set" and tired of Hollywood egos and Hollywood hype. Dick will have stories to tell his friends and relatives for a long time. He told us one about the first assistant director, who'd been directing an outdoor scene. Dick said, "There was a faint, high-pitched, mechanical sound in the background that was bothering her. She sent one of her people to find out what it was. I told him, and he told her, 'Dick Dabbs says it's a cotton picker, about two miles away.' She told him, 'Well, shut it off.'"

Although Dick found the director exasperating, she was well liked by the film crew, and Jasmin and Rebecca defended her. They were impressed with her confidence and lack of self-consciousness. She was like the trial lawyers when it came to spitting in public. Jasmin met her outside her trailer and gave her a vial. She took the vial and walked into the catering tent, where she sat, spitting into it and talking with crew members who were eating breakfast. One crew member looked aghast while watching her spit at the breakfast table, and Jasmin got the vial out of sight as soon as possible, but the assistant director was completely unperturbed.

We distributed peer-rating questionnaires to crew members, because we wanted to compare certain personality characteristics to the testosterone scores. The questionnaires were helpful, but Jasmin, Rebecca, Dick, and my cousins were more helpful. Dick spent a great deal of time with the crew, and he described some of the people before we took our saliva samples and some afterward. The people who impressed Dick as being most outrageous turned out be among those highest in testosterone. Although our individual test results were confidential, as they had been with the construction workers, a few minutes after the film crew got their scores, everybody seemed to know the results of everyone else's test. With the exception of one woman who scored high, people of both sexes were happy if they scored high and unhappy if they scored low. Mary took that as evidence that male values dominate our culture and make both men and women overvalue testosterone. I agreed with her, particularly when we heard that one man had been planning to call his wife and tell her his score, but because it turned out to be lower than the group average, decided not to call her. The fact that he had looked forward to telling his wife about his score meant to me that he had a good relationship with her, and that his testosterone level was just about right. Dick, who was not generous with praise for the movie people, said that man was good at his job and also pleasant and reasonable in his dealings with others. Dick said, "The difference I saw between the high group and the others is that the people in the high group seemed to be trying to prove something, and some of the men who weren't so high seemed to be more secure in their masculinity."

Observations about the differences between the high group and the others, along with data from our saliva samples, made the study a successful one. The samples were informative, even though we collected them on the morning after a party near the end of the shoot. Many of the crew members were tired, hungover, or a little worried about finding a new job, and there were too few people in our experiment to make adjustments allowing for differences in age. All of these factors would tend to bring the group average down, but nevertheless, the sample average was a little high compared to the general population. Interestingly, two men over fifty had very high scores and one older woman had a high score, which made us wonder how much higher they must have been when they were younger.

ALL THE JOBS IN THE COUNTRY

The lawyers, actors, ministers, production crew members, and others we studied represented only a few occupations, but I found scores for a wider range of jobs in the records of the 4,462 military veterans described in Chapter 4. The average age of the veterans was thirty-eight years, and they were like much of the rest of the United States population in age, race, and income. Information available on each man included his testosterone score and his civilian occupation.

The men represented more than five hundred occupations, ranging from bridge welder to state legislator. I examined the testosterone level for each occupation and came up with a number of findings that were quite interesting. For example, heavy truck drivers were 25 percent higher in testosterone than light truck drivers, advertising managers 46 percent higher than computer programmers, automotive salesmen 24 percent higher than high school teachers, financial managers 24 percent higher than other financial officers, butchers 29 percent higher than draftsmen, and construction laborers 24 percent higher than a combined group of trial and nontrial lawyers. There is also some data comparing the testosterone levels of women in various occupations. One researcher has found women lawyers as a group (both trial and nontrial) to be higher in testosterone than women athletes, nurses, or teachers.[27]

Using the veterans data, many of the apparent differences among occupations, because they involve small samples, will not be statistically significant. To minimize the element of chance, we grouped similar occupations together following a system used by the U.S. Census Bureau. We divided the occupations into seven groups: managerial and professional; technical, clerical, and sales; service; precision production and repair; laborer and operator; farmer; and unemployed.

Figure 6.2 shows the average testosterone levels for the seven groups, again with error bars at the top. Farmers were lowest, followed by white-collar workers, including managerial and professional, technical, clerical, and sales categories. Next came blue-collar workers, including workers in production and labor. Finally, highest of all, were unemployed men. Unemployed men may be depressed, impotent, and low in testosterone because they have been laid off, as described in Chapter 4. However, many of the unemployed veterans were only temporarily without work, and I think many of them were not simply "unemployed," but unable or unwilling to stay at the same job for very long.

Overall, blue-collar workers were about 8 percent higher in testosterone than white-collar workers. Blue-collar workers also had fewer years of education, and their records showed more delinquent behavior and trouble with the law. Mike Roseberry, the construction superintendent mentioned in previous chapters, said this sounded right to him. Like Mike, who'd been willing to start a fight for research purposes, con-

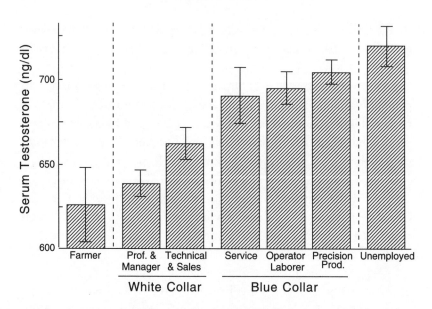

Figure 6.2. Testosterone levels among men in occupations defined by U.S. census categories. Testosterone was measured from serum, and the scale is the same as that in Figure 6.1.

struction workers take the direct approach to problem solving, and if the direct approach leads to a fight, they sometimes get into trouble. They like action and are interested in doing things, not thinking about them. In *Newsweek*, a "blue-collar guy" wrote about the energy of construction workers.[28] He said,

> ... they are always doing things that end up in the letter "n"— you know—huntin', fishin', workin' ... I have honest to God heard these things on Monday mornings about blue collar guy weekends: "I tore out a wall and added a room," "I built a garage," "I went walleye fishing Saturday and pheasant hunting Sunday," "I played touch football both days" (in January), "I went skydiving," "I went to the sports show and wrestled the bear."

Farmers are a special group, neither blue collar nor white collar. They are both managers and workers. Unlike other people, most farmers are born into their occupation. Land is expensive and the life is hard, and few people go into farming from the outside. Most people who are born into farming today leave when they grow up, but those who stay are part of a stable community. Farmers help each other, and they are seldom involved in one-on-one competition.

Some people call farmers "rednecks"; others call them "the salt of the earth." These mixed views, and the real lives of farmers, would not seem to suggest high levels of testosterone. It is a little-known fact that farming is one of the most dangerous occupations in the United States. Many farmers die in accidents, and in a group of farmers one is likely to notice arms or fingers missing. But in spite of the violence of life close to nature and heavy machinery, personal violence between farmers is rare. Farmers may have something in common with ministers, who are also low in testosterone. Both ministers and farmers have to be patient about things they cannot control. Ministers put up with sin and farmers put up with weather. Willa Cather wrote, "On the farm the weather was the great fact, and men's affairs went on underneath it, as the streams creep under the ice."[29]

Other investigators have studied testosterone in rural people. A study in Peru found farmers lower in testosterone than urban dwellers.[30] Current studies of men in Boston and of Ache hunter-gatherers and farmers in Paraguay have found men in Boston highest in testosterone and hunter-gatherers lowest.[31] The Ache, incidentally, are very violent in spite of their low testosterone levels. There is a great deal we do not know about how diet and lifestyle affect testosterone and how the presence of other people in a competitive city environment might raise testosterone levels. Among some birds, being among competitors in the mating season can raise testosterone levels.[32] Environmental factors might produce average testosterone differences among people within different cultures.

According to the veterans data, high testosterone levels do not bring money, prestige, and general success in our culture.[33] High-testosterone veterans left school sooner than did low-testosterone veterans, probably because they tended to be rambunctious and impatient. These tendencies interfere with getting an education, which is usually essential to white-collar success. High-testosterone boys don't like to sit and listen to the teacher day after day, and high-testosterone men find most white-collar work boring and confining. This makes it difficult for them to hold on to high-status jobs. Their excessive competitiveness might also interfere with white-collar success, where being a "team player" is at a premium. A study of success in the business world has shown that while the motive to achieve is helpful, the motive to compete interferes with achievement.[34] Maybe competition helps only when two people, like the Nobel prize—winning scientists mentioned earlier, want the same thing and push each other on to greater accomplishments.

The fact that higher testosterone correlates with lower status is surprising to many people, especially to successful business and professional men. Such men often regard themselves as macho and believe they are successful because their testosterone gives them a competitive edge. They do not have the story quite right. If they do in fact have high testosterone levels, which is not too likely, they should thank their parents and teachers for having been patient and skillful enough to civilize them.

THE IRONY OF TESTOSTERONE

Some occupations are supported by testosterone, some are in conflict with testosterone, and for some testosterone is irrelevant. When a friend of ours, Sharon Leventhal, was three, she said to her mother, "Mommy, I want to play the violin, because it's boo-tee-ful." She knew what she wanted, and she became a solo concert violinist. For most of us, finding an occupation comes at the end of a long path, and it is a compromise between what we want and what we can find.

Occupations are cultural creations, with ancient origins based on human needs and human nature. As we find more sophisticated ways to meet our needs, new jobs replace old ones. Occupations divide up the work that has to be done, and with technological advances, occupations have become more and more specialized. Ranchers have replaced hunters, as airplane mechanics have replaced blacksmiths and word processors have replaced scribes.

Modern and ancient forces come together in occupations. Ancient forces affect our temperament, testosterone levels, and even our enjoyment of our work.[35] High levels of testosterone evolved when the human race was young and people needed the skills of youth. High testosterone helped them compete, but it also led them to take risks, fight, get injured, and die young—and now it interferes with many modern activities. High-testosterone individuals are energetic but impatient; they do poorly in school and end up with fewer years of education; they can dominate others in face-to-face meetings, but they have trouble handling the complexities of business; they lean toward harsh and competitive activities and away from subdued and thoughtful ones. High testosterone is a drawback when careful planning, reliable work habits, and patience are needed, or when workers must attend to the needs of others. Except for a few of the top jobs in sports and acting, high testosterone, to my knowledge, does not contribute to financial success.

There is an irony to this. Natural selection gave an advantage to men with high levels of testosterone during thousands of years of violence and hardship. They developed muscular bodies and the skills needed for hunting and fighting, and now these qualities get them into trouble. It is understandable that high-testosterone men themselves would find little humor in this. Irony is for intellectuals with highly developed verbal skills. In the movie *Roxanne,* Steve Martin explained to Darryl Hannah about humor in Aspen, Colorado. He said, "Oh … irony … oh, no no, we don't get that here. See, people here ski topless while smoking dope, so irony is not really a top priority. We haven't had any real irony here since about '83, when I was the only practitioner of it, and I stopped because I was tired of being stared at."[36] If it's not funny in Aspen, it's hardly funny to an unemployed man.

Viewed more seriously, testosterone carries an element of tragedy that would appeal to the ancient Greeks. The Greeks saw tragedy in the mixed nature of human character, where strong individuals brought destruction upon themselves through their efforts to do what they thought was right. The classic tragic figure was Oedipus, who grew up believing he was an orphan. In a relentless search for truth, he found out that he was not an orphan and that he had unwittingly killed his own father and married his mother. He found the truth so awful that he blinded himself. Tragedy arises when testosterone is selected because it brings success in one-on-one encounters, and this sets the individual on a course of action that reduces the chance of more lasting success. High levels of testosterone brought the force and energy that helped to develop the modern world: bold traders, sailors, and explorers traveled and exchanged ideas and materials; shipwrights designed vessels for trade and exploration; copper miners and traders brought resources that made the bronze age possible. Life and ideas grew at the frontiers of experience, and restless individuals explored and mastered a material world that supports our intellectual world. High-testosterone individuals helped to build the modern world, and the modern world restricts them. High testosterone is close to the intersection of what is tragic and what is simply ironic. What evolved as an advantage so many generations ago is now often at cross-purposes with the demands of society.

Steve Olson, the "Blue Collar Guy" in *Newsweek*, saw the saga of human history repeated in his lifetime. He said:

> While we were building the world we live in, white-collar types were sitting on their ever-widening butts redefining the values we live by. One symbol of America's opulent wealth is the number of people who can sit and ponder and comment and write without producing a usable product or skill. Hey, get a real job—make something—then talk. These talkers are the guys we drove from the playgrounds into the libraries when we were young and now for 20 years or more we have endured the revenge of the nerds.[37]

Part Three
CIVILIZATION

7

Dear Ladies and Gentle Men

A KINDER AND GENTLER WORLD

Bruce Harvey, the high-testosterone defense lawyer described in Chapter 6, charmed Colleen Heusel. He was so pleasant and attentive when he interviewed prospective jurors that he changed the bad impression she had from seeing him on the news. Friendliness is not the distinguishing attribute of high-testosterone people, but it is a skill they can master along with good manners. High-testosterone people often excel at charm.

Although Harvey met the jury panel with an open and friendly manner, I know from seeing him in his adversarial role that he is not always so amiable. Another Harvey was nice all the time. He was the invisible talking rabbit in the play *Harvey*.[1] Harvey the rabbit brought happiness to everyone, and his main companion was Elwood Dowd, a gentle man. Elwood explained his philosophy to Dr. Chumley, a psychiatrist, "Dr. Chumley, my mother used to say to me, 'In this world, Elwood'—she always called me Elwood—she'd say, 'In this world, Elwood, you must be oh, so smart or oh, so pleasant.' For years I was smart. I recommend pleasant. You may quote me." Perhaps he depended on intelligence until he reached the age when a drop in testosterone made it possible for him to be consistently pleasant.

Elwood Dowd would have liked the song "Dear Hearts and Gentle People," which was popular in the 1950s. The words of this song do not have any ring of testosterone to them. Times change, and songs about gentle feelings are less common in today's world of violence, sophistication, and hard-driving achievement. They sound corny to us when we are used to seeing fast-paced violent film clips, such as those one television network runs to advertise "movies for guys who like movies."

With parents and grandparents all over America alarmed about school violence, there are signs that we might be ready for a "Dear Hearts and Gentle People" revival. George W. Bush has been talking about "compassionate conservatism," and Deborah Tannen has been writing and speaking in favor of good manners and consideration for others.[2] My students and I will know there's been a major turnaround when our subjects who learn that they are in the low-normal range for testosterone aren't disappointed. They shouldn't be disappointed at all, because as other chapters of this book have suggested, there are advantages to having low testosterone. As a group, low-testosterone people tend to be more friendly, more intellectual, and more interested in the welfare of others than are high-testosterone people. Low-testosterone people tend to do better in school, have higher-status occupations, feel closer to their friends and families, and have happier marriages. With all of this in their favor, it's not surprising that low-testosterone people smile more than high-testosterone people do.

SMILE! YOU'VE GOT LOW TESTOSTERONE!

My students and I began to notice that friendly and pleasant people were often low in testosterone. We checked this out by finding volunteers who seemed to be "nice guys" and collecting saliva samples from them for testosterone assay. For example, we selected one of the friendliest and most pleasant graduate students we knew. He was patient, considerate, calm, and likable. When we measured his testosterone level, we found it was low.

An important part of being friendly is having a nice smile, not the superficial kind of smile political observer Myra MacPherson describes as a "politician's smile—the kind that never reaches the eyes,"[3] but a sincere smile that makes crinkles around the corners of the eyes. In one study, we examined the facial expressions of 119 male and 114 female college students.[4] First we collected a saliva sample from each subject to measure testosterone. Then Paula Williams, a student assistant with a confident manner and an attractive smile herself, took two pictures of each subject. She took the first picture after telling the subject to relax and look toward the camera without smiling. Then she said, "Okay, now smile," and she smiled at the subject and took another picture.

We developed the pictures and lined them up on a tabletop from lowest to highest in testosterone. Among the females, there was no relationship between testosterone and facial expression. But among the males, the low-testosterone subjects looked more friendly to us. We examined the pictures in more detail, using the Facial Affect Coding System, which scores the muscle movements in facial expressions.[5] The analysis confirmed our hypothesis that low-testosterone males have more convincing smiles. The corners of their lips moved farther outward and upward, and the outer corners of their eyes crinkled more. Figure 7.1 shows the smile of a high- and the smile of a low-testosterone man. Figure 7.2 shows the nonsmiling expressions of the same two men.

The wide smiles and crinkles around the eyes, which indicate true enjoyment, were more typical of low-testosterone men.[6] The high-testosterone men may have been less happy, or they may have disliked being told to smile. Whatever the reason, their smiles showed less true enjoyment. Among the women there was no relation between their smiles and testosterone. Perhaps parents insist that their little girls smile and look pretty when they have their pictures taken, and by the time they grow up most of them have learned to smile convincingly at the camera.

When high-testosterone women are not posing for a picture, they are less likely to smile. At the University of Utah, anthropologist Eliza-

Figure 7.1. The smiling face of a high-testosterone man *(left)* and a low-testosterone man *(right)*.

Figure 7.2. The nonsmiling face of a high-testosterone man *(left)* and a low-testosterone man *(right)*.

beth Cashdan studied a group of women students who lived together. When Cashdan watched the women talking in informal groups, she found that those who were lower in testosterone smiled more often.[7] This is different from what we found in the photographs, but we had asked our subjects to smile, and Cashdan let hers smile or not as they wished. Women posing for photographs may smile because they are expected to smile, while in informal settings they may smile because of their true feelings, which are affected by testosterone.

Next we looked at smiles among college fraternity men. We counted smiles among members of the low- and high-testosterone college fraternities mentioned in Chapter 3. We did this by examining pictures of individual fraternity members in college yearbooks, as well as group pictures displayed in the fraternity houses. Fewer members were smiling in the higher-testosterone fraternities than in the lower-testosterone ones. In fraternities where testosterone scores were highest, a third of the members were smiling, and where they were lowest, two-thirds were smiling. In candid shots taken at social events, the difference among fraternities was less noticeable. One group photograph showed the members of a high-testosterone fraternity gathered with their dates before a party. All the men were smiling, but their smiles had a "wolfish" quality, with little of the crinkling around the eyes that especially indicates true enjoyment.

I've seen men, whose attention was fixed on macho activities, smile a gentle smile that I think can be related to both testosterone and pure enjoyment. At a party, Mary and I watched our son James and a friend talking about explosions. Our friend had been present as an invited observer at the demolition of a large building. He described watching the building collapse and seeing a massive black cloud rise above the rubble and roll toward him, blotting out the sun and covering him with dust and soot. When he finished the story, both he and James sat quietly for a moment, savoring the image of the grand event. Both had sweet, angelic smiles on their faces. Soon after that, Mary and I saw similar sweet smiles again. We were in a store watching a mega-TV demo about car racing. The video alternated between shots of speeding cars and close-ups of members of a pit crew watching the race. The crew members, almost surely a high-testosterone group, seemed absorbed by the race and unaware of the people around them, including the cameraman. Their smiles were not like the wolfish grins the fraternity boys put on for their party pictures. The pit crew members seemed to be smiling because they were truly enjoying themselves.

High-testosterone men look different from low-testosterone men whether or not they are smiling. In our Georgia State study, we found testosterone also related to the nonsmiling photographs Paula Williams took. The nonsmiling photographs were supposed to be neutral, not showing any particular expression. Among the women, when we looked at the pictures informally, the neutral pictures didn't suggest any difference between low and high testosterone. Among the men, however, those higher in testosterone looked more serious, tough, and hard. You can see this in the difference between the two men in Figure 7.2. We checked out our impressions by making two posters, one showing the twelve men highest in testosterone, and the other showing the twelve lowest. The posters did not identify which group was higher or lower in testosterone. Using three rating dimensions—power, activity, and goodness—developed by psychologist Charles Osgood and his colleagues, we asked seventy-two college students to look at the posters and tell us which group looked more strong and dominant, more active and energetic, and more good and friendly. Of the seventy-two students, fifty-nine thought the high-testosterone group looked more strong and dominant, and fifty-one thought it looked more active and energetic.

However, only eighteen thought the high-testosterone group looked more good and friendly. Fifty-four of the seventy-two students said that the low-testosterone group looked more good and friendly.

The high-testosterone group of nonsmiling men looked tough to us, but we had to study the pictures to figure out why. We saw no clear relationship between facial structure and testosterone level. Some researchers have suggested that testosterone shapes the faces of men and women differently, and there is a report, mentioned in Chapter 3, that men who are higher in testosterone have larger jaws.[8] The difference we saw between high- and low-testosterone men was not so much in facial structure but in expressiveness, which showed up especially around their eyes. High-testosterone men tended toward deadpan stares, while low-testosterone men were more expressive and generally more pleasant looking.

Related examples come from patients treated for prostate cancer. High testosterone is a risk factor for prostate cancer, and testosterone can make prostate cancer worse. Because of this, doctors treat prostate cancer patients with a testosterone-lowering medication. A side effect of lowered testosterone is that the men become more friendly, relaxed, sociable, and pleasant to deal with. They begin to smile more, and an aggressive and brusque edge to their behavior is reduced. They become more willing to engage in small talk.

Smiling promotes positive social relations because it is friendly and because it is responsive. People prefer responsive expressions to the deadpan stares we saw in our high-testosterone subjects. People want to see how others react when they open a gift, hear the punch line of a joke, or testify on the witness stand. Impassive faces bother everybody, even babies. A baby will look away if its mother stares at it with no expression or her face.[9] Writer Leslie Fiedler moved from the eastern United States to Montana, where he found impassive faces, and he wrote about the "Montana Face," built "not for sociability or feeling, but for facing into the weather."[10] In 1924, the author of one of the first textbooks on social psychology wrote, "The 'close-up' of the actor's face in the 'movie,' and the savage humor of the comic supplement indulge our craving to get a reaction, ludicrous or tragic, but always intense, from every situation."[11] Letters to the editor are popular newspaper features because they let readers know how other people are reacting to news.

Peggy Noonan, President Reagan's speechwriter, understood that people like personal reactions. She made sure that when Reagan made an announcement, he would say not just what was happening but also what he and Nancy thought about it.[12]

"GETTING TO LIKE YOU, GETTING TO HOPE YOU LIKE ME"

In *The King and I,* the musical version of the novel *Anna and the King of Siam,* the words "Getting to like you, getting to hope you like me" tell about the importance of getting along with others.[13] Smiling helps the process; it implies liking, and both smiling and liking are reciprocal. Smiles are contagious and sometimes automatic, as when we react to the wide, toothless grin of a baby. Smiling back is one of the earliest signs of sociability. Even infants smile back at people who smile at them.[14] It is interesting to note that while smiling is a universal expression for friendship and other happy feelings, there is no universal expression to indicate unhappiness. Anger, fear, sadness, and disgust all have their own individual expressions, but smiles can show friendship, amusement, pleasure, satisfaction, or happiness. With good feelings, it seems to be enough just to let others know that things are fine, and a smile does that.

Mary and I are convinced that our altered male dog, Bogart, can smile. His smile reaches up to his eyebrows and down to the tip of his wagging tail. He resembles a short-legged show horse as he trots along the sidewalk. He holds his head up and his tail up so high it looks like the plume on a drum major's hat. He stops to smile and wag at everyone— people, dogs, cats, old friends, and strangers. People smile back and usually stop to speak to him when they meet him on the sidewalk. At stoplights people smile at him from their car windows. With his contagious doggy smile, Bogart traffics in happiness.

Friendly gestures are common in species in which individuals depend on each other for survival. In the office or on the street, people and animals avoid violence by showing others that they are not threatening. Most other dogs are friendly to Bogart because he is friendly and shows no desire to fight. Like Bogart, low-testosterone people let others know they have no desire to fight. They are quick to smile, and their manner evokes friendliness in others. Whether smiles are automatic or calculated, the effect is the same: the smile indicates that there is no threat.

People smile to set a friendly tone for an encounter, thus minimizing the possibility that other people will be hostile. People, high or low in testosterone, who are at the receiving end of smiles usually smile back.

Smiles and friendliness are a part of the everyday social currency that people use to buy small favors and goodwill. They show that we are responsive, and they help us get things done. When people are smiling, their smiles stimulate their facial muscle nerves to send messages to emotional centers in their brains, telling these emotional centers that things are going well.[15] Both the person smiling and the person being smiled at feel better, and things go more smoothly. Smiles reduce hostility and make others like us. Low-testosterone people, who depend on cooperation from others, seem to use this strategy more often than high-testosterone people do. We all smile sometimes, but low-testosterone people smile most of all.

Smiles flatter and disarm people who might otherwise present a challenge. Smiling shows politeness, deference, and unaggressive intentions toward others, all of which are helpful to people who are "networking" their way to success. People who have reached positions of power smile less than those on their way up, maybe because they feel they don't have to ingratiate themselves with people who are paid to take orders. This may partly explain some contradictory findings on smiling, testosterone levels, and power. The two groups who smile least are people with high testosterone levels and people with power.[16] This is in spite of the fact that high-testosterone people do not, for the most part, have the power associated with high socioeconomic status in modern society.

A possible explanation for less smiling among high-status people is that most of those people are men. Women, who are less likely than men to be in high-status positions, smile more than men. There is strong social pressure on women to smile. A few years ago there was a poll reported on an Atlanta news program that showed "smiling" at the top of the list of what women did that men liked.[17]

As the gap between men's and women's status in society continues to close, it will be interesting to see whether men smile more and/or women smile less. Mary has noticed that in recent fashion ads, the female models aren't smiling as much as they used to, and in some of the ads, the models seem to be glowering at prospective customers. It remains to be seen whether this is part of a trend and whether it has anything to do with improved status for women.

TWO KINDS OF PEOPLE, TWO WAYS TO LIVE

Frank Sinatra sang, "I did it my way," and the Beatles sang, "I get by with a little help from my friends."[18] These are the ways in which high- and low-testosterone people approach the world. Sinatra's song is the self-congratulatory, high-testosterone way, while the Beatles' song is the congenial, low-testosterone way. They are opposing strategies, one based on dominance and the other on cooperation. The tough, high-testosterone person looks out for himself and competes for personal advantage, while the sociable, low-testosterone person avoids struggles for dominance and works with his associates for their mutual advantage.

While it is common to think of high-testosterone people as being simply independent, a study I did with my students indicates that this is not entirely true. We asked high- and low-testosterone men and women to carry beepers and diaries, and we beeped them at random intervals several times a day for four days.[19] We asked them to write down what they were doing and thinking each time they heard the beep. Examination of the diaries indicated that high-testosterone people, both men and women, depended on the company of others to make them happy. High-testosterone people seem to be unhappy when they are alone and happy when they are with people. They appear to need many friends and to spend a lot of time with them. Perhaps Animal and all his girlfriends, mentioned in Chapter 1, are examples of high-testosterone sociability. Low-testosterone people, on the other hand, seem to be less compulsively social. They like to spend more time alone or with intimate friends. Perhaps the relative solitude of farming is one thing that makes farming attractive to low-testosterone people.

Even though high-testosterone people seek companionship, they are more direct and confrontational in social situations. People with lower testosterone like to get along with others, and they are more pleasant, more polite, and more considerate. On the average, high-testosterone individuals are tougher, and low-testosterone individuals are friendlier. In real life there are many exceptions, of course, and on occasion anyone can be tough or friendly.

Nevertheless, most people lean more toward one strategy or the other. Low-testosterone people tend to prefer the kinder, gentler approach, and, except for unusual situations, they rely on it. Sticking with one strategy is simple and does not clutter the mind with too many possibilities. Some creatures are biologically programmed to prefer a particular strategy. The two types of males among the desert tree lizards described in Chapter 6 either competed to control territory or avoided competition and sought out uncontested territory. Both strategies allowed the males to survive, find mates, and reproduce. People tend toward one strategy over the other, but they are not as rigidly fixed as the lizards are.

Many people, including trial lawyers like Bruce Harvey who can be pleasant with jurors and tough with prosecutors, need to be flexible. With practice, they can learn to use both strategies with equal effect, but not necessarily with equal comfort. I have a woman friend who is a political activist. Her testosterone level is above the female average, but she prefers to be pleasant. She was brought up "to behave like a lady," and most of the time her upbringing influences her behavior more than her testosterone. Nevertheless, she can be tough, especially when "some officious jerk" tries to bully her. For a few seconds after she decides to get tough, she has stress symptoms: her throat tightens and blood rushes to her head. While the symptoms last, her activist friends say she has a wild look that scares people. She finds the symptoms unpleasant, but she thinks they work to her advantage.

Some people, like President Bush, are skilled enough to move back and forth between the two strategies with no apparent strain. In his political speeches, Bush called for a "kinder and gentler nation." Then he added a challenge—"Read my lips . . . No new taxes!"—imitating the actor Clint Eastwood's challenge, "Go ahead. Make my day." The comedian Rich Little said he impersonated President Bush by pretending to be Mr. Rogers imitating John Wayne. High-testosterone people have something in common with actors, as noted earlier, and they may find it easy to move back and forth between smiles and toughness. The high-testosterone individual can be friendly and pleasant when the occasion calls for it, but the low-testosterone individual finds it difficult, though not necessarily impossible, to be overtly aggressive. Assertiveness training classes are popular among people who don't want to be bulldozed by aggressive people. Assertiveness, like charm, can be learned.

Sometimes a change in strategy accompanies a change in testosterone. As we've discussed, polygamous male birds are high in testosterone throughout the breeding season, presumably because they compete continuously with other males over females. Monogamous male birds are high in testosterone only at the beginning of the breeding season, and then, as soon as they find mates, their testosterone levels drop. Males need a lot of testosterone to get a mate, but they need less to be good parents and caregivers.[20] The study of veterans mentioned in Chapter 5 showed that married men are lower in testosterone than single men, and a study of Air Force officers found that testosterone levels decreased when they married and increased when they divorced.[21] Men have also been found to have higher levels of prolactin and lower levels of testosterone immediately after they become fathers, as have the males in some species of small mammals, including gerbils and mice.[22] Perhaps these hormonal changes set them up for the gentler activities of parenthood.

All these findings come from studies of males. We don't know whether testosterone also drops in females when they become mothers. One of the oddest changes associated with testosterone is a sex-role reversal in the spotted sandpiper. Female sandpipers increase in testosterone sevenfold in the breeding season, while males decrease twenty-five-fold. After this change occurs, the males sit peaceably on the eggs in the nest, while the females wander off to their own affairs.[23]

WHEN YOUR LEVEL IS TOO LOW

Most of the studies of violence, divorce, and misbehavior indicate desirable effects of low-testosterone levels. In comparison with others, men in the bottom 10 percent of the testosterone distribution are about half as likely to have trouble with the police, use hard drugs, be divorced, or hit their mates.[24] Low testosterone does not make a person weak or cowardly, but it does takes away the combative "chip on the shoulder" that sometimes goes with very high testosterone. Men and women in the low-normal range of testosterone tend to be friendly and accommodating, but that tendency may not hold when testosterone is extremely low.

There is a floor, a minimum level of testosterone, below which problems begin to occur. Endocrinologists find that low testosterone has its greatest effect in lowering energy and reducing sexual activity. People with levels below the normal range are sometimes so deficient in energy that it is difficult for them to smile and be sociable or to otherwise show interest in people. Very low levels of testosterone may be related to clinical depression,[25] although most studies have not found this to be true.[26] Although it contributes to fatigue and reduced libido, a testosterone deficiency does not usually seem to make people particularly sad. Overall, the findings about negative effects of low testosterone are not clear.

Most people who are very low in testosterone appear normal. Prostate cancer patients whose testosterone levels are being lowered as part of their treatment appear good humored. I heard about a man who volunteered to be in a testosterone experiment. He agreed to have his testosterone temporarily reduced to almost zero, and he seemed not to mind when he lost his sex drive. He knew, of course, that the effect was temporary. Someone who lost his libido without knowing if or when he would get it back might feel quite differently.

Extremely low levels of testosterone affect women just as they affect men. Women have less testosterone than men, and their levels fall even lower after menopause, when the ovaries stop producing estrogen and testosterone. For quite a while, gynecologists have been prescribing estrogen to relieve menopausal symptoms, but recently they have begun to treat patients who do not respond well enough to estrogen alone with additional small doses of testosterone. Women who take both estrogen and testosterone report an increase in energy, strength, sexual interest, and general positive outlook. I know a woman who took only estrogen following surgical menopause, an operation in which her ovaries were removed. She said that after two years she had lost so much strength in her grip that she could barely hold a vacuum cleaner to do housework. Adding testosterone to her estrogen treatment corrected her problem.

RELATED HORMONES

This chapter is about kind and gentle behavior that goes with low levels of testosterone, but testosterone does not act alone. It interacts or coexists with other hormones and neurotransmitters, including cortisol, serotonin, and prolactin, which decrease testosterone and/or moderate its effects.

Cortisol, whether naturally produced or injected, is one of the hormones that lower testosterone in men.[27] Cortisol is part of the body's fight-or-flight response; it releases stored energy and helps us deal with emergencies, both those we run from and those we face head-on. Cortisol is normally associated with stressful situations, but in some individuals it is chronically high and chronically stressful. Low-testosterone men who are high in cortisol are not inclined to be aggressive or confrontational, but they are not as friendly and cheerful as other low-testosterone men. The stress associated with elevated levels of cortisol tends to make them anxious.

The effect of cortisol on testosterone is different in women than in men, probably because the adrenal cortex, which produces cortisol, also produces testosterone. In women, testosterone from the adrenals is roughly equal to the testosterone from the ovaries, but in men, testosterone from the adrenals is relatively unimportant compared to the amount that comes from the testes. In women, testosterone appears not to be lowered significantly by increases in cortisol.[28] Women may be more likely than men to be high or low in both hormones at the same time.

Serotonin is a neurotransmitter that affects some of the same aspects of mind and social behavior that testosterone does, but in a way that gives people a more pleasant demeanor. At present, it is not clear whether serotonin produces its effects on personality independently of testosterone, or somehow reduces the effects of testosterone, or does a little of each. Serotonin research, particularly on human subjects, is more expensive and more difficult than testosterone research, because serotonin is assayed from spinal fluid. Spitting is easy, giving blood is more difficult, and donating spinal fluid is beyond what almost anyone will do for science. In 1995, a military study of testosterone and serotonin in prison inmates was put on hold until researchers could find an easier way to collect serotonin samples.[29]

In the meantime, researchers can make some guesses based on indirect evidence. There are several studies in which fluoxetine, a drug known by its brand name, Prozac, has been administered to laboratory animals. Fluoxetine, which inhibits serotonin uptake and therefore keeps serotonin levels high, seems to be related to increased levels of prolactin, a hormone that is known to reduce testosterone levels.[30] Another study shows that large intravenous doses of the amino acid tryptophan, a precursor of serotonin, will increase prolactin levels.[31] These studies suggest to researchers that high serotonin levels may reduce testosterone, at least slightly, by raising prolactin levels.

Anyone with a friend who's been successfully treated with Prozac knows how elevated levels of serotonin affect personality. People who take Prozac are likely to be calmer, more confident, less irritable, more optimistic, less impulsive, and more pleasant to be around than they were before they started taking the drug. In some species of monkeys, alpha males are likely to be high in serotonin. As described in Chapter 5, female vervet monkeys like high-serotonin males and help them gain leadership roles. Such high-serotonin males are dominant, as high-testosterone males are, but they are calmer. Apparently the females appreciate the calmer and less violent leadership style of high-serotonin males. As far as peaceful behavior goes, the worst combination would seem to be low serotonin together with high testosterone. A person with this kind of mix would likely be both impulsive and dominant.[32]

Sometimes when we examine self-confident, dominant men, expecting them to be high in testosterone, we find they are not. For example, we studied an outdoorsman who lived in Alaska and spent weeks alone in the wilderness. He had a touch of vanity, and he always came back to civilization looking neat, with his beard and mustache in good shape. Suzanne Womack, who was a friend of his, said he had panache and sex appeal, and she thought he would be high in testosterone. We checked him out (after she collected saliva from him on a trip to Alaska) and found that his testosterone level was average. I suspect, but do not know, that his serotonin level was high. He had the kind of calm competence associated with leadership, the kind that makes high-serotonin male vervet monkeys attractive to females.[33] Two other people Suzanne checked out from Alaska were mountain climbers, both very high in testosterone. In exploring other characteristics with these men, she asked one to describe how high his sex drive was. He said, "Ballistic!"

We did not assay the mountain climber's other hormone levels, but it's safe to assume he was low in prolactin. Men with high levels of prolactin do not have "ballistic" sex drives. Prolactin, like cortisol, moderates the effects of testosterone, but unlike cortisol, it has a calming effect. Prolactin is generally known as the hormone that stimulates milk production in new mothers, but it is present in men and women and in vertebrates other than mammals. Often related to nesting and nurturing activity, elevated prolactin levels signal male penguins and both male and female pigeons to produce crop milk, a sort of nondairy creamer that nourishes their young. Although prolactin sometimes encourages nurturing behavior in new fathers, it rarely stimulates milk production in male mammals, but there are exceptions. In rare cases, when the milk-producing apparatus has been exposed to higher-than-normal levels of estrogen and progesterone, prolactin can stimulate milk production in males. Biologist Roger Short talks about Claymore, a remarkable goat with a high prolactin level who didn't let being male interfere with producing milk. Claymore liked his own milk and sometimes nursed himself; he also provided milk for billy goat milk cheese. He was a member of a small family of Scottish goats in which both males and females produced milk. Claymore's grandfather, who died of mastitis, had enough testosterone, in spite of his high prolactin levels, to achieve reproductive success.[34]

Above-average levels of prolactin have an effect on personality that is different from testosterone's, partly because it inhibits testosterone production. The simplest way to describe prolactin is to say that it makes people "nice." People with high levels of prolactin are agreeable, helpful, and do what they are asked. They have little interest in sex or in starting fights, but they do not hesitate to protect their young. Maternal aggression is triggered not by prolactin but by other factors, which include the hormone progesterone. It is easy to see how the offspring of mothers with proper levels of progesterone and prolactin had an evolutionary advantage. Progesterone would have come into play when it was necessary for mothers to fight off dangerous intruders. In the absence of danger, prolactin would have motivated our primitive female ancestors to take good care of their babies and not wander away looking for fights and sex. During most of human evolutionary history, young children could not survive without their mothers' care. Protective mothers who avoided unnecessary fights were more likely to pass on their genes to future generations than were mothers who risked their lives and the lives of their children with frequent fighting.[35]

Like the other hormones that gave our ancestors an evolutionary advantage, prolactin can sometimes be too much of a good thing. Every once in a while, something goes wrong with the pituitary gland, where prolactin is produced, and causes hyperprolactinemia, in which prolactin levels climb to five or six times normal and dramatically affect personality. I talked to two endocrinologists about hyperprolactinemia. One told me that hyperprolactinemia has similar effects on personality in both men and women. Hyperprolactinemia patients are polite, indirect, and unaggressive, sometimes to the point of obsequiousness. I asked the endocrinologist to give me an example of their behavior. He said, "If I am late for an appointment, most of my patients will show at least some sign of irritation, but not my hyperprolactinemia patients. There have been occasions when I've had emergencies that put me an hour or so behind schedule, and I've had two patients waiting, one with hyperprolactinemia and one with a thyroid disorder, and the one with hyperprolactinemia has the earlier appointment. I have to resist an impulse to see the thyroid patient first, because I know he or she is the one who is impatient. I know when I apologize to hyperprolactinemia patients for keeping them waiting, they'll say something like, 'Your time is more valuable than mine. All I have to do is sit.' "

I asked him if there was a difference between the way high-prolactin and other low-testosterone patients acted. He said that male patients in both categories tended to see him because they were concerned about libidinal changes and erectile dysfunction. Both want their problems fixed, but the person who is low in testosterone and normal in prolactin is more in a hurry about it. At his first appointment, such a person might say, "I want a testosterone shot today and every day until I'm better," or say, "I'm going on vacation in two weeks and I want to be cured by then." On the other hand, a high-prolactin patient would be more likely to say, "I'm supposed to go on vacation in two weeks. Maybe you'd like to start my treatment after that."

The endocrinologist also said that his new male hyperprolactinemia patients were generally not in a big hurry about seeing a doctor, and they tended to be more advanced in their condition when he first saw them than were their female counterparts—missed menstrual periods prompted women to seek treatment sooner. Even though he saw many women before their symptoms were advanced, their demeanor almost always revealed the elevated prolactin levels that laboratory tests would later confirm. In addition to being polite and unaggressive, these women were likely to express feelings of inadequacy and dependency.

The endocrinologist's adult male patients may have had similar feelings, but they kept those feelings to themselves. Social conditioning probably partly explains why the endocrinologist noticed that only men whose problems started before puberty were likely to reveal feelings of inadequacy and show dependency on others. For example, sexually immature young men and many women hyperprolactinemic patients would bring companions with them to their medical appointments, as if they depended on other people to make sure they did things right.

One such patient was a man whose condition resulted from a tumor on his pituitary gland. The tumor had interfered with his sexual development, and although he was a twenty-five-year-old man, he had the body and mind-set of a thirteen-year-old boy. His mother brought him for most of his appointments during the early stages of his treatment. At first he was a model patient, showing up on time for every appointment and following instructions exactly. As the tumor shrank, prolactin began to drop and testosterone began to rise, and he began to miss some of his appointments. At that point, the patient's mother told the endocrinologist that she was furious about what he had done to her boy. When he had started treatment, she said her son had been well-behaved. After treatment, he had begun to misbehave, and sometimes now he stayed out all night.

With treatment of hyperprolactinemia, it is not unusual to hear that when patients begin to produce testosterone, they get into trouble. The other endocrinologist I talked with told me about a nice married man whose prolactin level was too high. The endocrinologist lowered the man's prolactin level, and his marriage became unstable. The man worked as a traveling salesman, and in his new high-testosterone state he began to marry other women in other towns.

A final link between prolactin and testosterone has to do with smiles. Medical internists are taught that patients who are high in prolactin have wrinkles around the corners of their eyes, and this is usually assumed to be caused by the thinness of their skin; but prolactin wrinkles look like the crinkles around the eyes in the smiles of low-testosterone men. At this time, there have been no studies comparing the way high-prolactin and low-prolactin people smile, but a reasonable hypothesis is that high-prolactin people and low-testosterone people would have similar smiles.

Happy people have smile crinkles around their eyes, and they tend to be kind and helpful. Try the following experiment. Make a list of the ten people you know best. Put an H beside each one you believe is happy. Then put an U beside each one you believe is unselfish. When you look at the results, you will find that you often put H and U by the same person. Psychologist Bernard Rimland had two hundred students do this exercise. They marked about half the two thousand people they listed as happy, and they marked about half as unselfish. They marked the majority of the people, 79 percent, as unselfish and happy, or as self-ish and unhappy. Only 4 percent were both happy and selfish.[36]

A study at the University of Western Ontario showed a link between low testosterone and kind and gentle altruism.[37] Students answered questions about themselves and provided saliva samples for testosterone measurement. The questions measured empathy, helpful-ness, and concern for others, and together they produced an overall altruism score. The study found that lower-testosterone students were more altruistic. They were people who would appreciate the sentiment expressed in a popular bumper sticker: "Practice random kindness and senseless acts of beauty."

ALTRUISM AND MIXED MOTIVES

Perhaps kind and gentle altruism is purer when it is practiced by low-testosterone people. Altruism can take on some of the characteristics of a competitive sport when it is practiced by high-testosterone people.

Even though everybody knows "it is more blessed to give than receive," there's often a touch of genteel self-interest in altruistic ges-tures. A sociable person gives wedding gifts to his friends' children, and then, when his children marry, they get presents from his friends. With most people it's not exactly quid pro quo, but sometimes it comes close. Mary eloped to marry her first husband, and his mother was irate. She told the newlyweds, "I've been giving people wedding presents for years, and now it's their time to give the presents. Since you didn't have a wedding in Atlanta, you're just going to have to come to Jacksonville. I'm going to have a reception down here." Mary suspects that her first mother-in-law was a high-testosterone woman.

Humans, like Mary's first mother-in-law, aren't the only species to mix a little testosterone with altruism. Dr. Tim Clutton-Brock, a Cambridge University behavioral ecologist, can attest to the fact that meerkats have mixed motives, and his recent research on meerkats in southern Africa illustrates the point. For years, biologists have used meerkat sentinels as examples of animal altruism. The sentinels watch for hawks from high, seemingly vulnerable perches, providing security for other meerkats as they look for food and eat. But now Clutton-Brock, after he and thirty colleagues spent thousands of hours over a five-year period watching meerkats, questions the purity of the sentinels' altruism. Behind the altruism, they noticed some behavior that looked more like competitiveness. The scientists saw hawks kill other meerkats, but never a sentinel. The scientists also observed that meerkats volunteered for sentry duty only after they'd eaten well, and then they chose perches near hiding holes. Furthermore, well-fed meerkats sometimes fought over who got to be the sentinel, not surprising once it became evident that the first meerkat to spot a hawk would be the first one down the hiding hole. Nevertheless, the sentinels were altruistic enough to delay diving for cover long enough to shout a warning call. While not the heroes they were once thought to be, they did provide a valuable service to the meerkat community.

The mixed motives of meerkat sentinels do not negate the fact that among some other animals, including the dwarf mongoose, sentinel work is unselfish, heroic, and often deadly. Dwarf mongoose sentinels watch from behind as the rest of the group hunts for food. The sentinels' rearguard position makes them easy targets for predators.[38]

Whether altruism is selfless and pure or not, it is a good thing. Life is a tangled path. Altruism tainted with self-interest and competitiveness is better than no altruism at all. It is in the interest of civilization to promote and reward altruism, the kind and gentle variety as well as the heroic variety, which is the subject of the next chapter.

8

Heroic Altruism

A WALK ON THE CRUST OF HELL

In a steel mill in Pennsylvania, two hours before dawn on October 14, 1970, Joseph Wiest's partner was working with a furnace of molten steel. He was thrusting a rod through a hole in the furnace door to measure the temperature of the steel as he stood on a platform thirty feet above a pit that collected slag from the furnace. Suddenly the platform collapsed, and he fell to the bottom of the pit. He was badly injured and could not move. Wiest leaped down three flights of iron stairs to find his partner trapped in a corner behind a pool of slag. Below a thin crust that had hardened over its surface, the slag was red-hot and molten. If Wiest tried to walk across, he might break through the crust and be burned alive. He said later, "I didn't think, you just don't think." He walked as quickly and lightly as he could across the slag, the inch-thick soles of his boots beginning to smoke. His face felt as if it were frying. The fumes were choking, and the furnace of molten steel was hanging over his head. Wiest lifted his injured partner, a man taller than himself, and started back across. He could feel the crust cracking beneath his feet. He stumbled once and fell, landing on his left hip with the full weight of his partner across him. The crust did not break. He managed to lift his partner again and carried him off the slag. Other workmen came running and doused them with water. Wiest's trousers were burned away on the left side, and he had second-degree burns. A few days later, his partner died of multiple injuries. Wiest received the bronze Carnegie Hero Award medal for his action.[1]

When I read the story about Wiest, I was struck by his single-minded resolve, which reminded me of the focus and intensity I have come to associate with high levels of testosterone. His story prompted me to look for a connection between heroic altruism and testosterone. Years ago, when I began my research on testosterone, I was expecting to find selfishness and violence, and I did, but now I'm seeing generosity and altruism, too. Throughout this book I have presented a rather sorry view of men, especially men who are high in testosterone. They are often rough and callous, preoccupied with sex and dominance, and single-minded to the point of obsessiveness. Nevertheless, in the presence of strong social forces needed to civilize them and keep them out of trouble, men, in spite of their hormones, have the capacity to be thoughtful. They can stand out in goodness as well as badness; most work hard to support their families, and many, like Wiest, risk their lives to save the lives of others. David Gilmore, in studying different societies to write *Manhood in the Making*, was impressed with the selflessness of men and their willingness to give their lives for others. He said, "Real men give more than they take."[2] My research leads me to agree with him and draw the same conclusion about women: real women also give more than they take.

I'm not the first researcher to begin a project expecting the worst of human nature, only to become pleasantly surprised. Carl Sagan and Ann Druyan began *Shadows of Forgotten Ancestors*[3] concerned that selfishness and violence might be dominant, but they ended up convinced that generosity and altruism held their own. In their book, they explored the evolutionary family tree and found evidence that both the altruistic and selfish sides of human nature have prehuman roots.

In earlier chapters I visited the evolutionary family tree and described how the raw power of testosterone, an ancient and primitive hormone, interferes with success in modern life. This chapter is about how testosterone can transcend its origins and find a helpful role in civilized society. Altruism covers a wide range of behavior, from taking flowers to a friend to walking across a pool of hot slag to rescue an injured partner. It can be gentle or heroic, and there is evidence that testosterone plays a part especially in heroic altruism. The positive qualities associated with testosterone—strength and energy, focused attention, preference for action over thought, and a generally dominant manner—characterize heroic altruists.

LOCAL HEROES

There are many heroic altruists among firefighters, men and women who have chosen a career that is helpful to others and dangerous to themselves. When Noel Fannin, a student at Georgia State University, decided to study heroes, she printed a batch of the "I Spit for Science" badges that we give to volunteers who provide saliva samples for testosterone assays, and she headed for the fire station. First she collected saliva samples and other data from firefighters in DeKalb County, Georgia, which is near Atlanta, and then from firefighters in the city of Atlanta. She is studying how testosterone and personality relate to heroic altruism among firefighters.

Fannin collected data from two hundred DeKalb firefighters. Most of the firefighters were men, and it is the men we will discuss here. She studied their firefighting performance and the emergency medical technician (EMT) work that is so often required of firefighters today. They took personality tests, filled out questionnaires about themselves and their backgrounds, and donated saliva samples. Fannin asked six senior firemen who were familiar with the men to rate them as firefighters, and she asked two senior personnel who were familiar with their EMT work to also rate them in this area. All the ratings were on four-point scales, where one was a "check chaser," two was "average," three was a "real professional," and four was a bit excessive in energy and enthusiasm for the job. A four in firefighting was sometimes called a "hot dog," and a four in EMT work was sometimes called a "junior doc." Both types loved their work, but it was almost as if their motivation reflected too much of a good thing. Hot dogs sometimes took shortcuts when it came to safety, and they liked to borrow Crazy Horse's motto, "Today is a good day to die." Junior docs sometimes went beyond their job descriptions in administering treatment to injured people.

Two of the personality tests the firemen took turned out to be relevant to these ratings of firefighting and EMT work. One test measured personality traits described by psychologist David Bakan as "agency" and "communion."[4] Agency is associated with focus, getting the job done, and an urge to master. Communion is associated with openness, cooperativeness, and a willingness to be close to others. Agency and communion are different but not mutually exclusive. A person can be high, average, or low on both, or high on one and low on the other. The other test measured five normal personality traits frequently studied by psychologists today: neuroticism, extraversion, openness, agreeableness, and conscientiousness. As with agency and communion, a person can be high, average, or low on any combination of these five traits.

In examining the firefighting ratings, we found that firemen with the top ratings tended to be higher in agency than in communion. People high in agency, in addition to wanting to master situations, have tendencies to be self-protective, self-assertive, and self-expansive, tendencies that interfere with interpersonal closeness. In other words, the hotshot firefighters didn't stand out as being especially sensitive or sympathetic everyday companions. Fannin's data give support to the idea that wanting to get the job done is at least as important as wanting to help others in heroic altruism.

The top firemen also scored higher on extraversion and lower on openness* and agreeableness than did the other firemen. We found that testosterone predicted who would be hotshots, but only when considered in combination with agency. Hotshots were twice as likely as the other firemen to be above average in both testosterone and agency. The combination of agency and testosterone reminds me of a spelling rhyme I learned in school: "When two vowels go walking, the first one does the talking." When agency and testosterone go walking, agency does the talking, and testosterone encourages it along.

The relationships among agency, testosterone, and firefighting are shown in Figure 8.1. The main part of the figure shows testosterone enabling the link between agency and energetic firefighting (in statistical terms, testosterone "moderates" the link). The lower parts of the figure show that when testosterone levels are low, agency is not related to firefighting performance, but when testosterone levels are high, agency is related to high ratings on the four-point firefighting scale. Just being motivated toward getting the job done appears not to be enough; testosterone is needed to translate the motivation into action.

Firemen who are high in agency and testosterone have less interest than others in emergency medical work, which is an important part of

---

*Openness includes receptivity to new ideas and feelings.

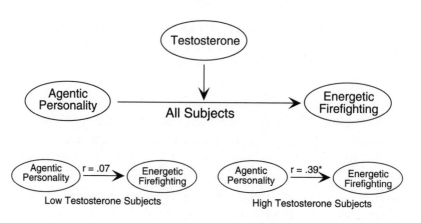

Figure 8.1. High levels of testosterone enable effects of agency on firefighting. An agentic (action-oriented) personality leads to energetic firefighting, but only among men who are also high in testosterone. Asterisk indicates a statistically significant relationship.

what present-day firemen are expected to do. On the other hand, firemen who scored high on communion, even those with above-average testosterone levels, found equal satisfaction in firefighting and emergency medical work.

In examining the EMT ratings, we again found testosterone playing a role, but this time in combination with conscientiousness instead of agency. The findings are summarized in Figure 8.2. Testosterone enables a link between personality and energetic EMT work. When testosterone levels are low, conscientiousness appears to have no effect. When levels are high, there is a positive relation between conscientiousness and EMT work. As with firefighting, motivation is important, but it alone is not enough. The addition of testosterone helps translate motivation into action, which can be excessive action. Sometimes the junior docs are so eager to help injured people that they go ahead with procedures that could more safely be postponed until paramedics or physicians are on the scene. These findings are reminiscent of other findings in the area of altruism, where empathy alone is a poor predictor of whether or not a person will actually offer help.

Fire Station #4 is a special unit of the Atlanta Fire Department. Firemen there are trained to deal with especially difficult or complicated fires and other emergencies, including gas leaks. Fannin collected

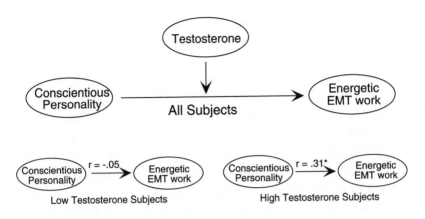

Figure 8.2. High levels of testosterone enable effects of conscientiousness on emergency medical technician (EMT) work. A conscientious personality leads to energetic EMT work, but only among men who are also high in testosterone. Asterisk indicates a statistically significant relationship.

spit for science from the firefighters at Fire Station #4 on quiet days and on days when there were fires. She rode with them in the fire truck and the HazMat (hazardous materials) truck several times. On one trip, she collected saliva samples en route, and then, to her surprise, the firefighters leaned back and dozed the rest of the way. Fannin took saliva samples before and after the fire. The assays showed that testosterone levels rose on the way to the fire and fell afterward.

On April 12, 1999, Fire Station #4 got a call. There was a huge, dangerous fire at an old cotton mill being renovated for loft apartments in Atlanta's Cabbagetown neighborhood. A man was trapped on top of a crane above the blaze. He'd escaped the heat in the crane's cab by climbing out to the end of the counterbalance shortly before the cab burst into flames, but he was by no means safe. Although the wind was blowing heat and smoke away from him, wind often changes. A weakening hot brick wall was standing perilously close to the crane's tower. There was also a limit to how much heat the tower could take before it would collapse. A helicopter rescue was the crane operator's only hope.

That was a challenge to the firefighters at Station #4, and there were plenty of volunteers. Matt Moseley had suited up first, making him the volunteer to get the job. Hanging from a rope beneath the rescue helicopter, he braved heat and smoke while the pilot, maneuvering through tricky air currents, made several passes before putting Moseley in position for a perfect landing on the counterbalance. When he reached the man he'd come to save, Moseley told him, "Your boss sent me to get you. He said you can go home early today."[5]

Matt Moseley's testosterone level is higher than average, but not extremely high. He is a good-looking, nice guy with lots of down-home wit and charm. Carmen Burns interviewed him on *Peachtree Morning*, a local television show, after the rescue and told him that a lot of young women wanted to know if he was available. He said he had to say he had a steady girlfriend, because if he didn't, his girlfriend would see to it that he became available immediately. Moseley is the kind of all-American hero who makes everybody feel wonderful.

Another kind of hero, one that is familiar to moviegoers, is more complicated, a mixture of good and bad. A reoccurring theme in Hollywood movies, including *The Dirty Dozen* and *The Assassin*, is the criminal turned hero. The premise of these movies is that under the right circumstances criminal audacity and derring-do can be transformed into selfless bravery and heroism.

Mitchell Murray, a twenty-year-old Georgia man, is a real-life example of a criminal turned hero. On April 29, 1999, Murray, a convicted car thief who was trained as a volunteer firefighter while in prison, was out on parole. He was staying with his grandmother, and was outside at two in the morning having a cigarette because she doesn't allow smoking in her house. That's when he heard shouting and saw his neighbor, clothes in flames, fleeing from his house. He was calling for someone to help his family trapped inside, and Murray rushed to help. When burglar bars kept him from getting into the burning house, he ran back home to wake his eighteen-year-old brother, and together the brothers found a way inside.

At the back of the house above a stone wall there was a boarded-up window that had no burglar bars. The brothers broke through it, and Murray climbed into a smoke-filled bedroom. He was able to get four members of the family, the mother and three daughters, out through the window to his brother, who lowered them to the ground. Murray came close to saving another sister, but an explosion blew the girl from his arms and knocked him to the floor. Before he could find her again, policemen pulled him from the fire and forcibly restrained him from going back into the house.[6]

Murray was modest about the rescue when he talked to reporters and to Noel Fannin. He was sad about not having been able to save the fourth sister and said he'd just done what God and circumstance put him in the right place to do, the same thing he thought anyone would have done. He never decided to go into the house. He did what he had to do without thinking about it. He heard the girls screaming and just went in. Murray agreed to give Fannin a saliva sample for her research project, and as she expected, his testosterone level was high.

Murray, who'd been having trouble finding regular work when he was on parole, spent the last few dollars he had on a doll he gave to one of the little girls he'd rescued from the fire.[7] After that he told Fannin he'd probably be back in jail within a year, then he disappeared and his parole was revoked. As he predicted, he was soon back in jail.

Rebecca Strong has no criminal record, but she is like Mitchell Murray in several ways: she is high in testosterone, she does what needs to be done without hesitating, and she has a soft spot for children. Rebecca was one of the student researchers on the movie crew project described in Chapter 6. Now she works with abused children and is committed to doing as much as she can to help them. Rebecca doesn't look tough, but she is. She is outgoing and bold, sometimes to the point of daring. Considering her interests, her testosterone level, and her personality, it is not surprising that she has put herself in potentially risky situations on more than one occasion to prevent children from being hurt. When she goes to the aid of children, she does it without making a conscious choice.

In 1994, Rebecca was a student, and she was recovering from a sledding accident that had broken her neck. She was walking through Central City Park in Atlanta during her lunch break. The park was crowded, and she heard someone say, "Did you see that man dragging that baby?" Rebecca looked around and saw a man, about six feet five inches tall and muscular, pulling a baby boy along by one hand. The baby, not much over a year old, could not walk fast enough to keep up with his long-legged father, and was alternately off the ground or dragging, whimpering with pain and distress. Immediately Rebecca moved toward the man and the baby, aware as she did so that she was putting herself into a precarious situation, especially so because her doctor had just removed the halo brace she had been wearing to protect her injured neck.

She caught up with the man, and walking along beside him she said,

"Excuse me, sir, but did you know that holding your baby that way could injure his shoulder?" The man answered Rebecca in obscene and abusive language, but she continued talking as calmly and reasonably as she could. She told him, "Lifting him by one arm could dislocate his shoulder now or cause him to have arthritis later on."

Rebecca knew the man was on the edge of violence, and that if he hit her, her neck could pop, leaving her dead or paralyzed. She backed away, but just a little bit. Her knees were shaking so much she was afraid they would collapse underneath her, but she didn't give up. She said, "It would really be better if you picked up your baby."

The man continued cursing her, but then he picked up his baby and walked away.

Rebecca most often goes to the rescue when children are in trouble, but she also helps adults. Once she pulled a severely injured truck driver out of his wrecked cab. A man who was rubbernecking at a safe distance refused to help. He told Rebecca he saw a stream of something blowing out the back of the cab, and he was afraid it might be gas and it might explode. After Rebecca pulled the truck driver to safety, she sat with him for forty-five minutes until an ambulance came and then visited him several times in the hospital.

VARIETIES OF HEROIC ALTRUISM

People like Wiest, Moseley, Murray, and Strong are just plain tough. Heroic altruism is risky; it involves power, force and gumption. Heroic altruism is a special event, a spectacular response to a crisis or an emergency, and it testifies to the fact that high-testosterone people can make important contributions to the modern world.

Although heroes share a willingness to step forward, take a chance, and act, not all heroes are the same, and they don't all have the same motivation. They can be motivated by love and compassion, by ethical, patriotic, or religious ideals, by fondness of adventure, by an absence of nonheroic options, or by several things at once. Altruism can be impulsive or deliberate. It can be a one-time thing or a prolonged effort. People show up at emergencies to help others threatened by fire, accident, and natural disaster. Soldiers throw themselves onto hand grenades to save their comrades. A third of the Medal of Honor winners in World War II

died when they threw themselves onto hand grenades or other explo-
sives, sacrificing their lives to save their fellows.[8] Volunteers teach school
in war zones and work in refugee camps around the world. Brave people
with varying motives helped slaves escape along the Underground Rail-
road before the Civil War, worked in leper colonies when leprosy was
thought to be highly contagious, and risked their lives and careers to
fight for civil rights.[9]

Psychologist Perry London reported that some of the people who
rescued Jews in Europe during World War II were motivated by both
altruism and a liking for excitement.[10] One rescuer from the Netherlands had a hobby of racing motorcycles, especially over narrow boards
across deep ditches. He and his friends would sabotage German trucks
by putting sugar in the gas tanks just for the fun of it, not as part of any
organized program. Later, he talked about his wartime activities as great
adventures, and he seemed unconcerned about danger.

Another study of motives and altruism involved people who rescued Jews during World War II. These people fell into two groups, with
differing moral priorities.[11] A sense of right and wrong motivated those
in the first group; they didn't like to see people treated unjustly. Sympathy motivated those in the second group; they didn't like to see people
suffer. The first group was concerned with justice, and the second with
care. The first group included more men and the second more women.

These two groups are very similar to the two groups psychologist
Carol Gilligan describes when she writes about moral thinking.[12] Gilligan believes there are two basic frames of reference for morality. One,
more common among men, is similar to what David Bakan calls agency,
which we studied in firefighters and which has to do with independence, autonomy, and justice. The other, more common among
women, is similar to what Bakan calls communion and has to do with
relationships, connection, and compassion. If testosterone works with
Gilligan's moral frames of reference as it works with agency and communion in firefighting and EMT work, it might translate a concern with
independence, autonomy, and justice or a concern with relationships,
connection, and compassion into action.

Gilligan has studied the differences between boys and girls in how
they relate to others. She says that even as children, boys are concerned
more with autonomy and girls more with connection. She tells the

story of two four-year-old children playing together. The girl said, "Let's play next-door neighbors." The boy said, "I want to play pirates." After they argued a bit, the girl said, "Okay, then you can be the pirate who lives next door." The girl wanted connection, and the boy wanted autonomy. Gilligan believes this boy-girl difference develops into an adult difference in morality. She believes women's interest in connection leads them to value caring for others, whereas men's interest in autonomy leads them to value impersonal justice.

The difference between men and women in their need for agency and communion is a classic theme in literature and mythology. Aeneas, driven by masculine values, fled westward at the end of the Trojan War. Following a message from a dream, he headed for the Tiber River, where he would found the city of Rome. During his travels he visited Carthage, where he fell in love with the beautiful Dido. She wanted him to stay with her at Carthage, but the god of war found him and made him move on. He continued to the banks of the Tiber River, fought battles and married a woman there, and founded Illium, which became Rome. Later, seeking his father in the underworld, he met Dido again. She had killed herself when he left Carthage. Aeneas was grief stricken; he had not wanted to hurt her. He left Carthage because he thought he had to. Many men, like Aeneas, see themselves in conflict with the demands of the world.

Most men are not as single-minded as Aeneas. They try to bring love and autonomy together. My great-grandfather, John Quincy Adams Dabbs, served as a private throughout the Civil War, working as a cannon loader. He gained a bit of glory when he took command and rallied his company after the officers were killed at Antietam, but apparently he had no grand vision of himself as a military leader. He was willing to do what needed to be done, and he wanted to get home alive. He was not on any heroic journey from Troy to Rome; he was homesick. From Camp Taylor, Virginia, in the winter of 1864, caught between his duty and the pull of home, he wrote to his beloved wife, Elizabeth Euphrasia Hoole: "My Darling I dreamed about you the other night and that I felt you all over. You was as round and plump as a butter ball. My bowels is not very well. I think cold has fall on them."[13]

I suspect that John Quincy had less testosterone than Aeneas, and the gods of macho morality demanded less of him. His drive toward war was tempered by love; nevertheless, he did his duty as he saw it. To him, serving in the army was a matter of doing his share. It was much like paying taxes.

THE ALTRUISM TAX

Paying tax is another way of thinking about altruism. Herbert Simon, a Nobel Prize-winning psychologist, writes about economics and decision making; he says altruism is like a tax that everybody pays to keep society running smoothly. I think our cat, Ivy, had an animal's grasp of this human concept, as she seemed to understand the reciprocal nature of altruism. She'd been a stray cat, and appreciated the nice life she had with us. Soon after we took Ivy in, Mary came home from the grocery store to find her waiting in the driveway. She led Mary to our front steps, where she had lined up a dead bird, a dead chipmunk, and a dead snake across the bottom step. She had paid her tax and made sure Mary knew it. Later Ivy brought live snakes into the house for us. It took us a long time to convince her that we wanted her to be a freeloader.

If everyone adds a little altruism to the communal pot, help gets spread around approximately where it is needed. Costs and benefits usually turn out more or less right when it comes to the kind of everyday altruism that brings pleasure and comfort to everyone's life. Heroic altruism is different: the tax is higher, and testosterone makes it easier to pay. Most people would prefer not to trade their lives for a posthumous medal, but some people do it. Testosterone makes people willing to face danger and narrows their focus to the task at hand, enabling high-testosterone people to help others without thinking about how much it will cost them. Every helpful action carries a cost. The cost may be small, as in the effort needed to visit a sick friend. It may be large, as when the German athlete Lutz Long helped the American Jesse Owens in the 1936 Olympics by pointing out an error in Owens's technique, and Owens, with his technique improved, went on to beat Long and win a gold medal.[14] The tax is highest when it costs a life, as when a soldier sacrifices himself for his comrades. Altruistic people either do not recognize the cost, or they do not care about it and want to help anyway.

Herbert Simon has a theory that explains why so many people behave altruistically and ignore the cost to themselves.[15] He was not writing about testosterone, but his theory applies to it. Putting things in economic terms, he says that in order for people to benefit from living in a civilized world, they have to pay their share. However, says Simon, people actually pay a little more than their share due to a pair of traits, which he calls "bounded rationality" and "docility," that work together toward that end. Bounded rationality comes into play when people are unable to figure out all the consequences of their actions. This is especially true in an emergency, when someone cries out for help and there is no time to think. Working in tandem with bounded rationality, docility means that people follow rules and support social values; they respond to calls for help. Being docile keeps people from having to figure out everything for themselves, but occasionally it makes them act against their self-interest. It is when they act against their self-interest that they are paying the altruism tax.

All civilized people must be docile to some extent, even high-testosterone people. Although high-testosterone people may be a little less docile than average, it is tempting to say that what they lack in docility they more than make up for with bounded rationality. There are two characteristics of high-testosterone people that should reinforce the effects of bounded rationality, making them willing to pay the heavy heroic altruism tax. The first is their focused attention, and the second is their quick action.

Testosterone increases focus, as indicated by the animal studies of persistence and as reported by the Dutch sex-change patient described in Chapter 3.[16] Focused attention makes people more likely to take risks without noticing that others are holding back. Testosterone is like the blinders that keep horses and mules from being frightened or distracted by things around them. A friend of mine who raises horses stated it this way: "When you put blinders on them, they go forward better."

Testosterone facilitates quick action and increases one's readiness to act. In emergencies, most people look to see what others are doing; they wait for someone else to help, and often as a result no one helps. A person who is more willing to act needs less guidance from others. In 1971, psychologist Bibb Latané and I had our students do a study on helping. Each student got on an elevator with other people and dropped a handful of pencils and waited to see who would help pick them up.[17] Among the hundreds of people they observed, one man of action was quick enough to see the pencils start to fall and grab them before they hit the floor. He saw what needed to be done, and he did it in a hurry. Whether or not grabbing pencils in midair reflects a penchant for heroic altruism, I can't say for sure, but I believe the man who did it has a better chance at it than the people who didn't.

Action also counts in long-term helping. In 1961, David Rosenhan, who was studying altruism, interviewed a group of civil rights activists. Some were more fully committed to the civil rights movement than others.[18] Fully committed activists had done more, including going on more freedom rides in the South, but when they were interviewed, they talked less about what they had done. Partially committed activists had done less, but they talked more. Their talk drifted from what they had done to the philosophy of civil rights. Their insights were good, but thinking so much seemed to interfere with their acting. The action orientation of high-testosterone individuals makes it easier for them to help where others hold back. Perhaps the extra risk works out to their advantage in the long run, keeping them from becoming extinct, because potential mates find their action attractive and thrilling.

THE MIXED VALUES OF LOVE AND WAR

Testosterone provides the energy for extreme behavior, but something more is needed to predict whether the behavior will be good, bad, or both. Testosterone is closely tied to autonomy, and autonomy can lead toward selfishness or toward a concern with justice. Among the military veterans in Chapter 4, we found testosterone related to psychopathy, the tendency to disregard others and treat them in careless and harmful ways.[19] The psychologist Scott Lilienfeld finds that psychopathic people are often helpful. He believes this is because they tend to be fearless, and fearless people feel free to do whatever they want. Fearlessness and high testosterone often go together, with fearlessness making it easier for a high-testosterone person either to mistreat others or to help them. If we want to know whether fearless people will be helpful or harmful, we need to know the values that motivate them.

Some personality traits are linked directly to testosterone. For example, high-testosterone people have an affinity for confrontation; they are quick to fight, and sometimes they help another person by fighting; they like action and are willing to take risks, which makes them likely to help in emergencies. High-testosterone delinquent youths say that seeing a person in authority pick on another person makes them very angry. Disturbed by the unfairness of what they see, both boys and girls who are high in testosterone might strike out to help a person who is being picked on.

I call Terry Banks, the student who did most of the work on our delinquency study, "the strobe light of my life." Banks was an excellent researcher and a high-testosterone woman who got into fights. She had to go to the penitentiary after one fight with a policeman over a drug bust, but mostly she got into fights to help her friends. Banks ended up with a broken arm after trying to protect a friend from an abusive boyfriend. During the time she was my student, she worked nights as a dancer at a local club. Once, after missing several days at school, she explained, "I had to go to court about a fight I got into. One of the girls at the club was picking on a friend of mine, and I made her stop. I slammed her head into the locker about nine times. She was too drunk to remember what happened, though, so the judge threw the case out."

Banks blurred the line between violence and heroic altruism. Another woman friend of mine, whose violent and heroic tendencies are more subdued, also dislikes bullies. Her testosterone is a little on the high side, and she suspects it was more so when she was younger. Once, when she was in grade school, a group of boys her age were teasing little girls and pulling up their dresses. My friend chased down one of the boys, wrestled him to the ground, and pulled off his pants.

Sometimes it is hard to tell if people who go to the aid of the underdog are more concerned about helping victims or punishing bullies. A study of Good Samaritans in California who tried to help crime victims indicated that many of them were more interested in getting the perpetrator than in helping victims. For example:

> ...a motorist saw a truck strike a pedestrian and then drive away. The motorist gave chase and forced the hit-and-run driver to the side of the road. He then took out a shotgun he had in his car and held the truck driver at gunpoint until the police arrived. Meanwhile, the woman who had been hit by the truck was left lying in the road and died an hour later in the hospital.[20]

Readiness to fight and punish bullies is related to upbringing and to high levels of testosterone. Older fighters are like older trial lawyers; they rely on skills they acquired when they were younger and higher in testosterone. That seems to be the case with my friend David, a survivor of prostate cancer, the scourge of high-testosterone men. He's eighty years old, and he's been taking testosterone-lowering drugs for eleven years. The drugs make him more friendly and sociable than he used to be, but they didn't make him stop fighting.

He was in his mid-seventies the last time he got into a fight. He was most likely to fight when somebody picked on someone he was close to, but sometimes he just liked to fight. His last fight was at a service station and pecan stand in Valdosta, Georgia. He filled up his car with gas and stayed by the pump waiting for his wife, who was buying pecans. The man behind him became impatient, shouted for David to move, and made an obscene gesture. Instead of moving, David challenged the man to fight. The man, who was middle-aged and overweight, wanted to fight, too. He got out of his car, took a swing at David, and missed. By the time the station owner and another customer stopped the fight, the man had swung and missed several times and David had knocked him down once. David's wife thwarted his efforts to arrange a rematch.

David's wife points out that although retired professional men don't usually get into fights, David grew up in a rough neighborhood and came from a tough family. David's older brother was a union organizer, and his father was a federal agent during Prohibition. David also grew up with strong altruistic feelings and sided with the underdogs, so much so that when he was fifteen, he wanted to fight for democracy against Fascist bullies in the Spanish Civil War. He tried to convince his brother that they should join up and go to Spain with the Abraham Lincoln Brigade, but his brother talked him out of it. David got his chance to fight Fascist bullies in Italy during World War II, and he fondly remembers his wartime adventures, including the discomforts and the narrow escapes. Later, as a federal employee, his job took him south to deal with racial discrimination in housing.

Audie Murphy, the war hero and actor mentioned in previous chapters, liked to fight. He was famous for loyalty to his men, and he repeatedly risked his life for them. Murphy was also famous for his ability to track down and kill enemy snipers. He killed 241 men in face-to-face combat in fighting that moved across Italy, France, Belgium, and Germany. When the war was over, he became a movie star and was frequently involved in troubles associated with women, gambling, fighting, addiction, and the IRS. His training and temperament put him at odds with peace and civilian life.[21]

Murphy was a complex mixture of heroic altruism, violence, and delinquency, and he, like others who share those characteristics with him, was often in the news. Psychologist David Lykken, author of *The Antisocial Personalities*, noticed news items about heroic criminals and criminal heroes so often that he began to save clippings about them. Among his clippings are stories about a most decorated police detective convicted of armed robbery, a Medal of Honor winner convicted of forgery, a Good Citizenship Award winner charged with attempted murder, and a gangster turned humanitarian. I read about another honored policeman arrested for murder and another Medal of Honor winner arrested for robbing a liquor store. Soldiers decorated for heroism often have criminal records, and police officers decorated for bravery have often been disciplined for use of excessive force. An investigation of the Los Angeles police department found that officers who got into the most trouble had good performance evaluations.[22] A Frenchman, who was a former armed robber, was director of a well-run refugee camp in Albania during the 1999 Kosovo war.[23] A man moved by religious convictions to save unborn children killed an abortion doctor in Florida. Soldiers pray for God to help them kill the enemy, and killing the enemy is a way of helping their friends. Whether people are heroic and law-abiding or heroic and delinquent depends largely on circumstance, motivation, and values.

VALUES SUPPORTING HEROIC ALTRUISM

Some values that give people the motivation they need to perform acts of heroic altruism come from initiations (described in the next chapter), which let them know how to act as members of the group. Initiations are less important now than in primitive times, but they still affect us. Marine boot camp and street gang initiations produce rough values, which include personal defense and the protection of comrades. Depending on individual character and circumstances, rough values can support criminal or heroic behavior or both.

Other values come from unique events, or epiphanies, sudden and clear visions of truth. Watching a hero in action, understanding a previously hidden pattern, or grasping a vision of the future can have the quality of an epiphany. A businessman named Cabell Brand discovered the War on Poverty while watching a segment of the *Today* show, and immediately he began to work toward employment and rights for the poor.[24] Many high-testosterone people begin as delinquents and end up as responsible adults. Sometimes they "see the light" and make changes in the way they live. Terry Banks saw the light when she was at the penitentiary. After her release, she got her GED, went to college, worked hard, and made the dean's list. She quit getting into fights unless she had to help a friend.

Still other values come from role models. Many heroic people have had important figures in their backgrounds who served as models for them. Martin Luther King, Jr., inspired John Lewis, as Mohandas Gandhi had inspired King. Lewis followed the examples of King and Gandhi, protesting injustice with nonviolent passive resistance. He went to jail frequently and endured many beatings in and out of jail. Lewis is a heroic altruist with a highly developed moral conscience and many traits, including fearlessness, intensity of focus, and an affinity for action, that make it all but certain that when he was a young man he would have had a higher-than-average level of testosterone.

On March 7, 1965, "Bloody Sunday" in Selma, Alabama, Lewis, standing in for King, who had to cancel at the last minute, was leading six hundred people in a peaceful march across the Edmund Pettus Bridge when an army of state troopers, local policemen, and members of the sheriff's posse attacked. A burly trooper clubbed Lewis, knocking him down with one blow and knocking him out with another. When Lewis woke up, he was lying on the bridge choking on tear gas fumes. Feeling "strangely calm" despite his pain, he managed to get up and walk to Brown's Chapel Church, where volunteer doctors were tending the wounded. Lewis postponed getting treatment for his injuries. "I wanted to do what I could to help with all this chaos. I was so much in the moment . . . ." He helped calm the crowd and organize a mass meeting, he gave a speech, and then he saw the doctors. They sent him to the Good Samaritan Hospital to be treated for a fractured skull and a severe concussion. Three days later, the doctors told him he needed to see some specialists in Boston for further treatment. He ignored the advice and went back to work.

The *New York Times* reported Lewis's speech in which he asked why President Lyndon Johnson could send troops to Vietnam but not to Selma, Alabama. That report and live television coverage of Bloody Sunday marked a turning point for the Alabama civil rights movement. The next day, the Justice Department decided to send FBI agents to find out if law-enforcement agencies had used "unnecessary force" in Selma.[25]

Lewis lived to have a successful political career, and now he jokes about having been in jail more times than anyone else in the United States House of Representatives. His wiry physique has left him, along with most of his hair, but his passionate commitment to justice and his focus on the task at hand remain. Before he picked King as a model for a life of heroic altruism, Lewis's basic character was set. Strong, loving parents reared him and nurtured the traits that enabled him to respond to King's message. Like most good people, Lewis developed a moral conscience early. He absorbed his core values day-by-day from the people he loved and who loved him.

Conscience and values can exist independently of testosterone. When they are present in a high-testosterone person, however, they provide direction and guidance to the focus, energy, and fearlessness of testosterone. To understand heroic altruism, we need to know how values, motives, and testosterone work together.

The core values people grow up with, including their moral conscience, point them toward helping or not helping. Values can promote thoughtful and deliberate altruism. Testosterone promotes spontaneity and impulsiveness, with a focus that disregards danger. Altruistic values and testosterone together produce an impressive mix of direction and drive. Testosterone can help a person who wants to do the right thing do it, especially when the right thing is difficult or dangerous. Core values have much to do with whether a high-testosterone individual will be a hero, a criminal, or both.

POSITIVE REINFORCEMENT

Based on his study of antisocial personalities, David Lykken has some ideas about how parents can be effective in instilling prosocial core values in fearless children. He thinks "the hero and the psychopath are twigs on the same genetic branch." He says:

> My theory of primary psychopathy … is that (at least some) primary psychopaths were born at the low end of the normal distribution of genetic fearfulness. Because most parents, teachers, and other socializing agents rely heavily on punishment in socializing kids, and because a relatively fearless youngster does not react well to punishment, many such kids do not develop an effective conscience, do not develop normal empathy, altruism, and responsibility. But they do well out on the street where their relative fearlessness makes them admired, a leader of the gang, and so on.
>
> A more fortunate child may have a skillful parent or parent surrogate who relies on positive reinforcement, who develops a warm, rewarding relationship with the child that the child values, and who manages to establish in the child a socialized self-concept—'you are such a good boy, helpful, courageous, truthful, strong, smart,' and so on—and who guides the child into activities where his relative fearlessness is an advantage but which are licit, and admirable, such as sports, acting, competitions, and so on. Even a relatively fearless child will work to avoid losing things that he values, such as that admirable self-concept, that warm relationship, the approval of people he admires. And such a youngster can grow up to be the kind of person one would want to have around when danger threatens, a cop, a soldier, a football hero, an explorer, an astronaut, etc.[26]

All children need loving guidance, and it is hard to overstate this need, especially when it comes to high-testosterone children, who have a greater-than-usual potential for heroism or delinquency. Although Lykken hasn't studied testosterone, research shows that bold and fearless children are likely to be high in testosterone.[27] That makes his advice about child rearing especially important to parents with high-testosterone boys and girls.

9

The Taming of Testosterone

ARES AT OLYMPUS

Ares was the Greek god of war. He could as well have been the god of testosterone. He lived on Mount Olympus with the other gods. He gave men the ferocity they needed to slay dragons, kill lions, father children, fight wars, and lay waste to the windy plains of Troy. Times have changed since Ares was young. Mount Olympus has been developed, its palaces converted to condos, its forests cut, its animals caged, its gods neglected. The world is more sophisticated, and the old warriors are hard to find. The Maasai have switched from lion hunting to the tourist trade. The Pequot Indians make money in their gambling casinos in Connecticut. Village gossip spreads through computer networks on the World Wide Web. People make their living from each other rather than from nature. Ares has traveled widely, but now he is back at Olympus. He lives among junked cars in the clear-cut stubble of the mountain forest, buying liquor from an encroaching mall, harassing goddesses wherever he finds them. He still enjoys life. He is a joker, and he sends random doses of high testosterone to middle-class children, to make life challenging for their parents and teachers.

ANCIENT AND MODERN TIMES

Ares and the other gods did not always live at Olympus. The Greeks believed that before the gods there were four great beings: earth, space, love, and the abyss, and before that there was nothing. Anthropologists believe that about four million years ago, the apelike ancestors of human beings began to stand and walk upright. A hundred thousand years ago, humanlike beings were on the scene. Forty to sixty thousand years ago, the beginnings of modern speech appeared. Skeletal remains from that time indicate that the throat and base of the skull were developing in a way that would produce the vocal sounds we use today.[1] No other creature, including our cousin Neanderthal, developed this vocal ability, which is probably one reason Neanderthal is extinct. Our voices made language possible, and language supported the growth of intelligence, philosophy, science, and modern civilization. Human beings emerged along with Ares and the other gods, companions in a forty-thousand-year journey to modern times.

As human beings found their voice and expanded their knowledge and intelligence, two important things happened: the population grew, and culture became more varied. Both of these affected the impact of testosterone.

World population grew slowly at first, but at an increasing rate. Forty thousand years ago, there were fewer than a million people on earth, living in groups of twenty-five to thirty people each.[2] Today there are more than six billion people, more than have lived in all of human history put together. When the population gets large, effects add up. People live in nations, cities, and other large groups. If one or two people out of a hundred in caveman times were unruly, violent, oversexed, suffering from "testosterone poisoning," or otherwise hard to control, they could not cause much trouble. The others in the group could handle them. But when one or two out of a hundred becomes one or two thousand out of a hundred thousand in a city, or one or two million out of a hundred million in a nation, the trouble starts. With this much testosterone, things operate on a new scale. People who are high in testosterone come together to join the same clubs, enter the same occupations, listen to the same radio talk shows, and support the same political candidates. They influence each other. Their special interests affect the overall tone of society. They begin to shape foreign and domestic policy.

This can cause problems. More men means more men who are high in testosterone. But there is another factor: culture modifies the effects of testosterone. Many cultures have developed in various parts of the world, and most of them channel the effects of testosterone toward specific goals. People are biological creatures who live in social settings, and any good explanation about how testosterone works must be a biosocial one. Biology provides the hormone and its potential effects on our action. But whether we act, and exactly how we act, depends on other factors, including culture.

Culture is the shared tradition of a group, passed down from one generation to the next. As the human population grew in ancient times, different cultures appeared. At first, people were limited to nearby food and supplies. Gradually they diversified, moving out to hunt animals, herd livestock, farm, develop their knowledge, and finally enter the occupations of the modern world. These developments took a long time. Many cultures rose and fell along the way, and testosterone has been there all along to play its role. Spatial skills at one time guided rocks and spears, and now they guide golf balls, basketballs, airplanes, and rockets. The sexual appetite of primitive man now directs and supports a sex industry. The old desire to dominate makes use of modern tools. A fondness for quick and lethal violence makes modern weapons attractive. The high-testosterone way of thought divides the world into camps of friends and enemies.

TRIBAL VALUES

Testosterone is more than an individual trait; it also affects groups of people. People are not solitary creatures, like bears or eagles; we evolved living together in families and tribes, and sociability is part of human nature. People still form groups—communities, cities, nations, denominations, clubs, associations, parties, regiments, families, and tribes—and we are more friendly and comfortable with members of our own group than with outsiders. When trouble arises, group members think in terms of "us" versus "them." Groups decide when to eat dinner, what kind of personal life or business practice will be acceptable, who must fight a war, when to celebrate holidays, and how to treat criminals. In comedian Lily Tomlin's words, "reality is a collective hunch." Groups create their own reality, and group members learn special truths from each other. Members must embrace the group's ideology or risk disapproval from the other members of the group. Reality varies from group to group, and the action it inspires sometimes surprises even the members of the group itself. A sports fan might go to the stadium not intending to fight, but there among his fellow fans and their collective testosterone load, he might get caught up in a brawl, and then later wonder why.

Group reality has a tribal quality. We usually think of tribes as made up of primitive people in less civilized parts of the world; but groups, everywhere in the world, have characteristics in common with tribes. Just as every person has an animal within, every group has a tribe within. Each tribe has its own way of doing things as well as its own reality, and in every tribe, the individual members want to be accepted and respected by the other members. John Keegan, a British military historian, said that British soldiers, officers as well as the men in the ranks, value being accepted by the other soldiers in the regiment above all other things.

Before Keegan went to teach at the Sandhurst Military Academy, he knew the retired soldiers who taught there would be different from other men. After all, the values of war are a world apart from the values of everyday life. Keegan expected the retired soldiers to be united by their association with the British army, and that was true to some extent, but what mattered to them more than the British army was their regiments. Keegan said, "Regimental loyalty was the touchstone of their lives." The regiments, some with roots in the seventeenth century, had strong separate traditions and distinctive uniforms. When the old soldiers dressed for evening mess at Sandhurst, each man wore on his regimental uniform the ribbons, medals, and crosses he'd earned in service to his country. The uniforms came in many colors, including scarlet, blue, black-green, and tartan plaid. Trim included heavy gold lace and purple facing. Cavalry officers wore fancy boots with spur slots, and gunners wore tight trousers. The old soldiers may have been rhinos on the battlefield, but they were peacocks at evening mess at Sandhurst.

Despite the emphasis on regimental affiliation, all the men were brothers-in-arms. They were friendly toward soldiers in other regiments, and they quickly forgave personal disagreements. Nevertheless, they would have never forgiven an insult to their regiment, if there had ever been such an insult. There wasn't, though, because everyone at Sandhurst knew a slur against a regiment would be a dangerous threat to the basic values of the group. When he learned about the intensity of regimental loyalty at Sandhurst, Keegan said, "Tribalism—that was what I had encountered."[3]

The distinction between us and them, between our people and everyone else, is a basic social distinction.[4] In colonial times, America consisted of a group of villages, each containing people who knew each other well and mistrusted outsiders.[5] We have advanced to larger units, and now we mistrust people outside our region, occupation, or social class. The distinction is emotionally loaded. Once we know "we" are different from "them," we conclude that we are better and that truth, virtue, and God are on our side. Much of the strife in the world results from this kind of thinking, which studies show is more common among men than women. In studying "Social Dominance Orientation," researchers found that men were more oriented toward social dominance than women. Survey data showed that more men than women favored inequality among social groups, military programs, and punitive public policy, whereas more women than men favored equal rights and social programs.[6] The sex difference raises the possibility that testosterone plays a part in "us-versus-them" thinking. Perhaps this is true because men have evolved over thousands of generations fighting each other, and the same hormone that contributes to their fighting makes them quick to label someone outside their group as inferior or as an enemy.

People are especially quick to divide others into friends and enemies in hard and threatening times. When the living is easy, people are more generous. In 1999, in anticipation of a Y2K disaster, late-night radio talk shows raised questions about how those who were prepared for the crisis should deal with those who were not. Should they share with neighbors who came to beg? Should they shoot beggars who might turn into thieves? In environments where resources are limited and threats from predators are frequent, nonhuman primates bond together more tightly within their groups and become more hostile to those outside their groups.[7] If high-testosterone individuals respond more readily to threat, they may become leaders and warlords in the fighting and violence that follows a national or ethnic threat.

Testosterone partly explains individual differences in violent behavior, but it can't explain why one group is more violent than another.

Cultural values and history are important in determining group behavior. For instance, the American South has a history different from that of the rest of the country, and for generations it has been more violent. There are many reasons for this, but psychologist Dick Nisbett has identified the Scotch-Irish herder ancestors of many Southerners as one of the reasons. Scotch-Irish herders held to a tradition that emphasized tribal values of personal honor and defense, which when transplanted into the South gave a boost to violent personal conflict.[8]

JOINING THE CLUB

Tribal values are not instincts; they have to be learned. In primitive tribes, there is no formal schooling, and people learn on the job. The hunter learns to hunt, the farmer to farm, and the physician to heal by watching others who can do these things. Tribal values are passed from one generation to the next. Without our history and the social rules of tribal values to guide us, we would be much like other animals. We would follow our natural inclinations and go off in our own directions. Some of us are naturally more happy, lazy, sad, sociable, creative, selfish, helpful, or competitive than others. Those of us with higher testosterone levels lean toward sex and dominance. Throughout long eras of human history, local initiations and social rules have kept societies stable and predictable. These forces have helped to control the high-testosterone individuals who might otherwise cause trouble.

The roles of men and women vary from tribe to tribe, but the role women have in bearing children and caring for them is important everywhere, no matter what needs or challenges face the tribe. The role of men in caring for children is less universally important, and a man's main usefulness to the tribe may come from hunting, fighting, fishing, traveling, or other activities. Because child bearing is important everywhere, the role of women is more predictable than the role of men.

This difference between the sexes is reflected in the initiation ceremonies of men and women, in what they must do to show they have "joined the club" and deserve to be treated as full-fledged members of society. Tribes, clubs, and other groups have initiations in which new members learn how to act, what to think, and what secrets they should know. They learn what is expected of them. In primitive tribes, initiations mark the beginning of adulthood, a time when the older generation passes its values on to the younger generation. In a book called *Manhood in the Making*, David Gilmore describes the difference between initiation ceremonies for males and females.[9] He says there are more initiations for males than for females, because the transition into adulthood is potentially less clear and more confusing for males than for females.

Nevertheless, many societies do have initiation ceremonies for girls, and the status of women in these societies is reflected in the initiation ceremonies. The festive Navajo Kinaalda is a menstruation ceremony. There is a great deal of singing and a ceremonial cake, and the honored girl runs as far as she can over the course of three days. For hundreds of years, the Navajos have been saying that the farther a girl runs during her Kinaalda, the longer and healthier her life will be.[10] In contrast to the Navajo, the Sabiny tribe in eastern Uganda celebrates a girl's passage into womanhood with a brutal ceremony that ends her ability to feel sexual pleasure. A "traditional surgeon" cuts away her clitoris and labia minor with a razor blade as the girl's friends and family watch. She endures the pain in silence, because if she cries out she becomes an embarrassment to her family.[11] Many girls throughout the world go through puberty without celebration or mutilation. For them, menstruation and the ability to have children mark the change from girlhood to womanhood. Biological markers and informal chats with their mothers are enough. Being able to have children is not all that defines a woman, but it is enough to let a girl into the club of women.

A boy's entry into the club of men is biologically less dramatic. Men have a fleeting role in the actual act of reproduction, and their responsibility for child rearing varies from society to society. In general, men spend more time on other roles and duties, which are defined by the needs and customs of their particular societies. Truk Island men fish on the open sea, and Samoan men fish in quiet lagoons. Not long ago, Masai men killed lions, and Samburu men stole cows. Manly skills vary from place to place and time to time, as do the ceremonies and rituals that underline their importance. Initiations do exist in the modern world, but they get less attention than they did in primitive society. Modern initiations today are pale remnants of old traditions. They exist in ceremonies like joining a fraternity, entering a new job, taking first communion, or having one's shirt bloodied after a deer hunt.

Manhood isn't automatic, and initiations help control the raw power of masculinity and convert it into manhood. Testosterone is close to masculinity, and the social rules of right behavior are close to manhood. Men tell each other what it means to be a man, and what they say differs from society to society. Boys learn to follow these rules as they grow up. They look to others for guidance, and in primitive societies initiations reveal the secrets of how they should act. Engaged Maasai men in Kenya get to wear red mud and feather headdresses. Except for an occasional bachelor party, engaged men in the United States are mostly ignored. Some problems of modern society arise because the old initiations and traditions are gone or no longer work. A movie called *Once Were Warriors* describes strong and spirited Polynesian Maori natives living in a poor area in the city of Wellington, New Zealand. In earlier traditional tribal life, the men would be warriors and use their physical power to serve the tribe. But they had moved to the city and abandoned most of their tribal customs, and their daily activities were marked by disorganized and random violence. Many of the adolescent boys got elaborate traditional Maori tattoos, but they belonged to street gangs instead of the old tribes.

Everywhere, all over the world, men learn to "be a man." Some are more successful than others. When my father was in the Army, waiting to go overseas and fight in World War I, there was a soldier in his company named Lou. Lou would get very drunk and talk to himself. One night my father heard him staggering down the line of tents, muttering to himself, "Be a man, Lou. Be a man." Lou headed for the latrine, made a wrong turn, went into the wrong tent, and urinated all over the captain sleeping there.

When I was growing up, all young men registered for the draft, and most of them served in the armed forces. This was a powerful experience. Military service became a common memory that men shared for the rest of their lives. Universal military service did not ensure a cohesive nation, but it was one of the things that helped define citizenship. Young men today receive less instruction on what they should do when they grow up. They pay more attention to each other than to adults, and they lose the benefit of prior history and experience. Youth gangs have replaced tribes. Young people are free to do many things they could not have done in the past, but they are short on guidance. As one of my female colleagues said, after hearing me talk about testosterone, "Men are like ships, with large sails and small rudders."

POWER AND LEGEND

Leaders often go a step beyond initiation into manhood or womanhood. The extra step, which usually involves overcoming extreme difficulties, transforms manhood or womanhood into something more. Transforming experiences are reflected in personal histories about the creation of new and stronger identities, and the backgrounds of many leaders contain stories that take on the character of legends, describing struggles and successes that mark transitions to greatness. A leader may have been a warrior, battled cancer, overcome poverty, or marched for civil rights in Alabama. Often leaders have humble beginnings but have been transformed and risen above those origins.[12] They are both "of the people and beyond the people," making it possible for others to identify with them and look up to them at the same time. People expect their leaders to be powerful and active, but not necessarily good. Many social and biological factors, including socialization, experience, and testosterone, conspire to make a leader a rogue or a hero, but somewhere along the line he or she will have become a person who is out of the ordinary.

Ashoka, a leader in India in the third century B.C., went a step beyond the experiences common to most men. As a young man, Ashoka went to war and led an army that killed a hundred thousand people. When he grew older, he decided that war was wrong and he would rule by right conduct alone, or "Dharma." His influence in promoting compassion, tolerance, gentleness, and truthfulness extended to the twentieth century and influenced the life of Mahatma Gandhi.[13]

South African President Nelson Mandela's prison experience transformed him. He is a contemporary example of a leader who has gone beyond the experience of ordinary men. Senator Bob Kerry is another. In 1969, recovering from war wounds in a Philadelphia naval hospital, Kerry made up his mind to do what he could to spare the next generation from what he'd been through in Vietnam.

BELONGING AND BEHAVING

Initiations controlled and shaped our impulses throughout much of history, but today something more is needed. Initiations work well when there are simple things to learn, such as whom to love or hate, what values to honor, how to act in important ceremonies, and how to treat one's enemy. As the world gets more complicated, it takes longer to learn all the things we need to know. It takes only a few hundred hours to master most complex skills. One can solo an airplane, for example, after ten to twelve hours of training and become a fair pilot after a hundred hours of practice. But learning to be an accountant, surgeon, lawyer, business executive, or college professor takes at least ten years of intensive study and practice to acquire the memory store to reach "world-class" performance.[14] Finding one's place in modern society is a long, drawn-out initiation rite that takes motivation, fortitude, years in school, and good control of rambunctious impulses. Strong and stable social institutions teach us what to do and how to control our impulses, including our impulses that come from testosterone.

The study of 4,662 military veterans showed how important social control is. In Chapter 4, I said that veterans in the top 10 percent of the testosterone distribution misbehaved more than others—they had more trouble with the law, hard drug use, and marijuana use. In order to see how social differences might affect these findings, I looked at education and income. People who have more education and higher incomes are said to be higher in socioeconomic status, or "SES." I classified veterans who were below average in both income and education as low in SES, and those who were above average in both as high in SES. I dropped about a third of the veterans who were above average on one and below average on the other, but the remaining two-thirds made up two distinctly different groups.

Overall, there was a negative relationship between testosterone and SES. High- testosterone men were twice as likely to be in the low than in the high SES group, as described in Chapter 6. Looking at the data further, I saw something even more interesting in the relation involving testosterone, SES, and delinquency. Although there were high-testosterone men in both SES groups, testosterone was more strongly related to delinquency in the low than in the high-SES group. Figure 9.1 shows risk ratios in the two groups. As in Chapter 4, the risk ratio indicates how much more likely a behavior is among men with high than with normal testosterone levels. Figure 9.1 shows risk ratios separately for men in the low- and high-SES groups. The risks of adult delinquency

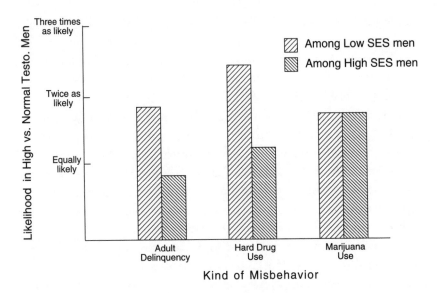

Figure 9.1. Relation of male testosterone levels to misbehavior among low- and high-socioeconomic-status (SES) men. The height of each column represents not the number of men who engage in the behavior, but the risk ratio indicating the likelihood of men in the top 10 percent of the testosterone distribution engaging in the behavior, relative to men in the remaining 90 percent of the distribution. The combination of high testosterone and low SES is associated with more delinquency and hard drug use, but not more marijuana use.

and of hard drug use related to testosterone were about twice as high among low- than among high-SES men. On the other hand, the risk of marijuana use related to testosterone was about the same among low- and high-SES men.

The greatest misbehavior came from a combination of high testosterone and low SES. This suggests that SES can modify the effect of testosterone. Men who are high in SES and also high in testosterone may restrain themselves because they know they have more to lose. This appeared true for general adult delinquency and hard drug use, but marijuana use was related to testosterone similarly in low- and high-SES groups. This is probably because marijuana is openly accepted by so many people at all levels of society. Everyone knows it is illegal, but it is less frowned upon than hard drug use. High-testosterone men are relatively free to follow their wilder inclinations and use marijuana, regardless of their SES status. Others studying this group of veterans have reached similar conclusions about how important social control forces are. Testosterone has fewer bad effects among men who are solidly embedded in social networks, men who grow up with strong parental support and have high levels of formal education, stable marriages, steady jobs, and numerous friends and social contacts.[15]

Social control forces may affect young people even more than adults, particularly adolescents who are in a state of transition when their physical growth is almost complete and their hormones are approaching adult levels. They are no longer children but not yet quite adults. Adolescents are at a stage when they are leaving their parents for longer periods of time and spending more time with others. There have been several studies of testosterone in adolescents. One, a Norwegian study of sixteen-year-old boys, found testosterone related to physical aggression, especially in response to threat.[16] A North Carolina study of fourteen- to sixteen-year-old boys found testosterone related to getting drunk, smoking cigarettes, cutting school, having sex, and smoking marijuana, but also found the effects of testosterone depended on the young person's background. Testosterone had a less negative effect among boys who were involved in school and community activities and had a positive attitude toward home.[17]

Testosterone may affect adolescents more because they have not yet learned to control it, which makes parental guidance and community involvement important to all young people, not just those with extremely high testosterone levels. A recent syphilis epidemic among upper-middle-class high school students in a metro-Atlanta county made this point dramatically. On a *Frontline* program titled "The Lost Children of Rockdale County," Dr. Claire Sterk[18] described a community that gave too little social support to its young people. There were too few after-school programs, too few community-sponsored activities for teens, and too little supervision from ambitious, hardworking parents. A group of Rockdale teens, with some of the girls as young as 13, were bored and rebellious, and they began congregating after school in homes where there were no adults present. The gatherings turned into drinking parties and then into large drunken sex orgies. At first, many of the girls viewed their initiation into sexual activity in the group setting as a coming-of-age event, which gave them special status. Later, as some of the older boys in the group instigated more extreme sexual behavior, including three boys having simultaneous sex with one girl, the girls became less comfortable with the parties. Even before the syphilis outbreak, the girls began to feel as though they'd lost control of the situation. Even if the leaders of the group were higher than average in testosterone, the extreme behavior of the group probably had much more to do with environmental than biological factors.

Perhaps parents in Rockdale County should consider what leaders in some African-American communities around the country are doing. They are adapting traditional rites of passage to contemporary American life. These rites-of-passage programs, with the goal of equating manhood with prosocial values, encourage high standards for behavior, wholesome activities, and community service. Psychologist Rhoderick Watts of DePaul University said, "Telling young black men what is needed to make the transition into manhood effectively contributes to their socialization process and gives them a sense of responsibility as they move into adulthood."[19] What he says applies to young people of all colors, and with "womanhood" substituted for "manhood," it applies to girls as well as boys.

In the absence of positive social influences, especially for adolescents, testosterone increases impulsiveness, interferes with self-control, and leads toward delinquency. Socializing forces are also important in determining whether adolescent misbehavior will lead to adult problems. The veterans data show that social integration had its greatest positive effect on high-testosterone men who had been juvenile delinquents.[20] Low-testosterone men tend to behave well regardless of their environment. High-testosterone men and boys need the social control that goes with family and community life. They will resist it, but they will benefit from it.

Belonging to a group makes one consider others in the group and try to do what the others think is right. Often this results in good behavior, but not always. The "lost children of Rockdale County" belonged to a group that encouraged risky behavior. Belonging to a criminal family or to a group of skinheads could make a person even more delinquent. Some male groups promote attitudes conducive to rape. Sexual assault is reported to be more common among athletes in team sports than among athletes in individual sports.[21] The pursuit of feelings of power and status in some fraternities has led to group sexual assault.[22] Belonging to a group means acting as the group thinks you should act. When an individual misbehaves according to the standards of the larger society, the behavior is often consistent with the standards of a nonconforming group.

Among college students, few studies have found testosterone related to aggression, violence, or other serious misbehavior, despite pockets of bad behavior in this population.[23] College students encounter many social control forces, which tend to restrain the effects of testosterone. Because of this, testosterone that might cause problems in a criminal population may have little effect among college students. At the other extreme from college students, individuals who are intoxicated, or too young to have learned how to behave, may show large effects of testosterone. In a preliminary study of a group of recovering alcoholics, I found that those who were higher in testosterone reported fighting more when intoxicated but not when sober. This is similar to what was found among squirrel monkeys, who fought more when they were given a combination of testosterone to make them aggressive and alcohol to reduce their inhibitions.[24] With animals or people, look out for high-testosterone drunks. I have also begun to examine children, who have very little testosterone but also very little experience in dealing with it. Initial findings, as reported in Chapter 4, indicate that testosterone can be related to aggressive behavior even among five- to eleven-year-old boys.[25]

TOO MANY MEN?

Sometimes in groups, particularly in informal and predominantly male groups, the effects of testosterone seem to be collective. The roughness of male life is indicated by fragments of pottery from American Indian villages. In permanent settlements, where women were present, there were a variety of bowls in different sizes. In war camps, where there were no women to bring refinement to the dinner hour, the men ate out of a few large bowls.[26] Sometimes in mostly male families, home life takes on some of the roughness of a war camp. When our boys were little, we had a neighbor with a husband and three sons. She really wanted a daughter. She once exclaimed to Mary, who had some sympathy for her point of view, "I get so tired of trains and trucks and guns and penises! I wish I had a little girl!"

The beneficial effects of belonging to a group, the increased tendency to defer to others and behave oneself, may be more difficult when there are more men around. Vigilante groups and street gangs are examples of especially rough predominantly male groups. The absolute number of men is important, and the ratio of men to women may be even more important.[27] In places where the army is in training, there will be more men. At a time when men have been killed in war, there will be more women. On the frontier, where settlements are sparse, work is hard, and danger is high, there will be fewer women than men. The writer Muriel Spark, living in Salisbury, Southern Rhodesia (now Harare, Zimbabwe), in 1937, said, "In the colony, there was one white woman to three white men, which led to violent situations—sometimes murder—among the men."[28]

The combination of too many men and too little control leads to violence. The historian David Courtwright writes that throughout history, whenever there have been large numbers of "loose" men around, not caught up in social relationships and obligations, there has been trouble.[29] He believes that much of the violence in America comes from the frontier history of the nation. On a frontier there is usually a culture of honor, in which a man's reputation depends on his willingness to fight to defend himself. There are many single men, much alcohol use, and few religious and civic activities. Tendencies to engage in violence, including violence related to testosterone, are given free rein. Violence is historically high among men returning from war, unless care is taken to bring them back into the life of the nation, as was done by the G.I. Bill after World War II.

Men's violence toward other men flows over into violence toward women. Men are more violent toward women in cultures where there is war, interpersonal violence, and an ideology of male toughness.[30] This pattern brings to mind the relationship between sports and sexual violence. College records show more sexual assault by male athletes than by other students, highest among athletes in team sports as previously mentioned, but high even among those in individual sports.[31] Athletes have the double problem of being high in testosterone and being involved in competitive and often violent sports, where controls on their behavior are loose. An interesting natural experiment is working its way out today in China, where more boys than girls are being born. It is estimated that within twenty-five years there will be two million more men than women entering the marriage market in China.[32] One wonders how much restraint there will be among these "undomesticated" men.

"BUT WE HAVE FREE WILL"

Mary sometimes sleeps with a small radio under her pillow. Sounds from the radio blend with her leftover thoughts of the day to provide her with entertaining dreams. Sometimes she remembers bits from news reports and late-night talk shows, which she tells me about in the morning. One such item is appropriate here: a woman called a talk show because she had thoughts of killing her child, and it worried her. The impatient talk jockey said, "Come on, now. I know this happens in the animal kingdom. A new horse will take over a herd and kick the mares to make them abort, so he can father his own children. Animals act like that. We all have those impulses. But we have free will! We can do better than that!"

Mary wondered whether the caller was suffering from postpartum depression. It seemed to Mary that free will wouldn't help the caller much until she got medical treatment and help with child care. Effectively treating postpartum depression, like treating hypothyroidism and diabetes, starts with understanding how hormones work within the human body.

Although high testosterone is not usually a condition that requires medical treatment, understanding how it works is a first step toward directing its energy and focus toward prosocial goals. A high-testosterone student I know has told me how hard he has to work to avoid misbehaving. In the past he was delinquent, but now he is law-abiding. He has many tattoos—from ferocious fighting dragons on his back to a friendly Kermit the Frog on the calf of his leg—that chart the changes he has made in his life. He runs his own business now and leads a steady life with a girlfriend to whom he is faithful. Even though he is happy with his present life, he knows he could backslide and put his relationship with his girlfriend at risk. He handles temptation by focusing his attention on positive activities and telling himself to behave. His strategy for dealing with the antisocial aspects of high testosterone combines understanding and will, the strategy Patrick Henry used to deal with the threat of war. Henry said, "I am willing to know the whole truth; to know the worst, and provide for it."[33]

Thomas Henry Huxley said, "To a person uninstructed in natural history, his country or seaside stroll is a walk through a gallery filled with wonderful works of art, nine-tenths of which have their faces turned to the wall."[34] Understanding hormones, too, provides us with a better grasp of the richness of our lives, and beyond that, provides us with practical guidance on how to control our behavior. Sociobiologists like E. O. Wilson believe that understanding the relationship between our animal qualities and our behavior frees us to improve our behavior, similar to the way that understanding the relationship between tubercule bacilli and disease freed us to find effective treatment for tuberculosis. Knowledge of chemistry makes anesthesia possible, knowledge of DNA makes treating genetic diseases possible, and knowledge of nutrition makes a healthy diet more likely. Beyond the medical area, knowledge of our biological limits has encouraged us to transcend these limits by building rockets to fly into space, submarines to swim to the ocean floor, and computers to calculate sums imponderable to human minds. Knowledge of the innate reactions of others lets people know that attacking them will be dangerous and smiling at them will be rewarded. Knowledge of the weather tells us to prepare for a hurricane, and knowledge of heavy traffic tells us to seek a road less traveled. Free will, like art appreciation in Huxley's natural gallery, works better in partnership with knowledge than with ignorance.

In a smoothly functioning society there are many restraints on antisocial behavior, and as my high-testosterone student discovered for himself, some of the most effective are internal. The things we do to control ourselves we call free will, which is what it feels like, but it varies to a remarkable degree with our background, training, and environment. We control ourselves with skills we learn from our families and our communities.

These controls especially come from parents, who teach children how to behave. Parents sometimes worry about restricting the masculinity of their sons. They shouldn't worry. With a million years of evolution behind them, most boys will be masculine no matter what their parents do. If they are not masculine, it is more likely because of physiology than parenting. General Douglas MacArthur's mother wanted to guide him so carefully that she moved to West Point to watch over him when he was a cadet. MacArthur is not the only manly hero who had an "overprotective" mother.

When families are fragmented and parents spend little time with their children, formal schooling becomes more important. Programs like Headstart take on special value. Lynn Curtis, President of the Milton Eisenhower Foundation and lead author of a thirty-year update of a report by the National Commission on the Causes and Prevention of Violence, said, "Headstart is one of the most successful crime prevention programs around."[35] He reported that Headstart decreases drug use and criminal behavior, and it increases the odds of finishing school and finding employment. Edward Zigler, the founder of Headstart, believes Headstart and similar programs are successful largely because they engage the parents' attention and interest in the children.[36] Headstart integrates parents, teachers, and students into a functioning social group with shared goals and values; it sets the stage for the process of socialization, civilizing masculinity and femininity and transforming them into manhood and womanhood.

The sociologist Émile Durkheim described socialization as binding the individual to the group, "by making his society an integral part of him, so that he can no more separate himself from it than from himself."[37] Socialization is particularly important if the raw masculine qualities associated with testosterone are to be transformed into the protective, altruistic, and even heroic aspects of manhood. Manhood draws upon the qualities of testosterone and masculinity tamed. Male human beings have to learn to be men. They have to come under the influence of social values. Females have to learn to be women and learn prosocial values, too, but most women don't have to work as hard as men to curb violent tendencies. Many men carry within them, more or less socialized and under control, a potential for violent destruction. The potential for violence, along with other qualities related to testosterone, including persistence, boldness, competitiveness, fearlessness, and risk taking, helped create the modern world. These qualities are essential human characteristics, but they need to be held in check. Given the social conflicts and danger of violence today, we may need to spend more time developing traits and skills, including cooperativeness and empathy, that come more naturally to most women than to men.

This final chapter has described the need to control testosterone to keep it from doing too much damage. After thinking about the matter, Mary reached a conclusion about testosterone. She said, "It's 'guystuff,' and guystuff seems to be about building stuff, fixing stuff, and blowing stuff up." She went on to say, "A mother's job is to encourage the building and fixing, and discourage the blowing up." We learned the importance of controlling human nature while we were raising our two sons. We are proud to say they grew up to be fairly well civilized, even the one who lives part-time in the jungle. Civilizing is a job for fathers and mothers. Delinquent behaviors are more common among children raised by one parent alone, even allowing for differences in income and education.[38] I suspect that absent parents have an especially bad effect on high-testosterone children, either boys or girls, because the rambunctious nature of these children demands more guidance and control.

Without the civilizing effects of mothers, fathers, laws, customs, and societies, we fall quickly into a savage state.[39] King Arthur's polite court at Camelot controlled the wilder impulses of his knights, and when the court began to fall apart, his knights looked forward to the freedom to go to war again. Sir Bors was enthusiastic about the prospect. He said, "No offense to you ladies, but this time it will be a man's world, absolutely uninspired, unrefined, and unencumbered. Please God!"[40] It was his testosterone talking, and the royal court had been restraining its effects.

Fortunately for the citizens of modern democratic societies, it doesn't take a royal court to restrain the more rambunctious effects of testosterone. Loving families, good schools, and stable communities can channel the energy of the Sir Borses still among us into positive activities. Trial lawyers, athletes, actors, construction workers, soldiers, and heroes still have jobs to do.

EPILOGUE

The Circle

THE SECRET

Robert Frost was a farmer, a poet, and a seeker of truth. He was skeptical about how much he could learn. He believed he would always circle the truth and never exactly find it. He wrote a two-line poem about a children's game, called "The Secret Sits." It says, "We dance round in a ring and suppose, / But the Secret sits in the middle and knows."[1]

This poem describes children at play. It also describes scientists at work. Science does not always advance steadily, bit by bit, with scientists busy in their laboratories, carefully doing their experiments and filling in details, according to a schedule. Scientists often advance erratically, with pauses and leaps of faith. They are like the children in the poem moved to a rock pile, inching their way along and leaping to new ledges, hanging by their fingers as they steady themselves. They cannot be sure of the best way of moving across the rocks. Their friends watch, waiting for a fall, thinking they could probably do it better themselves.

Scientists advance by making guesses. They get hunches and try new ideas. They circle the truth. They occasionally leap and scramble, filling in the details later. Sometimes they slip and fall. It is a while before they know they've taken the right path. The best they can do at any moment is to show that the facts fit their theories, that they are not obviously wrong. They can never prove with absolute certainty that they are right. They can expect that sooner or later other scientists will come along, with new findings and new ways of looking at them, and others will think the new ways make more sense.

This book has circled testosterone, sex differences, and social forces. It has dealt with aggression, love, work, heroism, violence, and altruism. It has dealt with men, women, and the relationship between them. Many of the findings are clearly established. There is agreement that testosterone increases muscle strength and sexual activity. There is little doubt that it is related to such things as delinquency and marital instability. Other findings are more tentative, such as those dealing with thought, occupations, sex differences, and the nature of heroism and altruism. We do not know for sure that people who throw themselves onto hand grenades are high in testosterone. Such people are hard to study.

The book has moved between science and anecdote, example and principle, theory and fact. It has circled testosterone, itself a molecule made up of circles of atoms. Scientific studies, case histories, chance meetings, public events, salivary assays, and characters from literature and history have been landmarks in the circle. The circle we've been following around testosterone is itself a landmark in the circle surrounding human nature.

THE STAR-SPLITTER

I would like to end with thoughts from two poets, T. S. Eliot and Robert Frost. Both saw life as a long, circling journey. Eliot looked back nostalgically toward old England and the town of Little Gidding, where he thought all the important things had been learned long ago. He said that at the end of the road we would find ourselves back where we had started, and then we would see things as they really are.[2] He overstated it, though there is truth in what he said. The general effects of testosterone were discovered a century and a half ago by Professor Berthold of Goettingen, who performed experiments on roosters. In 1849, Berthold began a paper with the words, "On August 2 last year I caponized six young cockerals," meaning he castrated six young roosters. He reported that the cockerals failed to develop normally, but that if he transplanted new testes into them they "exhibited the normal behavior of uncastrated fowls; they crowed lustily, often engaged in battle with each other and the other cockerals, and showed the usual reactions to hens."[3] T. S. Eliot might say this is close to what we now know about high-testosterone men, with their crowing, battles, and "usual reactions," and Berthold knew about it in 1849.

Robert Frost was friendlier toward new knowledge, but even he was skeptical about how much we can learn. He described a New Hampshire farmer named Brad McLaughlin, a man slow to get things done, who worked outdoors after dark by the light of a "smokey lantern chimney," while the stars and the gods watched him and laughed at him. Disgusted with where his life was going, McLaughlin burned his house down for the fire insurance and used the money to buy a telescope, the better to understand his place in the universe. On winter nights he and a friend would set up the telescope, and as his friend said, "We spread our two legs as we spread its three, / Pointed our thoughts the way we pointed it, / And standing at our leisure till the day broke, / Said some of the best things we ever said." They called the telescope the "star-splitter," because it was so unsteady that it shook and split the image of a star into many tiny pieces. They learned little about the stars, despite the pleasure they gained, and in the end the poet asked, "We've looked and looked, but after all where are we? / Do we know any better where we are, / And how it stands between the night tonight / And a man with a smokey lantern chimney? / How different from the way it ever stood?"[4]

The Star-Splitter is a caution against too much certainty. Our tools are imperfect, our telescopes shake, and our words do not capture exactly what we mean. Beyond the words we use to describe it, testosterone is part of the animal within us, and it has its own reality, following its own ancient rules worked out before words existed. It is a part of the natural world, acting on and being acted upon by the other parts in complicated ways we only partly understand. With every scientific advance we know a little better where and how to look for answers.

NOTES

PART ONE: HUMAN NATURE
Chapter 1. The Animal Within

1. This story is from Irwin S. Bernstein, "Taboo or Toy," in *Play—Its Role in Development and Evolution*, eds. Jerome S. Bruner, Alison Jolly, and Kathy Sylvia (New York: Basic Books, 1976), pp. 194–197.

2. "Confucian Principles," host Bob Edwards, *Morning Edition* (Washington, D.C.: National Public Radio, 1 April 1999). Reid's book is *Confucius Lives Next Door* (New York: Viking, 2000).

3. I am indebted to Joe McGrath for describing this process of understanding, which he refers to as "knowledge accrual." See Joseph E. McGrath, Joanne Martin, and Richard A. Kulka, "Some Quasi-Rules for Making Judgment Calls in Research," in *Judgment Calls in Research*, eds. Joseph E. McGrath, Joanne Martin, and Richard A. Kulka (Beverly Hills, CA: Sage, 1982), pp. 103–118.

4. Alan Alda, "What Every Woman Should Know About Men," *MS Magazine*, October 1977, pp. 15–16.

5. *Newsweek*, 19 July 1999.

6. Daniel Malamud and Lawrence Tabak, *Saliva as a Diagnostic Fluid* (New York: New York Academy of Sciences, 1993).

7. Constance R. Martin, *Endocrine Physiology* (New York: Oxford University Press, 1985), p. 4.

8. Rupert P. Amann, "Physiology and Endocrinology," in *Equine Reproduction*, eds. Angus O. McKinnon and James L. Voss (Philadelphia: Lea & Febiger, 1993), pp. 658–684. Amelie Bartolino, "Salivary Hormone Levels, Anxiety and Self Confidence Indices in Collegiate Football and Basketball Players over a Season of Play" (Ph.D. diss., University of Texas, 1996). Information on rattlesnake hormones comes from Dr. Gordon Shuett at Arizona State University.

9. An excellent overview of the nature and effects of hormones is provided

by Randy J. Nelson, *An Introduction to Behavioral Endocrinology* (Sunderland, MA: Sinauer Associates, 1995).

10. See Natalie Angier, "Hyenas' Hormone Flow Puts Females in Charge," *New York Times*, 1 September 1992, pp. C1 ff. Sex hormones and hyenas are discussed at more length in Chapter 4.

11. Natalie Angier, "Canary Chicks: Not All Created Equal," *New York Times*, January 25, 1994, pp. C1 ff.

12. Elizabeth Culotta, "St. Louis Meeting Showcases 'Creature Features,'" *Science*, Vol. 267, January 20, 1995, pp. 330–331. Janet Raloff, "The Gender Benders: Are Environmental 'Hormones' Emasculating Wildlife?" *Science News*, Vol. 145 (8 January 1994), pp. 24–27.

13. J. Richard Udry, Naomi M. Morris, and Judith Kovenock, "Androgen Effects on Women's Gendered Behaviour," *Journal of Biosocial Science*, Vol. 27 (1995), pp. 359–368.

14. Mertice M. Clark, Peter Karpiuk, and Bennett G. Galef, Jr., "Hormonally Mediated Inheritance of Acquired Characteristics in Mongolian Gerbils," *Nature*, Vol. 364 (1993), p. 712.

15. See Valerie J. Grant, "Maternal Dominance and the Conception of Sons," *British Journal of Medical Psychology*, Vol. 67 (1994), pp. 343–351. Two earlier researchers who have worked extensively in this area are Marianne Bernstein and William H. James. See Marianne E. Bernstein and Milciades Martinez-Gustin, "Physical and Psychological Variation and the Sex Ratio," *Journal of Heredity*, Vol. 52 (1961), pp. 109–112; and William H. James, "The Hypothesized Hormonal Control of Human Sex Ratio at Birth—An Update," *Journal of Theoretical Biology*, Vol. 143 (1990), pp. 555–564.

16. The person known for linking waist-to-hip ratio to interpersonal attraction is psychologist Devendra Singh. See Devendra Singh, "Is Thin Really Beautiful and Good? Relationship between Waist-to-Hip Ratio (WHR) and Female Attractiveness," *Personality and Individual Differences*, Vol. 16 (1994), pp. 123–132.

17. Jonathan Bassett and James M. Dabbs, Jr., "Do Women with High Testosterone Have More Boy Babies?" Poster presented at the American Psychological Society annual meeting, June 1999.

18. *Extra* [television show], rep. Gina Silva reporting (24 June 1999).

19. Gene P. Sackett, "Receiving Severe Aggression Correlates with Fetal Gender in Pregnant Pigtailed Monkeys," *Developmental Psychobiology*, Vol. 14 (1980), pp. 267–272.

20. Henry S. Kupperman, "Male Sex Hormones," in *Drill's Pharmacology in Medicine*, ed. Joseph R. DiPalma (New York: McGraw-Hill, 1971), pp. 1366–1386.

21. The information on sexual dimorphism in this paragraph comes from Martin Daly and Margo Wilson, *Sex, Evolution, and Behavior: Adaptations for Reproduction* (North Scituate, MA: Duxbury Press, 1978); from Alfred Glucks-

mann, *Sex Determination and Sexual Dimorphism in Mammals* (London: Wykeham Publications, 1978); and from *Sexual Dimorphism in Homo Sapiens: A Question of Size*, ed. Roberta Hall (New York: Praeger, 1982).

22. S. L. Klein and R. J. Nelson, "Adaptive Immune Responses are Linked to the Mating System of Arvocine Rodents," *American Naturalist*, Vol. 151 (1998), pp. 59–67.

23. Claude Bouchard, Jean-Pierre Deprés, Pascale Mauriège, Martine Marcotte, Monique Chagnon, France T. Dionne, and Alain Bélaanger, "The Genes in the Constellation of Determinants of Regional Fat Distribution," *International Journal of Obesity*, Vol. 15 (1991), pp. 9–18.

24. David J. Evans, Raymond G. Hoffman, Ronald K. Kalkhoff, and Ahmed H. Kissebah, "Relationship of Androgenic Activity to Body Fat Topography, Fat Cell Morphology, and Metabolic Aberrations in Premenopausal Women," *Journal of Clinical Endocrinology and Metabolism*, Vol. 57 (1983), pp. 304–310.

25. Changes in testosterone levels due to environmental factors are reviewed in Benjamin C. Campbell and Paul W. Leslie, "The Reproductive Ecology of Human Males," *Yearbook of Physical Anthropology*, Vol. 38 (1995), pp. 1–26.

26. Peter T. Ellison, S. F. Lipson, R. G. Bribiescas, G. R. Bentley, B. C. Campbell, C. Panter-Brick, "Inter- and Intra-population Variation in the Pattern of Male Testosterone by Age," paper presented at meeting of the American Association of Physical Anthropologists, Salt Lake City, April 1998. Figure 1.3 is used with the permission of Peter Ellison.

27. Hannu Saloniemi, Kristiina Wähälä, Päivi Nykänen-Kurki, Karlo Kallela, and Ilkka Staastomoinen, "Phytoestrogen Content and Estrogenic Effect of Legume Fodder," *Proceedings of the Society for Experimental Biology and Medicine*, Vol. 208 (1995), pp. 13–18. A good book on chemical competition between plants and animals is Gerald A. Rosenthal and Daniel H. Janzen, eds., *Herbivores: Their Interaction with Secondary Plant Metabolites* (New York: Academic Press, 1979). A good book on reproductive biology is F. H. Bronson, *Mammalian Reproductive Biology* (Chicago: University of Chicago Press, 1989)

28. For the effects on quail and voles, see A. Starker Leopold, Michael Erwin, John Oh, and Bruce Browning, "Phytoestrogens: Adverse Effects on Reproduction in California Quail," *Science*, 191 (1976), pp. 98–100; and Patricia J. Berger, Norman C. Negus, Edward H. Sanders, and Pete D. Gardner, "6-Methoxybenzoxazolinone: A Plant Derivative that Stimulates Reproduction in *Microtus montanus*," *Science*, 214 (1981), p. 67

29. Patricia L. Whitten, Elizabeth Russell, and Frederick Naftolin, "Effects of a Normal, Human-Concentration, Phytoestrogen Diet on Rat Uterine Growth," *Steroids*, Vol. 57 (1992), pp. 98–106.

30. Fritz H. Schräder, "Impact of Ethnic, Nutritional and Other Environmental Factors on Prostate Cancer," in Shalender Bhasin, Henry L. Gabelnick, Jeffrey M. Spieler, Ronald S. Swerdloff, and Christiana Wang, *Pharmacology, Biology, and Clinical Applications of Androgens: Current Status and Future*

Prospects (New York: Wiley-Liss, 1996), pp. 121–135. One of the most remarkable recent papers in the area of nutrition is a report that eating moderate amounts of licorice can lower testosterone levels by about 30 percent; see Decio Armanini, Guglielmo Bonanni, and Mario Palermo, "Reduction of Serum Testosterone in Men by Licorice," *New England Journal of Medicine*, Vol. 341 (1999), p. 1158.

31. Earl Mindell, *Earl Mindell's Food as Medicine* (New York: Simon & Schuster, 1994), p. 176.

32. Richard M. Sharpe and Niels S. Skakkebaek, "Are Oestrogens Involved in Falling Sperm Counts and Disorders of the Male Reproductive Tract?" *The Lancet*, Vol. 341 (1993), pp. 1392–1395.

33. Chandra M. Tiwary, "Premature Sexual Development in Children Following the Use of Placenta and/or Estrogen Containing Hair Product(s)," *Pediatric Research*, Vol. 35, No. 4, Part 2 (1994), p. 108A.

34. Janet Raloff, "The Feminine Touch: Are Men Suffering from Prenatal or Childhood Exposure to 'Hormonal' Toxicants?" *Science News*, Vol. 145 (22 January 1994), pp. 56–58. A recent review of this research is provided by Gillian R. Bentley, "Environmental Pollutants and Fertility," in eds. G. R. Bentley and N. Mascie-Taylor, *Infertility in the Modern World: Present and Future Prospects* (New York: Cambridge University Press, 2000).

35. Johannes D. Veldhuis, John C. King, Randall J. Urban, Alan D. Rogol, William S. Evans, Lisa A. Kolp, and Michael L. Johnson, "Operating Characteristics of the Male Hypothalamo-Pituitary-Gonadal Axis: Pulsatile Release of Testosterone and Follicle-Stimulating Hormone and Their Temporal Coupling with Luteinizing Hormone," *Journal of Clinical Endocrinology and Metabolism*, Vol. 65 (1987), pp. 929–941.

36. S. K. Finley and M. F. Kritzer, "Immunoreactivty for Intracellular Androgen Receptors in Identified Subpopoulations of Neurons, Astrocytes, and Oligodendrocytes in Primate Prefontal Cortex," *Journal of Neurobiology*, Vol.15 (1999), pp. 446–457.

37. Robert Frost, "The Star-Splitter," in Edward Connery Latham, ed., *The Poetry of Robert Frost* (New York: Holt, Rinehart and Winston, 1969), p. 178.

38. This is from Sherrington, quoted in Vincent G. Dethier, *To Know a Fly* (San Francisco: Holden-Day, 1962), p. 109.

39. A good example from baseball of how small effects add up to something big is provided by Robert P. Abelson, "A Variance Explanation Paradox: When a Little is a Lot," *Psychological Bulletin*, Vol. 97 (1985), pp. 129–133.

Chapter 2. Two Sexes

1. The issue of why there are varying numbers of sexes, why two is most common, and when the mitochrondia will compete is discussed by Alun Anderson, "The Evolution of Sexes," *Science*, Vol. 257 (1992), pp. 324–328.

Also see Laurence D. Hurst and William D. Hamilton, "Cytoplastic Fusion and the Nature of Sexes," *Proceedings of the Royal Society of London* B, Vol. 247 (1992), pp. 189—194; and Laurence D. Hurst, "Intragenomic Conflict as an Evolutionary Force," *Proceedings of the Royal Society of London*, Vol. 248 (1992), pp. 135—140.

2. Variety is especially important in protecting the organism against parasites. For information on how increasing pressure from parasites leads to more use of sexual rather than asexual reproduction, see Natalie Angier, "Parasites Take the Biological Spotlight," *New York Times*, 17 July 1990, pp. C1—C2.

3. Lewis Thomas, "Notes of a Biology Watcher: A Fear of Pheromones," *New England Journal of Medicine*, Vol. 285 (1971), pp. 292—293. Copyright © 1971 Massachusetts Medical Society. All rights reserved.

4. Stephen J. Gould, *Wonderful Life: The Burgess Shale and the Nature of History* (New York: Norton, 1989).

5. Donald T. Campbell, "On the Conflicts Between Biological and Social Evolution and Between Psychology and Moral Tradition," *American Psychologist*, Vol. 30 (1975), pp. 1103—1126.

6. George P. Murdock, "The Common Denominator of Culture," in *The Science of Man in the World Crisis*, ed. R. Linton (Pittsburgh: University of Pittsburgh Press, 1945), pp. 123—142. Also see Martin Daly and Margo Wilson, *Sex, Evolution, and Behavior: Adaptations for Reproduction* (North Scituate, MA: Duxbury Press, 1978), p. 315.

7. Jan M. Gero and Margaret W. Conkey, eds., *Engendering Archaeology: Women in Prehistory* (Oxford: Blackwell, 1991).

8. Joshua Fischman, "Hard Evidence," *Discover*, February 1992, pp. 44—51.

9. M. Rebuffé-Scrive, P. Marin, and P. Björntorp, "Effect of Testosterone on Abdominal Adipose Tissue in Men," *International Journal of Obesity*, Vol. 15 (1991), pp. 791—795. See also, M. Krothiewski and P. Björntorp, "The Effects of Estrogen Treatment of Carcinoma of the Prostate on Regional Adipocyte Size," *Journal of Clinical Investigation*, Vol. 1 (1978), pp. 365—366.

10. Elizabeth R. McCown, "Sex Differences: The Female as Baseline for Species Description," in *Sexual Dimorphism in Homo Sapiens: A Question of Size*, ed. Roberta L. Hall (New York: Praeger, 1982), pp. 37—83.

11. This is contrary to a view that men evolved to bond especially closely to one another, because of the demands of their hunting backgrounds, as presented by Lionel Tiger, *Men in Groups* (New York: Random House, 1969). I believe there is little evidence that men bond together more closely than women.

12. Grover S. Krantz, "The Fossil Record of Sex," in *Sexual Dimorphism in Homo Sapiens: A Question of Size*, ed. Roberta L. Hall (New York: Praeger, 1982), pp. 85—105.

13. Sandra L. Bem, "Androgyny and Gender Schema Theory: A Conceptual and Empirical Integration," in *Nebraska Symposium on Motivation: Psy-*

chology and Gender, eds. R. A. Nienstbier and T. B. Donderroger (Lincoln: University of Nebraska Press, 1987), pp. 179–226.

14. J. Richard Udry, "The Nature of Gender," *Demography*, Vol. 31 (1994), pp. 561–573. Also see Martin Daly and Margo Wilson, *Sex, Evolution, and Behavior: Adaptations for Reproduction* (North Scituate, MA: Duxbury Press, 1978), p. 319.

15. Elizabeth R. McCown, "Sex Differences: The Female as Baseline for Species Description," in *Sexual Dimorphism in Homo Sapiens: A Question of Size*, ed. Roberta L. Hall (New York: Praeger, 1982), pp. 37–83.

16. Richard Dawkins, *The Selfish Gene* (New York: Oxford University Press, 1976).

17. Alfred M. Dufty, Jr., "Testosterone and Survival: A Cost of Aggressiveness?" *Hormones and Behavior*, Vol. 23, (1989), pp. 185–193. Also, Ellen D. Ketterson and Val Nolan, Jr., "Hormones and Life Histories: An Integrative Approach," *The American Naturalist*, Vol. 140 (1992), pp. S33–S62.

18. C. A. Marler and M. C. Moore, "Evolutionary Costs of Aggression Revealed by Testosterone Manipulations in Free-Living Male Lizards," *Behavioral Ecology and Sociobiology*, Vol. 23 (1988), pp. 21–26.

19. The relation between castration and longevity is discussed by Malcolm Potts and Roger Short in *Ever Since Adam and Eve: The Evolution of Human Sexuality* (New York: Cambridge University Press, 1999), p. 257, where it is noted that refraining from smoking increases life expectancy by 4.9 years, while getting castrated increases it by 13.6 years. Papers on the topic include James B. Hamilton and Gordon E. Mestler, "Mortality and Survival: Comparison of Eunuchs with Intact Men and Women in a Mentally Retarded Population," *Journal of Gerontology*, Vol. 24 (1969), pp. 394–411; James B. Hamilton, Ruth S. Hamilton, and Gordon E. Mestler, "Duration of Life and Causes of Death in Domestic Cats: Influence of Sex, Gonadectomy, and Inbreeding," *Journal of Gerontology*, Vol. 24 (1969), pp. 427–437; Peter A. Jewell, "Survival and Behaviour of Castrated Soay Sheep (*Ovis aries*) in a Feral Island Population on Hirta, St. Kilda, Scotland," *Journal of Zoology*, Vol. 243 (1997), pp. 623–636.

20. See J. Biasiotto and A. Ferrardo, "What's the Attraction?" *Muscle & Fitness*, March 1991, pp. 101 ff. See also, P. J. Lavrakas, "Female Preference for Male Physiques," *Journal of Research in Personality*, Vol. 9 (1975), pp. 324–334.

21. Michael J. Raleigh and Michael T. McGuire, "Social Influences on Endocrine Function in Male Vervet Monkeys," in *Socioendocrinology of Primate Reproduction*, eds. Toni E. Ziegler and Fred B. Bercovitch (New York: John Wiley & Sons, 1990), pp. 95–111.

22. Edward M. Miller, "Parental Provisioning versus Mate Seeking in Human Populations," *Personality and Individual Differences*, Vol. 17 (1994), pp. 227–255.

23. T. S. Eliot, "The Love Song of J. Alfred Prufrock," *Collected Poems: 1909–1935* (New York: Harcourt, Brace and Company, 1936).

24. Deborah Tannen, *You Just Don't Understand: Women and Men in Conversation* (New York: Ballantine, 1991).

25. www.wendy.com/women/quotations.html.

26. Quoted by Nancy Collins, "Wolf, Man, Jack," *Vanity Fair*, Vol. 57 (April 1994), pp. 118 ff.

27. Julianne Imperato-McGinley, Luis Guerrero, Teofilo Gautier, and Ralph E. Peterson, "Steroid 5-Alpha-Reductase Deficiency in Man: An Inherited Form of Male Pseudohermaphroditism," *Science*, Vol. 186 (1974), pp. 1213–1215.

28. Jlang-Ning Zhou, Michel A. Hofman, Louis J. G. Gooren, and Dick F. Swaab, "A Sex Difference in the Human Brain and its Relation to Transsexuality," *Nature*, Vol. 378 (1995), pp. 68–70.

29. The story of Gordon Langley Hall/Dawn Hall Simmons was summarized by Molly Parkin, "The Life and Love of a Trans-sexual," *London Sunday Times*, March 7, 1971, and by Virginia Spencer Carr, *The Lonely Hunter: A Biography of Carson McCullers* (New York: Carroll & Graf Publishers, 1975), p. 520. There is an interesting article about female-to-male transsexuals by Amy Bloom, "The Body Lies," *New Yorker*, July 18, 1994, pp. 38–49.

30. D. R. Robertson, "Social Control of Sex Reversal in a Coral-reef Fish," *Science*, Vol. 177 (1972), pp. 1007–1009.

31. Oscar Lewis, "Manly-Hearted Women Among the North Piegan," *American Anthropologist*, Vol. 43 (1941), pp. 173–187.

32. *500 Nations* [video], narr. Kevin Costner (Washington, D.C.: Public Broadcasting System, 1994).

Chapter 3. Testosterone, Mind, and Behavior

1. Stephanie van Goozen, *Male and Female: Effects of Sex Hormones on Aggression, Cognition, and Sexual Motivation* (Amsterdam: University of Amsterdam, 1994), p. 173.

2. Helen Fisher, *The First Sex: The Natural Talents of Women and How They Are Changing the World* (New York: Ballantine Books, 1999).

3. C. Davatzikos and S. M. Resnick, "Sex Differences in Anatomic Measures of Interhemispheric Connectivity: Correlations with Cognition in Women but not Men," *Cerebral Cortex*. Vol. 8 (1998), pp. 634–640.

4. William Shakespeare, *Henry V*, Act IV, Scene 1.

5. John Erskine, *Galahad: Enough of His Life to Explain His Reputation* (Indianapolis: The Bobbs-Merrill Company, 1926), p. 200.

6. Antoine de Saint-Exupéry, "Flight to Arras," *Airman's Oddesy* (New York: Harcourt Brace, 1942), p. 319.

7. Larry McMurtry, *Lonesome Dove* (New York: Pocket Books, 1985), p. 780.

8. John Archer, "Testosterone and Persistence in Mice," *Animal Behaviour*, Vol. 25 (1977), pp. 478–488. Also, R. L. Andrew and L. Rogers, "Testosterone, Search Behaviour, and Persistence," *Nature*, Vol. 237 (1972), pp. 343–346. Also, D. M. Broverman, I. K. Broverman, W. Vogel, R. D. Palmer, and E. L. Klaiber, "The Automatization of Cognitive Style and Physical Development," *Child Development*, Vol. 35 (1964), pp. 1343–1349.

9. *Creative Loafing,* June 17, 1995.

10. James Lee Burke, *The Neon Rain* (New York: Pocket Books, 1987), p. 263.

11. Evidence of the link between low testosterone and high verbal ability is given by Stephanie H. M. van Goozen, Peggy T. Cohen-Ketenis, Louis J. G. Gooren, Nico H. Frijda, and Nanne E. van de Poll, "Activating Effects of Androgens on Cognitive Performance: Causal Evidence in a Group of Female-to-Male Transsexuals," *Neuropsychologia*, Vol. 32 (1995), pp. 1153–1157.

12. Melissa Hines, "Gonadal Hormones and Human Cognitive Development," in J. Balthazart, ed., *Hormones, Brain and Behaviour in Vertebrates. I. Sexual differentiation, Neuroanatomical Aspects, Neurotransmitters and Neuropeptides. Comparative Physiology* (Basel: Karger, 1990), pp. 51–63.

13. Sue W. Kirkpatrick, P. Samuel Campbell, Rhonda E. Wharry, and Shirley L. Robinson, "Salivary Testosterone in Children With and Without Learning Disabilities," *Physiology and Behavior*, Vol. 53 (1993), pp. 583–586.

14. James M. Dabbs, Jr., "Testosterone and Occupational Achievement," *Social Forces*, Vol. 70 (1992), pp. 813–824.

15. James Lee Burke, *The Neon Rain* (New York: Pocket Books, 1987), pp. 163–164.

16. Tom Wolfe, *The Right Stuff* (New York: Farrar, Straus and Giroux, 1979), p. 144.

17. Walter Weintraub, *Verbal Behavior: Adaptation and Psychopathology* (New York: Springer, 1981).

18. "Women Veterans," host Linda Wertheimer, *All Things Considered* (Washington, D.C.: National Public Radio, 11 November 1991).

19. John T. Cacioppo, Richard E. Petty, Jeffrey Feinstein, and Blair Jarvis, "Dispositional Differences in Cognitive Motivation: The Life and Times of Individuals Varying in Need for Cognition," *Psychological Bulletin*, Vol. 19 (1995), pp. 197–253.

20. "Women Legislators make up 40 Percent of the Washington State Legislature," rep. Wendy Kaufman, *Morning Edition* (Washington, D.C.: National Public Radio, 23 February 1999).

21. Cormac McCarthy, *The Crossing* (New York: Random House, 1995), p. 189.

22. Lynn Liben, "Psychology Meets Geography: Exploring the Gender

Gap on the National Geography Bee," *Psychological Science Agenda*, Vol. 8 (1995, January/February), pp. 8–9.

23. J. A. Cross, "Factors Associated with Students' Place Location Knowledge," *Journal of Geography*, Vol. 86 (1987), pp. 59–63.

24. Ellen D. Ketterson and Van Nolan Jr., "Hormones and Life Histories: An Integrative Approach," *The American Naturalist*, Vol. 140 (1992), pp. S33–S62.

25. Roxane E. Osborne, Iwona Niekrasz, David Domek, Yaolong Zhang, Adolfo Garnica, and Thomas W. Seale, "Acute Anxiolytic-Like Behavioral Effects of Testosterone, its Metabolites, and Related Steroids," unpublished paper from the University of Oklahoma Health Sciences Center, 1995.

26. S. Goldberg and M. Lewis, "Play Behavior in the Year-old Infant," *Child Development*, Vol. 40 (1969), pp. 21–31.

27. Several studies here have produced uncertain results. Recent work by Irwin Silverman and his colleagues, however, finds testosterone correlated with mental rotation scores and explains some of the ambiguities in prior data. See Irwin Silverman, D. Kastuk, J. Choi, and K. Phillips, "Testosterone and Spatial Ability in Men," *Psychoneuroendocrinology*, Vol. 24 (1999), pp. 813–822.

28. Stephanie H. M. van Goozen, Peggy T. Cohen-Ketenis, Louis J. G. Gooren, Nico H. Frijda, and Nanne E. van de Poll, "Activating Effects of Androgens on Cognitive Performance: Causal Evidence in a Group of Female-to-Male Transsexuals," *Neuropsychologia*, Vol. 32 (1995), pp. 1153–1157.

29. Neil V. Watson and Doreen Kimura, "Nontrivial Sex Differences in Throwing and Intercepting: Relation to Psychometrically-Defined Spatial Functions," *Personality and Individual Differences*, Vol. 12 (1991), pp. 375–381. The information on computer target tracking tests comes from Dr. Earl Hunt at the University of Washington.

30. Lauren A. Baker and James M. Dabbs, Jr., "Gender Difference in Preference for Photographs," poster presented at the June 1999 meeting of the American Psychological Society.

31. Marion Eals and Irwin Silverman, "The Hunter-Gatherer Theory of Spatial Sex Differences: Proximate Factors Mediating the Female Advantage in Recall of Object Arrays," *Ethology and Sociobiology*, Vol. 15 (1994), pp. 95–105.

32. Liisa A. M. Galea and Doreen Kimura, "Sex Differences in Route-Learning," *Personality and Individual Differences*, Vol. 14 (1993), pp. 53–65. Also Silverman, Choi; sex differences in route learning.

33. George P. Murdock, "Comparative Data on the Division of Labor by Sex," *Social Forces*, Vol. 15 (1937), pp. 551–553.

34. Sheri A. Berenbaum and Melissa Hines, "Early Androgens are Related to Childhood Sex-Typed Toy Preferences," *Psychological Science*, Vol. 3 (1992), pp. 203–206.

35. Richard Preston, *American Steel* (New York: Prentice-Hall Press, 1991), p. 191.

36. See Elizabeth Hampson and Doreen Kimura, "Sex Differences and Hormonal Influences on Cognitive Function in Humans," in *Behavioral Endocrinology*, eds. Jill B. Becker, S. Marc Breedlove, and David Crews (Cambridge, MA: MIT Press, 1992), pp. 357–398.

37. Doreen Kimura, *Sex and Cognition* (Cambridge, MA: MIT Press, 1999).

38. Stephanie van Goozen, *Male and Female: Effects of Sex Hormones on Aggression, Cognition and Sexual Motivation* (Amsterdam: University of Amsterdam, 1994).

39. "A Look Back at the Development of the First Atomic Bomb," rep. Dan Charles, *Morning Edition* (Washington, D.C.: National Public Radio, 14 July 1995).

40. Shalender Bhasin, Thomas W. Storer, Nancy Berman, Carlos Callegari, Brenda Clevenger, Jeffrey Phillips, Thomas J. Bunnell, Ray Tricker, Aida Shirazi, and Richard Casaburi, "The Effects of Supraphysiologica Doses of Testosterone on Muscle Size and Strength in Normal Men," *New England Journal of Medicine*, Vol. 335 (1996), pp. 1–7.

41. Charles J. Lumsden and Edward O. Wilson, *Genes, Mind, and Culture: The Coevolutionary Process* (Cambridge, MA: Harvard University Press, 1981).

42. E-mail communication from Michio Kaku, 31 March 1999.

43. Richard Preston, *American Steel* (New York: Prentice Hall Press, 1991), p. 228.

44. Katherine Dunn, "The Badder, the Better," *Esquire*, February 1995, p. 95.

45. Cormac McCarthy, *The Crossing* (New York: Random House, 1995), p. 321.

46. John Erskine, *Galahad: Enough of His Life to Explain His Reputation* (Indianapolis: The Bobbs-Merrill Company, 1926), p. 170.

47. A. Wallace, *Homicide: The Social Reality* (Sydney: New South Wales Bureau of Crime Statistics and Research, 1986).

48. Eleanor E. Maccoby, "Gender and Relationships: A Developmental Account," *American Psychologist*, Vol. 45 (1990), pp. 513–520.

49. Dane Archer and Patricia McDaniel, "Violence and Gender: Differences and Similarities Across Societies," in *Interpersonal Violent Behavior: Social and Cultural Aspects*, eds. R. Barry Ruback and N. A. Weiner (New York: Springer, 1995), pp. 63–87.

50. W. J. Jeffcoate, N. B. Lincoln, C. Selby, and M. Herbert, "Correlation Between Anxiety and Serum Prolactin in Humans," *Journal of Psychosomatic Research*, Vol. 30 (1986), pp. 217–222.

51. Richard Lynn, "Sex Differences in Intelligence and Brain Size: A Developmental Theory," *Intelligence*, Vol. 27 (1999), pp. 1–12.

52. Lee Willerman, R. Schultz, J. M. Rutledge, and E. D. Bigler, "In Vivo Brain Size and Intelligence," *Intelligence*, Vol. 15 (1991), pp. 223–228.

53. Sandra F. Witelson, Debra L. Kigar, and Thomas Harvey, "The Exceptional Brain of Albert Einstein," *Lancet*, Vol. 353 (1999), pp. 2149–2153. See also Steven Levy, "The Roots of Genius? The Odd History of a Famous Old Brain," *Newsweek*, 28 June 1999, p. 32.

54. This view is also expressed by Richard Lynn, "Sex Differences in Intelligence and Brain Size: A Developmental Theory," *Intelligence*, Vol. 27 (1999), pp. 1–12.

55. This view is expressed in Roberta L. Hall and Henry S. Sharp, eds., *Wolf and Man: Evolution in Parallel* (New York: Academic Press, 1978).

56. This is the research of Sandra Wittleson, reported in the *New York Times*, February 28, 1995, p. C1 ff. Also, Herbert Haug, "Brain Sizes, Surfaces, and Neuronal Sizes of the Cortex Cerebri: A Stereological Investigation of Man and His Variability and a Comparison with Some Mammals (Primates, Whales, Marsupials, Insectivors, and One Elephant)," *American Journal of Anatomy*, Vol. 180 (1987), pp. 126–142.

57. See the Witelson *et al.* and Levy references four notes above.

58. Elizabeth R. McCown, "Sex Differences: The Female as Baseline for Species Description," in *Sexual Dimorphism in Homo Sapiens: A Question of Size*, ed. Roberta L. Hall (New York: Praeger, 1982), pp. 37–83.

59. G. Turbervile, *The Noble Arte of Venerie or Hunting* (Oxford: Clarendon Press, 1908, facsimile 1576 edition). Quoted in Roger Short, "Deer: Yesterday, Today, and Tomorrow," *Biology of Deer Production* (Royal Society of New Zealand, Bulletin 22, 1985), pp. 461–469.

60. James M. Dabbs, Jr., Denise de La Rue, and Paula M. Williams, "Testosterone and Occupational Choice: Actors, Ministers, and Other Men," *Journal of Personality and Social Psychology*, Vol. 59 (1990), pp. 1261–1265.

61. Sekou Sundiata, on "Fresh Air with Terry Gross" (Washington, D.C.: National Public Radio, 11 May 1994).

62. Audie Murphy quotations are from Don Graham, *No Name on the Bullet: A Biography of Audie Murphy* (New York: Viking Penguin, 1989), p. 59.

63. Terry Banks and James M. Dabbs, Jr., "Testosterone and Cortisol in a Delinquent and Violent Urban Subculture," *Journal of Social Psychology*, Vol. 136, (1996), pp. 49–56.

64. Gary Wills is quoted in Neal Gabler, "Male Bonding," *Modern Maturity* (January–February 2000), p. 54.

65. James M. Dabbs, Jr., Frank J. Bernieri, Rebecca K. Strong, Rhonda Milun, and Rebecca Campo, "Going on Stage: Testosterone in Greetings and Meetings," unpublished manuscript, Georgia State University, 2000.

66. Roxane E. Osborne, Iwona Niekrasz, David Domek, Yaolong Zhang, Adolfo Garnica, and Thomas W. Seale, "Acute Anxiolytic-Like Behavioral Effects of Testosterone, its Metabolites, and Related Steroids," unpublished paper from the University of Oklahoma Health Sciences Center, 1995.

67. A. Boissy and M. F. Bouissou, "Effects of Androgen Treatment on Behav-

ioral and Physiological Responses of Heifers to Fear-Eliciting Situations," *Hormones and Behavior*, Vol. 28 (1944), pp. 66–83.

68. Harry C. Triandis, *Culture and Social Behavior* (New York: McGraw-Hill, 1994), p. 29.

69. Stephen Potter, *The Complete Upmanship* (New York: Holt, Rinehart and Winston, 1970), p. 14.

70. *The Kennedys* [video] (Washington, D.C.: Public Broadcasting System, 1999).

71. Eugene S. Morton and Jake Page, *Animal Talk: Science and the Voices of Nature* (New York: Random House, 1992).

72. This work is by Dr. A. G. Alias, Chester Mental Health Center, Chester, IL.

73. A German study reports a lower ratio of testosterone to estradiol among tenors than among baritones and basses. See W. Meuser and E. Nieschlag, "Sexualhormone und Stimmlage des Mannes," *Deutsche Medizinische Wochenschrift*, Vol. 102 (1977), pp. 261–264.

74. James M. Dabbs, Jr., and Alison Malinger, "High Testosterone Levels Predict Low Voice Pitch Among Males," *Personality and Individual Differences*, Vol. 27 (1999), pp. 801–804.

75. Pat Conroy, *The Great Santini* (Boston: Houghton Mifflin, 1976).

76. See Randy Thornhill and A. P. Moller, "Developmental Stability, Disease and Medicine," *Biological Reviews of the Cambridge Philosophical Society*, Vol. 72 (1977), pp. 497–548. The information on jaw size comes from A. R. Gage, John T. Manning, D. Scutt, M. J. Diver, and W. D. Fraser, "Testosterone, Cortisol and Jaw Size in Men," unpublished manuscript, University of Liverpool, 1999.

77. Allan Mazur and Ulrich Mueller, "Channel Modeling: From West Point Cadet to General," *Public Administration Review*, Vol. 56 (1996), pp. 191–198. See also, Allan Mazur, Julie Mazur, and Caroline Keating, "Military Rank Attainment of a West Point Class: Effects of Cadet's Physical Features," *American Journal of Sociology*, Vol. 90 (1984), pp. 125–150.

78. Madeline E. Heilman and Lois R. Saruwatari, "When Beauty Is Beastly: The Effects of Appearance and Sex on Evaluations of Job Applicants for Managerial and Nonmanagerial Jobs," *Organizational Behavior and Human Performance*, Vol. 25 (1979), pp. 360–372.

79. This example of a cultural hero in a corporation comes from Terrence E. Deal and Allan A. Kennedy, *Corporate Cultures: The Rites and Rituals of Corporate Life* (Reading, MA: Addison-Wesley, 1982), p. 54.

PART TWO: SOCIAL LIFE
Chapter 4. Ruthless Creatures

1. http://www.geocities.com/RainForest/Vines/8591/hyena/hyenas.htm

2. Tamer M. Yalcinkaya, Pentti K. Siiteri, Jean-Louis Vigne, Paul Licht,

Sushama Pavgi, Laurence G. Frank, and Stephen E. Glickman, "A Mechanism for Virilization of Female Spotted Hyenas in Utero," *Science*, Vol. 260 (1993), pp. 1929–1931. Paul Licht, Laurence G. Frank, Sushama Pavgi, Tamar M. Yalcinkaya, Pentti K. Siiteri, and Stephen E. Glickman, "Hormonal Correlates of 'Masculinization' in Female Spotted Hyenas (*Crocuta crocuta*). 2. Maternal and Fetal Steroids," *Journal of Reproduction and Fertility*, Vol. 95 (1992). pp. 463–474. Also, Natalie Angier, "Hyenas' Hormone Flow Puts Females in Charge," *New York Times*, September 1, 1992, pp. C1 ff.

3. Laura Smale, Kay E. Holekamp, Mary Weldele, Laurence G. Frank, and Stephen E. Glickman, "Competition and Cooperation Between Litter-mates in the Spotted Hyaena, *Crocuta crocuta*," *Animal Behavior*, Vol. 50 (1995), pp. 671–682.

4. http://www.geocities.com/RainForest/Vines/8591/hyena/hyenas.htm

5. James M. Dabbs, Jr., Timothy S. Carr, Robert L. Frady, and Jasmin K. Riad, "Testosterone, Crime, and Misbehavior Among 692 Male Prison Inmates," *Personality and Individual Differences*, Vol. 18 (1995), pp. 627–633.

6. James M. Dabbs, Jr., Robert L. Frady, Timothy S. Carr, and Norma F. Besch, "Saliva Testosterone and Criminal Violence in Young Adult Prison Inmates," *Psychosomatic Medicine*, Vol. 49 (1987), pp. 174–182.

7. Immanuel Kant, "Eternal Peace," in *Immanuel Kant's Moral and Political Writings*, ed. Karl J. Frederick (New York: Modern Library, 1949), p. 436.

8. These findings are reported by James M. Dabbs, Jr., R. Barry Ruback, Robert L. Frady, Charles H. Hopper, and Demetrios S. Sgoutas, "Saliva Testosterone and Criminal Violence Among Women," *Personality and Individual Differences*, Vol. 9 (1988), pp. 269–275, and by James M. Dabbs, Jr. and Marian F. Hargrove, "Age, Testosterone, and Behavior among Female Prison Inmates," *Psychosomatic Medicine*, Vol. 59 (1997), pp. 477–480.

9. *The American Heritage Dictionary of the English Language* (New York: Houghton-Mifflin, 1969).

10. James M. Dabbs, Jr., and Robin Morris, "Testosterone, Social Class, and Antisocial Behavior in a Sample of 4,662 Men," *Psychological Science*, Vol. 1 (1990), pp. 209–211.

11. Terry Banks and James M. Dabbs, Jr., "Testosterone and Cortisol in a Delinquent and Violent Urban Subculture," *Journal of Social Psychology*, Vol. 136 (1990), pp. 49–56.

12. James M. Dabbs, Jr., Marian F. Hargrove, and Colleen Heusel, "Testosterone Differences Among College Fraternities: Well-Behaved vs. Rambunctious," *Personality and Individual Differences*, Vol. 20 (1996), pp. 157–167.

13. Michael D. Lemonick, "Young, Single and out of Control," *Time*, 13 October 1997, p. 68.

14. J. Richard Udry, "Biosocial Models of Adolescent Problem Behaviors," *Social Biology*, Vol. 37 (1990), pp. 1–10.

15. Dan Olweus, Åke Mattsson, Daisy Schalling, and Hans Läw, "Circulat-

ing Testosterone Levels and Aggression in Adolescent Males: A Causal Analysis," *Psychosomatic Medicine*, Vol. 50 (1986), pp. 261–272.

16. Sue W. Kirkpatrick, P. Samuel Campbell, Rhonda E. Wharry, and Shirley L. Robinson, "Salivary Testosterone in Children With and Without Learning Disabilities," *Physiology and Behavior*, Vol. 53 (1993), pp. 583–586.

17. Susan E. Chance, Ronald T. Brown, James M. Dabbs, Jr., and Robert Casey, "Testosterone, Intelligence, and Behavior Disorders in Young Boys," *Personality and Individual Differences*, Vol. 28 (2000), pp. 437–445.

18. Rebecca K. Strong and James M. Dabbs, Jr., "Testosterone and Behavior in Normal Young Children," *Personality and Individual Differences*," Vol. 28 (2000), pp. 905–915.

19. Michael S. Bahrke, Charles E. Yesalis III, and James E. Wright, "Psychological and Behavioral Effects of Endogenous Testosterone Levels and Anabolic-Androgenic Steroids among Males: A Review," *Sports Medicine*, Vol. 10 (1990), pp. 303–337.

20. Irwin S. Bernstein, Robert M. Rose, and Thomas P. Gordon, "Behavioral and Environmental Events Influencing Primate Testosterone Levels," *Journal of Human Evolution*, Vol. 3 (1974), pp. 517–525.

21. D. J. Albert, R. H. Jonik, M. L. Walsh, and D. M. Petrovic, "Testosterone Supports Hormone-dependent Aggression in Female Rats," *Physiology and Behavior*, Vol. 46 (1989), pp. 185–199.

22. Natalie Angier, "In Fish, Social Status Goes Right to the Brain," *New York Times*, 12 November, 1991, pp. C1 ff. This article cites especially the work of Dr. Russell Fernald.

23. Natalie Angier, "Pit Viper's Life: Bizarre, Gallant, and Venomous," *New York Times*, 15 October 1991, pp. B5 ff. See also Gordon W. Shuett, H. J. Harlow, J. D. Rose, E. A. Van Kirk, and W. J. Murdoch, "Levels of Plasma Corticosterone and Testosterone in Male Copperheads (*Agkistrodon contortrix*) following Staged Fights," *Hormones and Behavior*, Vol. 30 (1996), pp. 60–68; and Gordon W. Shuett, "Fighting Dynamics of Male Copperheads, *Agkistrodon contortrix* (*Serpentes, Viperidae*): Stress-induced Inhibition of Sexual Behavior in Losers," *Zoo Biology*, Vol. 15 (1998), pp. 209–221.

24. Wendy M. Thompson, James M. Dabbs, Jr., and Robert L. Frady, "Changes in Saliva Testosterone Levels During a 90-Day Shock Incarceration Program," *Criminal Justice and Behavior*, Vol. 17 (1990), pp. 246–252.

25. L. E. Kreuz, R. M. Rose, and R. Jennings, "Suppression of Plasma Testosterone Levels and Psychological Stress," *Archives of General Psychiatry*, Vol. 26 (1971), pp. 479–482.

26. Richard H. Rahe, Samuel Karson, Noel S. Howard, Jr., Robert T. Rubin, and Russell E. Poland, "Psychological and Physiological Assessments on American Hostages Freed from Captivity in Iran," *Psychosomatic Medicine*, Vol. 52 (1980), pp. 1–16.

27. Alan Booth, Greg Shelley, Allan Mazur, Gerry Tharp, and Roger Kittok, "Testosterone, and Winning and Losing in Human Competition," *Hormones and Behavior*, Vol. 23 (1989), pp. 556–571.

28. Allan Mazur, Alan Booth, and James M. Dabbs, Jr., "Testosterone and Chess Competition," *Social Psychology Quarterly*, Vol. 55 (1992), pp. 70–77.

29. Neil S. Jacobson, John M. Gottman, and Joann Wu Shortt, "The Distinction Between Type 1 and Type 2 Batterers—Further Considerations: Reply to Ornduff et al. (1995), Margolin et al. (1995), and Walker (1995)," *Journal of Family Psychology*, Vol. 9 (1995), pp. 272–279.

30. Paul C. Bernhardt, James M. Dabbs, Jr., Julie A. Fielden, and Candice Lutter, "Testosterone Changes During Vicarious Experiences of Winning and Losing among Fans at Sporting Events," *Physiology and Behavior*, Vol. 65 (1998), pp. 59–62.

31. G. F. White, J. Katz, and K. E. Scarborough, "The Impact of Professional Football Games upon Violent Assaults on Women," *Violence and Victims*, Vol. 7 (1992), pp. 157–171.

Chapter 5. Love and Sex

1. There is an engaging description of this study in Arthur Aron and Elaine N. Aron, *The Heart of Social Psychology: A Backstage View of a Passionate Science* (Lexington MA: Lexington Books, 1989), pp. 104–107. For the original study, see Donald Dutton and Arthur Aron, "Some Evidence for Heightened Sexual Arousal under Conditions of High Anxiety," *Journal of Personality and Social Psychology*, Vol. 30 (1974), pp. 510–517.

2. Dolf Zillmann, "Transfer of Excitation in Emotional Behavior," in John T. Cacioppo and Richard E. Petty, eds., *Social Psychophysiology: A Source Book* (New York: Guilford, 1983), pp. 215–240.

3. "Prairie Vole Study May Hold Key to Human Love," rep. Michelle Trudeau, *All Things Considered* (Washington, D.C.: National Public Radio, 12 February 1993). For other work on hormones and pair bonding, see James T. Winslow, Nick Hastings, C. Sue Carter, Carroll R. Harbaugh, and Thomas R. Insel, "A Role for Central Vasopressin in Pair Bonding in Monogamous Prairie Voles," *Nature*, Vol. 365 (1993), pp. 545–548.

4. Elaine Hatfield and Richard L. Rapson, *Love, Sex, and Intimacy: Their Psychology, Biology, and History* (New York: Harper Collins College, 1993), p. 42.

5. Joseph Mitchell, "A Mess of Clams," in *Up in the Old Hotel, and Other Stories* (New York: Pantheon, 1992), p. 324.

6. David Hamilton, *The Monkey Gland Affair* (London: Chatto and Windus, 1986). See also John H. Hoberman and Charles E. Yesalis, "The History of Synthetic Testosterone," *Scientific American*, Vol. 272 (February 1995), pp. 76–81.

7. Stephen Lock, " 'O that I were young again': Yeats and the Steinach Operation," *British Medical Journal*, Vol. 287 (1983), pp. 1864–1868.

8. See Carrie J. Bagatell, Julia R. Heiman, Jean E. River, and William J. Bremner, "Effects of Endogenous Testosterone and Estradiol on Sexual Behavior in Normal Young Men," *Journal of Clinical Endocrinology and Metabolism*, Vol. 78 (1994), pp. 711–716. Also, Julian M. Davidson, Carlos A. Camargo, and Erla R. Smith, "Effects of Androgen on Sexual Behavior in Hypogonadal Men," *Journal of Clinical Endocrinology and Metabolism*, Vol. 48 (1979), pp. 955–958.

9. However, it should be noted that variations in testosterone level across the menstrual cycle within a woman are generally much smaller than mean differences between women. Because of this, even if a researcher ignores the menstrual cycle in measuring testosterone, there is not likely to be confusion in distinguishing between low- and high-testosterone women. See James M. Dabbs, Jr., and Denise de La Rue, "Salivary Testosterone Measurements among Women: Relative Magnitude of Daily and Menstrual Cycles," *Hormone Research*, Vol. 35 (1991), pp. 182–148.

10. Naomi M. Morris, J. Richard Udry, Firyal Khan-Dawood, and M. Yusoff Dawood, "Marital Sex Frequency and Midcycle Female Testosterone," *Archives of Sexual Behavior*, Vol. 16 (1987), pp. 27–37.

11. See H. A. Feldman, I. Goldstein, D. G. Hatzichristou, R. J. Krane, and J. B. McKinlay, "Impotence and its Medical and Psychosocial Correlates: Results of the Massachusetts Male Aging Study," *Journal of Urology*, Vol. 151 (1994), pp. 54–61.

12. Elizabeth Cashdan, "Hormones, Sex, and Status in Women," *Hormones and Behavior*, Vol. 29 (1995), pp. 354–366.

13. These findings are discussed by Del Thiessen, "Hormonal Correlates of Sexual Aggression," in Lee Ellis and Harry Hoffman, eds., *Crime in Biological, Social and Moral Contexts* (New York: Praeger, 1990), pp. 153–161.

14. See Randy Thornhill and Craig T. Palmer, *A Natural History of Rape: Biological Bases of Sexual Coercion* (Cambridge, MA: MIT Press, 2000).

15. Barbara B. Sherwin, M. Gelfand, and W. Brender, "Androgen Enhances Sexual Motivation in Females: A Prospective, Crossover Study of Sex Steriod Administration in the Surgical Menopause," *Psychosomatic Medicine*, Vol. 47 (1985), pp. 339–351. Also, Adriaan Tuiten, Jack Van Honk, Hans Koppeschaar, Coen Bernaards, Jos Thijssen, and Rien Verbaten, "Time Course of Effects of Testosterone Administration on Sexual Arousal in Women," *Archives of General Psychiatry*, Vol. 57 (2000), pp. 149–153.

16. Anonymous, "Effects of Sexual Activity on Beard Growth in Man," *Nature*, Vol. 226 (1970), pp. 869–870.

17. This experiment, along with citations regarding sexual anticipation and testosterone in animals, is reported in James M. Dabbs, Jr., and Suzanne Mohammed, "Male and Female Salivary Testosterone Concentrations Before and After Sexual Activity," *Physiology and Behavior*, Vol. 52 (1992), pp. 195–197.

Recent research has linked specific brain areas to male sexual behavior, identifying places where brain activation is correlated with increasing testosterone levels among men viewing sexually explicit films; see S. Stoleru et al., "Neuroanatomical Correlates of Visually Evoked Sexual Arousal in Human Males," *Archives of Sexual Behavior,* Vol. 28 (1999), pp. 1—21.

18. Samuel Yochelson and Stanton E. Samenow, *The Criminal Personality* (New York: J. Aronson, 1976).

19. Alfred, Lord Tennyson, "Locksley Hall."

20. James M. Dabbs, Jr., "Age and Seasonal Variation in Serum Testosterone Concentration among Men," *Chronobiology International*, Vol. 7 (1990), pp. 245—249.

21. Richard J. Levine, "Season Variation in Human Semen Quality," in *Temperature and Environmental Effects on the Testis*, ed. A. W. Zorgniotti (New York: Plenum Press, 1991), pp. 89—96. Also, Leonidas Politoff, Martin Birkhauser, Alfonso Almendral, and Alain Zorn, "New Data Confirming a Circannual Rhythm in Spermatogenesis," *Fertility and Sterility*, Vol. 52, 1989, pp. 486—489.

22. Walter Randall, "A Statistical Analysis of the Annual Pattern in Births in the USA, 1967 to 1976," *Journal of Interdisciplinary Cycle Research*, Vol. 18 (1987), pp. 179—191.

23. The information on rattlesnakes and copperheads comes from Dr. Gordon Shuett at Arizona State University. See Gordon W. Shuett, H. J. Harlow, J. D. Rose, E. A. Van Kirk, and W. J. Murdoch, "Annual Cycle of Plasma Testosterone in Male Copperheads, Agkistrodon contortrix (Serpentes, Viperidae): Relationship to Spermatogenesis, Mating, and Agonistic Behavior," *General and Comparative Endocrinology*, Vol. 105 (1997), pp. 417—424. See also Natalie Angier, "Pit Viper's Life: Bizarre, Gallant, and Venomous," *New York Times,* October 15, 1991, pp. B5 ff.

24. For a wide-ranging discussion of how light affects people, see John N. Ott, *Health and Light: The Effects of Natural and Artificial Light on Man and Other Living Things* (Old Greenwich, CT: Devin-Adair, 1973).

25. J. Richard Udry and Naomi M. Morris, "The Distribution of Events in the Human Menstrual Cycle," *Journal of Reproduction and Fertility*, Vol. 51 (1977), pp. 419—425.

26. Jared Diamond, "The Accidental Conqueror," *Discover,* December 1991, pp. 71—76. See also Jared Diamond, *Guns, Germs, and Steel: The Fates of Human Societies* (New York: W.W. Norton & Co., 1999), pp. 157—175.

27. "The Better Sex," host Dan Rather, *48 Hours* (New York: NBC News, 20 July 1994).

28. Michael J. Raleigh and Michael T. McGuire, "Social Influences on Endocrine Function in Male Vervet Monkeys," in Toni E. Ziegler and Fred B. Bercovitch, eds., *Socioendocrinology of Primate Reproduction* (New York: John Wiley & Sons, 1990), pp. 95—111.

29. Alvin M. Josephy, Jr., *500 Nations: An Illustrated History of North American Indians* (New York: Alfred A. Knopf, 1994), p. 50.

30. Teresa Julian and Patrick C. McKenry, "Relationship of Testosterone to Men's Family Functioning at Mid-Life: A Research Note," *Aggressive Behavior*, Vol. 15 (1989), pp. 281–289.

31. Stacy J. Rogers, "The Nexus of Job Satisfaction, Marital Satisfaction and Individual Well-Being: Does Marriage Order Matter?" *Research in the Sociology of Work*, Vol. 5 (1999), pp. 141–167.

32. Alan Booth and James M. Dabbs, Jr., "Testosterone and Men's Marriages," *Social Forces*, Vol. 72 (1993), pp. 463–477.

33. Roland J. Erwin, Ruben C. Gur, Raquel E. Gur, Brett Skolnick, Maureen Mawhinney-Hee, and Joseph Smailis, "Facial Emotion Discrimination: I. Task Construction and Behavioral Findings in Normal Subjects," *Psychiatry Research*, Vol. 42 (1992), pp. 231–240.

34. David M. Buss, *The Evolution of Desire: Strategies of Human Mating* (New York: Basic Books, 1994).

35. Cynthia Gimbel and Alan Booth, "Who Fought in Vietnam?" *Social Forces*, Vol. 74 (1996), pp. 1137–1157.

36. Barbara Kantrowitz and Pat Wingert, "The Science of a Good Marriage," *Newsweek*, 19 April 1999, p. 54.

37. David M. Buss, "The Strategies of Human Mating," *American Scientist*, Vol. 82 (1994), pp. 238–249.

38. Shakespeare, *Othello*, Act I, Scene iii.

39. David D. Gilmore, *Manhood in the Making* (New Haven: Yale University Press, 1990), pp 138–139.

40. David Attenborough, *The Life of Birds* (Princeton: Princeton University, 1998). See also *The Life of Birds* [video], narr. David Attenborough (Washington, D.C.: Public Broadcasting System).

41. Paul Spencer, *The Samburu: A Study of Gerontocracy in a Nomadic Tribe* (Berkeley: University of California Press, 1965), p. 127.

42. David M. Buss, "Human Mate Selection," *American Scientist*, Vol. 73 (1985), pp. 47–51.

43. This information was provided by Dr. Udry. It comes from J. Richard Udry, Naomi M. Morris, and Judith Kovenock, "Androgen Effects on Women's Gendered Behaviour," *Journal of Biosocial Science*, Vol. 27 (1995), pp. 359–368.

44. This story is from Eugene J. Webb and Jerry R. Salancik, "The Interview or The Only Wheel in Town," *Journalism Monographs*, November 1966.

45. *Encyclopaedia Britannica*, 15th edition.

46. Caryl E. Rusbult and John M. Martz, "Remaining in an Abusive Relationship: An Investment Model Analysis of Nonvoluntary Dependence," *Personality and Social Psychology Bulletin*, Vol. 21 (1995), pp. 558–571.

47. Kim Hill and Hillard Kaplan, "Tradeoffs in Male and Female Repro-

ductive Strategies Among the Ache: Part 2," in Laura Betzig, Monique Borgerhoff Mulder, and Paul Turke, eds., *Human Reproductive Behavior: A Darwinian Perspective* (Cambridge: Cambridge University Press, 1988), pp. 291–305.

48. David Attenborough, *The Life of Birds* (Princeton: Princeton University, 1998). See also *The Life of Birds* [video], narr. David Attenborough (Washington, D.C.: Public Broadcasting System).

49. Steven W. Gangestad and Jeffry A. Simpson, "The Evolution of Human Mating: Trade-offs and Strategic Pluralism," *Behavior and Brain Sciences,* in press.

50. Ellen D. Ketterson and Van Nolan Jr., "Hormones and Life Histories: An Integrative Approach," *The American Naturalist*, Vol. 140 (1992), pp. S33–S62.

51. K. E. Hunt, T. P. Hahn, and J. C. Wingfield, "Endocrine influences on parental care during a short breeding season; testosterone and male parental care in Lapland longspurs (Calcarius lapponicus)," *Behavioral Ecology and Sociobiology*, Vol. 45 (1999), pp. 360–369.

52. R. Knapp, J. C. Wingfield, and A. H. Bass, "Steroid Hormones and Paternal Care in the Plainfin Midshipman Fish (*Porichthys notatus*)," *Hormones and Behavior*, Vol. 35 (1999), pp. 81–89.

53. Alan Booth and James M. Dabbs, Jr., "Testosterone and Men's Marriages," *Social Forces*, Vol. 72 (1993), pp. 463–477. Also see Elizabeth Cashdan, "Hormones, Sex, and Status in Women," *Hormones and Behavior*, Vol. 29 (1995), pp. 354–366.

54. Allan Mazur and J. Michalek, "Marriage, Divorce, and Male Testosterone," *Social Forces*, Vol. 77 (1998), pp. 315–320.

55. D. J. Gubernick, C. M. Worthman, and J. F. Stallings, "Hormonal Correlates of Fatherhood in Men: A Preliminary Report," presented at the International Society for Developmental Psychobiology meeting, Newport Beach, October, 1992. See also, Carol M. Worthman, J. F. Stallings, and D. Gubernick, "Measurement of Hormones in Blood Spots: A Non-isotopic Assay for Prolactin," *American Journal of Physical Anthropology (Supplement No. 12)* (1991), pp. 186–187.

56. See Beth Azar, "Sex Differences May Not Be Set at Birth," *APA Monitor*, October, 1998; S. M. Breedlove, "Sex on the Brain," *Nature*, Vol. 389 (1997), p. 801; and B. M. Cooke, G. Tabibnia, and S. M. Breedlove, "A Brain Sexual Dimorphism Controlled by Adult Circulating Androgens," *Proceedings of the National Academy of Science*, Vol. 96 (1999), p. 7538–7540.

57. See Sharon M. Pearcey, Karen J. Docherty, and James M. Dabbs, Jr., "Testosterone and Sex Role Identification in Lesbian Couples," *Physiology and Behavior,* Vol. 60 (1996), pp. 1033–1035; and Devendra Singh, M. Vidaurii, R. J. Zambarano, and James M. Dabbs, Jr., "Behavioral, Morphological, and Hormonal Correlates of Erotic Role Identification Among Lesbian Women," *Journal of Personality and Social Psychology*, Vol. 76 (1999) pp. 1035–1049.

58. A. G. Alias, "Incongruous Correlations Among Three Androgenic Tissue Effects and Their Peculiar Relationship to Psychological Parameters: A Pilot Study," paper presented at meeting of the International Society for the Study of Individual Differences, 1995.

59. Simon LeVay and Dean H. Hamer, "Evidence for a Biological Influence in Male Homosexuality," *Scientific American,* May 1994, pp. 44–49.

60. Richard Dawkins, *The Selfish Gene* (New York: Oxford University Press, 1976).

61. The idea that fathers are more faithful in providing resources in cold than in warm climates is presented in detail by Edward M. Miller, "Parental Provisioning versus Mate Seeking in Human Populations," *Personality and Individual Differences,* Vol. 17 (1994), pp. 227–255.

62. This contrast between science and art is suggested by Peter Vaill, former dean of the business school at George Washington University, who said that "art is the attempt to wrest coherence and meaning out of reality than we ordinarily deal with," quoted in Karl Weick, *The Social Psychology of Organizing (2nd edition)* (Reading, MA: Addison-Wesley, 1979), p. 234.

Chapter 6. Earning a Living

1. David Margolick, "At the Bar," *New York Times,* 2 November 1990, p. B 12.

2. I am indebted to Colleen Heusel for this story.

3. *New York Times,* 2 November 1990, p. B 12.

4. David Noonan, "The Lone Ranger Lawyer," *Esquire,* May 1981, pp. 80–87.

5. Dashiell Hammett, *The Maltese Falcon* (New York: Modern Library, 1934). Dashiell Hammett gives this description of Sam Spade in the introduction to the book.

6. These words are attributed to Sir Ian Hamilton by W. W. Suojanen and N. P. Johannesen, "Leadership and Human Minds," *OE Communique,* No. 4 (1982), pp. 40–45.

7. Cynthia Gimbel and Alan Booth, "Who Fought in Vietnam?" *Social Forces,* Vol. 74 (1996), pp. 1137–1157.

8. Cynthia Gimbel and Alan Booth, "Who Fought in Vietnam?" *Social Forces,* Vol. 74 (1996), pp. 1137–1157.

9. The life and character of John Paul Vann is described by Neil Sheehan, *A Bright Shining Lie: John Paul Vann and America in Vietnam* (New York: Random House, 1988).

10. James M. Dabbs, Jr., "Testosterone and Occupational Achievement," *Social Forces,* Vol. 70 (1992), pp. 813–824.

11. Nicholas Wade, "Guillemin and Schally: A Race Spurred by Rivalry," *Science,* Vol. 200 (1978), pp. 510–513.

12. Diana Lutz, "The Personality of Physicists Measured," *American Scientist*, Vol. 82 (July–August, 1984), pp. 324–325.

13. Sharon Traweek, *Beamtimes and Lifetimes* (Cambridge, MA: Harvard University Press, 1988).

14. "U.S. Marshal," rep. Steve Kroft, *60 Minutes* (Washington, D.C.: CBS News, 5 May 1991).

15. "Bruce Ford Rodeo School Teaches Them How to Hang On," rep. Mark Roberts, *Morning Edition* (Washington, D.C.: National Public Radio, 22 July 1994).

16. D. W. Maurer, *The American Confidence Man* (Springfield, IL: Charles C. Thomas, 1974), p. 177.

17. D. W. Maurer, *The American Confidence Man* (Springfield, IL: Charles C. Thomas, 1974), p. 162.

18. Oscar Lewis, "Manly-Hearted Women Among the North Piegan," *American Anthropologist*, Vol. 43 (1941), pp. 173–187.

19. Sam Moses, "The Best Man for the Job Is a Woman," *Sports Illustrated*, 22 June 1981, pp. 71–84.

20. Information about Muldowney can be found at: www.mshf.com/hof/muldowney.htm

21. Pam Postema and Gene Wojciechowski, *You've Got to Have Balls to Make It in This League: My Life As an Umpire* (New York: Simon & Schuster, 1992).

22. Anna Quindlen, "Women in Combat," *New York Times*, 8 January 1992, p. A15.

23. Christopher W. Thompson and Michael C. Moore, "Behavioral and Hormonal Correlates of Alternative Reproductive Strategies in a Polygynous Lizard: Tests of the Relative Plasticity and Challenge Hypotheses," *Hormones and Behavior*, Vol. 26 (1992), pp. 568–585. Although the two types do not differ in testosterone level as adults, changing their testosterone levels early in life can lead to the adult development of one or the other of the two types.

24. James M. Dabbs, Jr., Denise de La Rue, and Paula M. Williams, "Testosterone and Occupational Choice: Actors, Ministers, and Other Men," *Journal of Personality and Social Psychology*, Vol. 59 (1990), pp. 1261–1265.

25. Stanley Karnow, *In Our Image: America's Empire in the Philippines* (New York: Random House, 1989), p. 271–275.

26. "Charles Dutton," rep. Meredith Vieira, *60 Minutes* (New York: CBS News, 16 September 1990).

27. Gail L. Schindler, "Testosterone Concentration, Personality Patterns, and Occupational Choice in Women" (Ph.D. diss., University of Houston, 1979).

28. Steve Olson, "Year of the Blue-Collar Guy," *Newsweek*, 6 November 1989, p. 16.

29. Willa Cather, *My Antonia* (New York: Houghton-Mifflin, 1918; New York: Quality Paperback, 1995), p. 206.

30. C. M. Beall, C. M. Worthman, J. Stallings, K. P. Strohl, G. M. Brittenham,

and M. Barragan, "Salivary Testosterone Concentration of Aymara Men Native to 3600 m," *Annals of Human Biology*, Vol. 19 (1992), pp. 67–78.

31. Richard G. Bribiescas, "Testosterone Levels among Ache Hunter/Gatherer Men: A Functional Interpretation of Population Variation among Adult Males," *Human Nature*, Vol. 7 (1975), pp. 163–188.

32. For more information on the challenge hypothesis, see John C. Wingfield, Robert E. Hegner, Alfred M. Dufty, Jr., and Gregory F. Ball, "The 'Challenge Hypothesis': Theoretical Implications for Patterns of Testosterone Secretion, Mating Systems, and Breeding Strategies," *American Naturalist*, Vol. 136 (1990), pp. 829–846. See also Ellen D. Ketterson and Van Nolan Jr., "Hormones and Life Histories: An Integrative Approach," *The American Naturalist*, Vol. 140 (1992), pp. S33–S62. For the argument that a similar challenge hypothesis applies to people, see Theodore D. Kemper, *Social Structure and Testosterone* (New Brunswick, NJ: Rutgers University), 1990.

33. James M. Dabbs, Jr., "Testosterone and Occupational Achievement," *Social Forces*, Vol. 70 (1992), pp. 813–824.

34. Janet T. Spence and Robert L. Helmreich, "Achievement-Related Motives and Behaviors," in *Achievement and Achievement Motives*, ed. Janet T. Spence (San Francisco: Freeman, 1983), pp. 7–73.

35. Richard D. Arvey, Thomas L. Bouchard, Jr., Nancy L. Segal, and Lauren M. Abraham, "Job Satisfaction: Environmental and Genetic Components," *Journal of Applied Psychology*, Vol. 74 (1989), pp. 187–192.

36. *Roxanne*, Columbia Pictures Industries, 1987.

37. Steve Olson, "Year of the Blue-Collar Guy," *Newsweek*, 6 November 1989, p. 16.

PART THREE: CIVILIZATION
Chapter 7. Dear Ladies and Gentle Men

1. Mary Chase, *Harvey* (New York: Oxford University Press, 1943). Act III.

2. Deborah Tannen, *The Argument Culture: Moving from Debate to Dialogue* (New York: Random House, 1998).

3. Myra MacPherson, *The Power Lovers: An Intimate Look* (New York: G. P. Putnam's Sons, New York, 1975), p. 43.

4. James M. Dabbs, Jr., "Testosterone, Smiling, and Facial Appearance," *Journal of Nonverbal Behavior*, Vol. 21 (97), pp. 45–55.

5. I am indebted to Paul Ekman and Mark Frank for scoring these facial expressions.

6. Paul Ekman, Richard Davidson, and W. V. Friesen, "Emotional Expression and Brain Physiology II: The Duchenne Smile," *Journal of Personality and Social Psychology*, Vol. 58 (1990), pp. 342–353.

7. Elizabeth Cashdan, "Hormones, Sex, and Status in Women," *Hormones and Behavior*, Vol. 29 (1995), pp. 354–366.

8. See Albert R. Thornhill and A. P. Moller, "Developmental Stability, Disease and Medicine," *Biological Reviews of the Cambridge Philosophical Society*, Vol. 72 (1977), pp. 497–548. The information on jaw size comes from A. R. Gage, John T. Manning, D. Scutt, M. J. Diver, and W. D. Fraser, "Testosterone, Cortisol and Jaw Size in Men," unpublished report, University of Liverpool, 1999.

9. E. Tronick, H. Als, L. B. Adamson, S. Wise, and T. B. Brazelton, "The Infant's Response to Entrapment Between Contradictory Messages in Face-to-Face Interaction," *Journal of the American Academy of Child Psychiatry*, Vol. 17 (1980), pp. 1–3.

10. Leslie Fiedler, "Montana; or The End of Jean-Jacques Rousseau," in Leslie Fiedler, A Fiedler Reader (New York: Stein and Day, 1977), pp. 13–23. (Originally published in *Partisan Review*, June 1948.)

11. Floyd H. Allport, *Social Psychology* (Cambridge, MA: Riverside Press, 1924), p. 287.

12. Peggy Noonan, *What I Saw at the Revolution: A Political Life in the Reagan Era* (New York: Random House, 1990).

13. Richard Rogers and Oscar Hammerstein II, *The King and I* (1951).

14. A. N. Metzoff and M. K. Moore, "Imitation of Facial and Manual Gestures by Human Neonates," *Science*, Vol. 198 (1977), pp. 74–78. Also, A. N. Metzoff and M. K. Moore, "Newborn Infants Imitate Adult Facial Gestures," *Child Development*, Vol. 54 (1983), pp. 702–709.

15. Fritz Strack, Leonard L. Martin, and Sabine Stepper, "Inhibiting and Facilitating Conditions of the Human Smile: A Nonobtrusive Test of the Facial Feedback Hypothesis," *Journal of Personality and Social Psychology*, Vol. 54 (1988), pp. 768–777.

16. Findings on the relation of social status to smiling are mixed. People with more power need to smile less to get what they want, and it is widely believed that they do smile less, but studies often show similar smiling at low and high levels in the status hierarchy. See Judith A. Hall and Gregory B. Friedman, "Status, Gender, and Nonverbal Behavior: A Study of Structured Interactions Between Employees of a Company," *Personality and Social Psychology Bulletin*, Vol. 25 (1999), pp. 1082–1091.

17. "Noonday" (Atlanta, GA: WXIA television, 21 February 1999).

18. John Lennon and Paul McCartney, "A Little Help from My Friends" (England: Northern Songs Ltd., 1967).

19. James M. Dabbs, Jr., Rebecca K. Strong, and Rhonda Milun, "Exploring the Mind of Testosterone: A Beeper Study," *Journal of Research in Personality*, Vol. 31 (1997), pp. 577–587.

20. John C. Wingfield, Robert E. Hegner, Alfred M. Dufty, Jr., and Gregory F. Ball, "The 'Challenge Hypothesis': Theoretical Implications for Patterns of Testosterone Secretion, Mating Systems, and Breeding Strategies," *American Naturalist*, Vol. 136 (1990), pp. 829–846. Also, Ellen D. Ketterson and Van

Nolan, Jr., "Hormones and Life Histories: An Integrative Approach," *The American Naturalist*, Vol. 140 (1992), pp. S33–S62.

21. Allan Mazur and Joel Michalek, "Marriage, Divorce, and Male Testosterone," *Social Forces*, Vol. 77 (1998), pp. 315–330.

22. David J. Gubernick, Carol M., and Joy F. Stallings, "Hormonal Correlates of Fatherhood in Men: A Preliminary Report," paper presented at the meeting of the International Society for Developmental Psychobiology, Newport Beach, 1992. The results are also reported in Carol M. Worthman, Joy F. Stallings, and David J. Gubernick, "Measurement of Hormones in Blood Spots: A Non-isotopic Assay for Prolactin," *American Journal of Physical Anthropology (Supplement No. 12)*, (1991), pp. 186–187. Similar results are reported by Anne E. Storey, Carolyn J. Walsh, Roma L. Quinton, and Katherine E. Wynne-Edwards, "Hormonal Correlates of Paternal Responsiveness in New and Expectant Fathers," *Hormones and Behavior*, in press. There are also indications of higher prolactin in new fathers than in expectant fathers among mice, reported by D. J. Gubernick and R. J. Nelson, "Prolactin and Paternal Behavior in the Biparental California Mouse, Peromyscus Californicus," *Hormones and Behavior*, Vol. 23 (1989), pp. 203–210; and of higher prolactin and lower testosterone levels among male gerbils who are living with a mate and pups than among those who are not, reported by R. E. Brown, T. Murdoch, P. R. Murphy, and W. H. Moger, "Hormonal Responses of Male Gerbils to Stimuli from their Mate and Pups," *Hormones and Behavior*. Vol. 29 (1995), pp. 474–491.

23. Randy J. Nelson, *An Introduction to Behavioral Endocrinology* (Sunderland, MA: Sinauer, 1995), p. 86. Also see A. J. Fivizzani, and L. W. Oring, "Plasma Steroid Hormones in Relation to Behavioral Sex Role Reversal in the Spotted Sandpiper, *Actitis macularia*," *Biological Reproduction*, Vol. 35 (1986), pp. 1195–1201.

24. This conclusion comes from a reanalysis of the data reported by James M. Dabbs, Jr., and Robin Morris, "Testosterone, Social Class, and Antisocial Behavior in a Sample of 4,662 Men," *Psychological Science*, Vol. 1 (1990), pp. 209–211.

25. A. Steiger, U. von Bardeleben, K. Wiedemann, and F. Holsboer, "Sleep EEG and Nocturnal Secretion of Testosterone and Cortisol in Patients with Major Endogenous Depression During Acute Phase and after Remission," *Journal of Psychiatric Research*, Vol. 25 (1991), pp. 169–177.

26. Robert T. Rubin, Russell E. Poland, and Ira M. Lesser, "Neuroendocrine Aspects of Primary Endogenous Depression VIII. Pituitary-Gonadal Axis Activity in Male Patients and Matched Control Subjects," *Psychoneuroendocrinology*, Vol. 14 (1989), pp. 217–229.

27. D. C. Cumming, M. E. Quigley, and S. S. C. Yen, "Acute suppression of circulating testosterone levels by cortisol in men," *Journal of Clinical Endocrinology and Metabolism*, Vol. 57 (1983), pp. 671–673.

28. Very little is known about the relation between testosterone and corti-

sol levels in normal women. The study by Banks and Dabbs (1996) indicated a positive correlation between levels of the two hormones.

29. Julia Ross, "Clues Sought in Brain's Physiology," *U. S. Medicine*, May 1995, pp. 3 ff.

30. William W. Morgan and Damon C. Herbert, "Elevation of Serum Prolactin Levels after the Inhibition of Serotonin Uptake," *Endocrinology*, Vol. 103 (1978), pp. 1016–1022.

31. D. S. Charney, G. R. Henninger, J. F. Reinhard, D. E. Sternberg, and K. M. Hafstead, "The Effect of IV L-Tryptophan on Prolactin, Growth Hormones and Mood in Healthy Subjects," *Psychopharmacology*, Vol. 78 (1982), pp. 38–45. This study is cited in Eric R. Braverman with Carl C. Pfeiffer, *The Healing Nutrients Within: Facts, Findings and New Research on Amino Acids* (New Canaan, CT: Keats Publishing, 1987), p. 74.

32. Paul C. Bernhardt, "Influence of Serotonin and Testosterone in Aggression and Dominance: Convergence with Social Psychology," *Current Directions in Psychological Science*, Vol. 6 (1997), pp. 44–48.

33. Michael J. Raleigh and Michael T. McGuire, "Social Influences on Endocrine Function in Male Vervet Monkeys," in Toni E. Ziegler and Fred B. Bercovitch, eds., *Socioendocrinology of Primate Reproduction* (New York: John Wiley & Sons, 1990), pp. 95–111.

34. Roger Short, now at Monash University in Melbourne, Australia, studied Claymore's milk production, milk composition, and testosterone levels throughout an entire year. He suspects Claymore's disorder arose from a single gene defect involving aromatization of testosterone to estrogen in the mammary tissue, as has been described among men with gynecomastia.

35. Anne Campbell, "Staying Alive: Evolution, Culture, and Women's Intrasexual Aggression," *Behavioral and Brain Sciences*, Vol. 22 (1999), pp. 203–252.

36. Bernard Rimland, "The Altruism Paradox," *Psychological Reports*, Vol. 51 (1982), pp. 551–552.

37. Julie A. Harris, J. Philippe Rushton, Elizabeth Hampson, and Douglas N. Jackson, "Salivary Testosterone and Self-report Aggressive and Pro-social Personality Characteristics in Men and Women," *Aggressive Behavior*, Vol. 22 (1996), 321–331.

38. Carol Kaesuk Yoon, "Study Exposes Craven Motive of the Brave Meerkat Sentry," *New York Times on the Web*, 8 June 1999.

Chapter 8. Heroic Altruism

1. Jack Markowitz, *A Walk on the Crust of Hell* (Brattleboro, VT: Stephen Greene Press, 1973).

2. David D. Gilmore, *Manhood in the Making* (New Haven: Yale University Press, 1990), p. 229.

3. Carl Sagan and Ann Druyan, *Shadows of Forgotten Ancestors* (New York: Random House, 1992).

4. David Bakan, *The Duality of Human Existence* (Chicago: Rand McNally, 1966), p. 15.

5. *Peachtree Morning* (Atlanta, GA: WXIA television, 13 April 1999).

6. R. Robin McDonald, "The Happenstance Heroes," *Atlanta Journal-Constitution*, 30 April 1999, p. C1.

7. R. Robin McDonald, "Despite Heroic Rescue, Heartache," *Atlanta Journal-Constitution*, 2 May 1999, p. E9.

8. Joseph A. Blake, "Death by Hand Grenade: Altruistic Suicide in Combat," *Suicide and Life-Threatening Behavior*, Vol. 8 (1978), pp. 46–59.

9. These and other examples of helping behavior come from David Rosenhan, "The Natural Socialization of Altruistic Autonomy," in *Altruism and Helping Behavior*, eds. Jacqueline Macaulay and Leonard Berkowitz (New York: Academic Press, 1970), pp. 251–268.

10. Perry London, "The Rescuers: Motivational Hypotheses about Christians Who Saved Jews from the Nazis," in *Altruism and Helping Behavior*, eds. Jaqueline R. Macaulay and Leonard Berkowitz (New York: Academic Press, 1970), pp. 241–250.

11. Eva Fogelman and Valerie Lewis Wiener, "The Few, The Brave, The Noble," *Psychology Today*, August 1985, pp. 61–66.

12. Carol Gilligan,. "Remapping the Moral Domain: New Images of Self in Relationship," in *Mapping the Moral Domain: A Contribution of Women's Thinking to Psychological Theory and Education*, eds. Carol Gilligan, Janie V. Ward, Jill M. Taylor, and Betty Bardige (Cambridge, MA: Harvard University Press, 1988), pp. 3–19.

13. The letters of John Quincy Adams Dabbs are in the Caroliniana Library, University of South Carolina.

14. Daniel Goleman, "Brutal Sports and Brutal Fans," *New York Times*, 13 August 1985, p. 19.

15. Herbert Simon, "A Mechanism for Social Selection and Successful Altruism," *Science*, Vol. 250 (1990), pp. 1665–1668.

16. John Archer, "Testosterone and Persistence in Mice," *Animal Behaviour*, Vol. 25 (1977), pp. 478–488. Also, R. L. Andrew and L. Rogers, "Testosterone, Search Behaviour, and Persistence," *Nature*, Vol. 237 (1972), pp. 343–346. Also, Stephanie van Goozen, *Male and Female: Effects of Sex Hormones on Aggression, Cognition, and Sexual Motivation* (Amsterdam: University of Amsterdam, 1994), p. 173.

17. Bibb Latané and James M. Dabbs, Jr., "Sex, Group Size, and Helping in Three Cities," *Sociometry*, Vol. 38 (1975), pp. 180–194.

18. David Rosenhan, "The Natural Socialization of Altruistic Autonomy," in *Altruism and Helping Behavior*, eds. Jacqueline Macaulay and Leonard Berkowitz (New York: Academic Press, 1970), pp. 251–268.

19. James M. Dabbs, Jr., Charles H. Hopper, and Gregory J. Jurkovic, "Testosterone and Personality among College Students and Military Veterans," *Personality and Individual Differences*, Vol. 11 (1990), pp. 1263–1269.

20. Ted L. Huston, Gilbert Geis, and Richard Wright, "The Angry Samaritans," *Psychology Today* (June 1976), pp. 61 ff.

21. Don Graham, *No Name on the Bullet: A Biography of Audie Murphy* (New York: Viking, 1989).

22. Warren Christopher, "Report of the Independent Commission on the Los Angeles Police Department," 9 July 1991.

23. "Refugees offer their Reactions to Serb Withdrawal from Kosovo," rep. Sarah Chayes, *Weekend Edition* (Washington, D.C.: National Public Radio, 12 June 1999).

24. Ann Colby and William Damon, *Some Do Care: Contemporary Lives of Moral Commitment* (New York: Free Press, 1992).

25. John Lewis with Michael D'Orso, *Walking with the Wind: A Memoir of the Movement* (New York: Simon & Schuster, 1998), pp. 327–335.

26. E-mail communication from David Lykken, 9 June 1999.

27. Rebecca Strong and James M. Dabbs, Jr., "Testosterone and Behavior in Normal Young Children," *Personality and Individual Differences*, Vol. 28 (2000), pp. 905–915.

Chapter 9. The Taming of Testosterone

1. Philip Lieberman, "Hominid Evolution, Supralaryngeal Vocal Tract Physiology, and the Fossil Evidence for Reconstructions," *Brain and Language*, Vol. 7 (1979), pp. 101–126.

2. Experts are in general agreement regarding these estimates, although there is much guesswork involved. A good background is provided by Fekri A. Hassan, *Demographic Archaeology* (New York: Academic Press, 1981).

3. John Keegan, *A History of Warfare* (New York: Alfred A. Knopf, 1993), p. xv.

4. Henri Tajfel, *Human Groups as Social Categories* (Cambridge: Cambridge University Press, 1981).

5. D. Rothman, *The Discovery of the Asylum: Social Order and Disorder in the New Republic* (Boston: Little, Brown, 1971).

6. See F. Pratto, J. M. Stallworth, and J. Sidanius, "The Gender Gap: Differences in Political Attitudes and Social Dominance Orientation," *British Journal of Social Psychology*, Vol. 36 (1997), pp. 49–68.

7. John H. Crook, "The Socio-ecology of Primates," in *Social Behavior of Birds and Mammals*, ed. John H. Crook (New York: Academic Press, 1970), pp. 103–166.

8. Richard E. Nisbett, "Violence and Regional Culture," *American Psychologist*, Vol. 48 (1993), pp. 441–449.

9. David D. Gilmore, *Manhood in the Making* (New Haven: Yale University Press, 1990).

10. Tony Hillerman, *Listening Woman* (New York: Harper Paperbacks, 1978), pp. 135–157.

11. Louise Gubb-Saba, "A Painful Tradition," *Newsweek*, 5 July 1999, pp. 32–33.

12. " 'Log Cabin Stories: Candidates' Tales," rep. Ira Glass, *Morning Edition* (Washington, D.C.: National Public Radio, 14 January 1992).

13. "India: The Empire of the Spirit," narr. Michael Wood, *Legacy* [video series] (Maryland Public Television, 1991).

14. Herbert A. Simon, "The Information-Processing Theory of Mind," *American Psychologist*, Vol. 50 (1995), pp. 507–508.

15. Alan Booth and D. Wayne Osgood, "The Influence of Testosterone on Deviance in Adulthood: Assessing and Explaining the Relationship," *Criminology*, Vol. 31 (1993), pp. 93–117. Also, Alan Booth, John N. Edwards, and David R. Johnson, "Social Integration and Power," *Social Forces*, Vol. 70 (1991), pp. 207–224.

16. Dan Olweus, Åke Mattsson, Daisy Schalling, and Hans Läw, "Circulating Testosterone Levels and Aggression in Adolescent Males: A Causal Analysis," *Psychosomatic Medicine*, Vol. 50 (1986), pp. 261–272.

17. J. Richard Udry, "Biosocial Models of Adolescent Problem Behaviors," *Social Biology*, Vol. 37 (1990), pp. 1–10.

18. Dr. Claire Sterk of the Emory University School of Public Health and member of the team that investigated the syphilis outbreak, in an interview made as part of the Public Television Service *Frontline* program, "The Lost Children of Rockdale County." The interview is published at http://pbs.org/wgbh/pages/frontline/shows/georgia/interviews/sterk.html.

19. Erin Burnette, "Black Males Retrieve a Noble Heritage," *APA Monitor*, Vol. 26 (June 1995), pp. 1 ff.

20. Alan Booth and D. Wayne Osgood, "The Influence of Testosterone on Deviance in Adulthood: Assessing and Explaining the Relationship," *Criminology*, Vol. 31 (1993), pp. 93–117.

21. "Athletes and Sexual Crimes Against Women," comm. Frank Deford, *Morning Edition* (Washington, D.C.: National Public Radio, 24 March 1994).

22. Peggy Reeves Sanday, *Fraternity Gang Rapes: Sex, Brotherhood, and Privilege on Campus* (New York: New York University Press, 1990).

23. James M. Dabbs, Jr., Charles H. Hopper, and Gregory J. Jurkovic, "Testosterone and Personality among College Students and Military Veterans," *Personality and Individual Differences*, Vol. 11 (1990), pp. 1263–1269.

24. James T. Winslow, James Ellingboe, and Klaus A. Miczek, "Effects of Alcohol on Aggressive Behavior in Squirrel Monkeys: Influence of Testosterone and Social Context," Psychopharmacology, Vol. 95 (1988), pp. 356–363.

25. Susan E. Chance, Ronald T. Brown, James M. Dabbs, Jr., and Robert Casey, "Testosterone, Intelligence, and Behavior Disorders in Young Boys," *Personality and Individual Differences*, Vol. 28 (2000), pp. 437–445.

26. Roy S. Dickens, Jr., "Ceramic Patterning and Social Structure at Two Late Upper Creek Sites in Alabama," delivered at the 33rd Southeastern Archaeological Conference, Tuscaloosa, AL, November 6, 1976.

27. An extensive discussion of the relation between sex ratios and power is provided by Marcia Guttentag and Paul F. Secord, *Too Many Women? The Sex Ratio Question* (Beverly Hills, CA: Sage Publications, 1983).

28. Muriel Spark, "Personal History: Venture into Africa," *The New Yorker*, 2 March 1992, p. 75.

29. David T. Courtwright, *Violent Land: Single Men and Social Disorder from the Frontier to the Inner City* (Cambridge, MA: Harvard University Press, 1996).

30. Peggy Reeves Sanday, "The Socio-Cultural Context of Rape: A Cross-Cultural Study," *Journal of Social Issues*, Vol. 37 (1981), pp. 5–27.

31. Todd W. Crosset, Jeffrey R. Benedict, and Mark A. McDonald, "Male Student-Athletes Reported for Sexual Assault: A Survey of Campus Police Departments and Judicial Affairs Offices," *Journal of Sport and Social Issues*, Vol. 19 (1995), pp. 126–140.

32. Jeff Nesmith, "China's Surplus of Bachelors Could Breed Chaos," *Atlanta Journal-Constitution*, 27 January 1995, p. A12; Shripad Tuljapurkar, Nan Li, and Marcus W. Feldman, "High Sex Ratios in China Future," *Science*, Vol. 267 (1995), pp. 874–876.

33. Patrick Henry, from a speech in Virginia Convention on March 23, 1775, in *Bartlett's Familiar Quotations*.

34. Thomas Henry Huxley, from "On the Educational Value of the Natural History Sciences" (1854), in *Bartlett's Familiar Quotations*.

35. "Violent Crime Report Update," host Alex Chadwick, *Morning Edition* (Washington, D.C.: National Public Radio, 10 December 1999).

36. Edward Zigler, Cara Taussig, and Kathryn Black, "Early Childhood Intervention: A Promising Prevention for Juvenile Delinquency," *American Psychologist*, Vol. 47 (1992), pp. 996–1006.

37. Émile Durkheim, *Moral Education: A Study of the Theory and Application of the Sociology of Education* (New York: Free Press, 1961), p. 277.

38. Sara McLanahan, "The Consequences of Single Motherhood," *American Prospect*, Vol. 18 (1994), pp. 48–58. See also Sara McLanahan and Gary Sandefur, *Growing Up with a Single Parent: What Hurts, What Helps* (Cambridge, MA: Harvard University Press, 1994).

39. William Golding, *Lord of the Flies* (New York: Coward-McCann, 1962).

40. John Erskine, *Galahad: Enough of His Life to Explain His Reputation* (Indianapolis: The Bobbs-Merrill Company, 1926), p. 324.

Epilogue. The Circle

1. Robert Frost, "The Secret Sits," in Edward Connery Lathem, ed., *The Poetry of Robert Frost* (New York: Holt, Rinehart and Winston, 1969), p. 362.

2. T. S. Eliot, "Little Gidding," in *Four Quartets* (New York: Harcourt Brace Javonovich, 1971), p. 59.

3. Arnold A. Berthold, "Transplantation of Testes," translated by D. P. Quiring, *Bulletin of the History of Medicine*, Vol. 16 (1944), pp. 399–401.

4. Robert Frost, "The Star-Splitter," Edward Connery Lathem, ed., *The Poetry of Robert Frost* (New York: Holt, Rinehart and Winston, 1969), p. 179

REFERENCES

Abelson, Robert P. "A Variance Explanation Paradox: When a Little Is a Lot." *Psychological Bulletin* 97 (1985): 129–33.

Albert, D. J., R. H. Jonic, M. L. Walsh, and D. M. Petrovic. "Testosterone Supports Hormone-Dependent Aggression in Female Rats." *Physiology and Behavior* 46 (1989): 185–89.

Alda, Alan. "What Every Woman Should Know About Men." *MS Magazine*, October 1977, pp. 15–16.

Alias, A. G. "Incongrous Correlations Among Three Androgenic Tissue Effects and Their Peculiar Relationship to Psychological Parameters: A Pilot Study." *Paper Presented at the International Society for the Study of Individual Differences Meeting* (1995).

Allport, Floyd H. *Social Psychology.* Cambridge, MA: Riverside Press, 1924.

Amann, Rupert P. "Physiology and Endocrinology." In *Equine Reproduction.* Eds. Angus O. McKinnon, and James L. Voss, 658–85. Philadelphia: Lea & Febiger, 1993.

Anderson, Alun. "The Evolution of Sexes." *Science* 257 (1992): 324–28.

Andrew, R. L. "Increased Persistence of Attention Produced by Testosterone, and Its Implications for the Study of Sexual Behavior." In *Biological Determinants of Sexual Behavior.* Ed. J. B. Hutchison, 255–75. New York: Wiley, 1978.

Andrew, R. L., and L. Rogers. "Testosterone, Search Behaviour, and Persistence." *Nature* 237 (1972): 343–46.

Angier, Natalie. "Parasites Take the Biological Spotlight." *New York Times,* 17 July 1990, sec. C, pp. 1–2.

———. "Pit Viper's Life: Bizarre, Gallant, and Venomous." *New York Times,* 15 October 1991, sec. B, p. 5 ff.

———. "In Fish, Social Status Goes Right to the Brain." *New York Times,* 12 November 1991, sec. C, p. 1 ff.

_____. "Hyenas' Hormone Flow Puts Females in Charge." *New York Times,* 1 September 1992, sec. C, p. 1 ff.

_____. "Canary Chicks: Not All Created Equal." *New York Times,* 25 January 1994, sec. C, p. 1 ff.

Anonymous. "Effects of Sexual Activity on Beard Growth in Man." *Nature* 1970 (226): 869–70.

Archer, D., and P. McDaniel. "Violence and Gender: Differences and Similarities Across Societies." In *Interpersonal Violent Behavior: Social and Cultural Aspects.* Eds. R. B. Ruback, and N. A. Weiner, 63–87. New York: Springer, 1995.

Archer, John. "Testosterone and Persistence in Mice." *Animal Behaviour* 25 (1977): 477–78.

Armanini, Decio, Guglielmo Bonanni, and Mario Palermo. "Reduction of Serum Testosterone in Men by Licorice." *New England Journal of Medicine* 341 (1999): 1158.

Aron, Arthur, and Elaine N. Aron. *The Heart of Social Psychology: A Backstage View of a Passionate Science.* Lexington, MA: Lexington Books, 1989.

Arvey, Richard D., Thomas L. Bouchard, Jr., Nancy L. Segal, and Lauren M. Abraham. "Job Satisfaction: Environmental and Genetic Components." *Journal of Applied Psychology* 74 (1989): 187–92.

Attenborough, David. *The Life of Birds.* Princeton, NJ: Princeton University Press, 1998.

Atwood, Margaret. *Cat's Eye.* Boston: G. K. Hall, 1990.

Azur, Beth. "Sex Differences May Not Be Set at Birth." *APA Monitor,* October 1998.

Bagatell, Carrie J., Julia R. Heiman, Jean E. River, and William J. Bremner. "Effects of Endogenous Testosterone and Estrodial on Sexual Behavior in Normal Young Men." *Journal of Clinical Endocrinology and Metabolism* 78 (1994): 711–16.

Bahrke, Michael S., Charles E. Yesalis III, and James E. Wright. "Psychological and Behavioural Effects of Endogenous Testosterone Levels and Anabolic-Androgenic Steroids Among Males: A Review." *Sports Medicine* 10 (1990): 303–37.

Bakan, D. *The Duality of Human Existance.* Chicago: Rand McNally, 1966.

Baker, Lauren, and James M. Dabbs, Jr. "Gender Difference in Preference for Photographs." *Poster Presented at American Psychological Association Annual Meeting* (1999).

Banks, Terry, and James M. Dabbs, Jr. "Salivary Testosterone and Cortisol in a Delinquent and Violent Urban Subculture." *Journal of Social Psychology* 136 (1996): 49–56.

Bartolino, Amelie. "Salivary Hormone Levels, Anxiety and Self-Confidence Indices in Collegiate Football and Basketball Players over a Season of Play." Ph.D. diss., University of Texas, 1996.

Bassett, Jonathan F., and James M. Dabbs, Jr. "Do Women With High

Testosterone Have More Boy Babies?" *Poster Presented at American Psychological Society Annual Meeting* (1999).

Baumeister, Roy F. *Meanings of Life.* New York: Guilford, 1991.

Beall, C. M., C. M. Worthman, J. Stallings, K. P. Strohl, G. M. Brittenham, and M. Barragan. "Salivary Testosterone Concentration of Aymara Men Native to 3600 m." *Annals of Human Biology* 19 (1992): 67–78.

Bem, Sandra L. "Androgyny and Gender Schema Theory: A Conceptual and Empirical Integration." In *Nebraska Symposium on Motivation: Psychology and Gender.* Eds. R. A. Nienstbier, and T. B. Donderroger, 179–226. Lincoln: University of Nebraska Press, 1987.

Bentley, Gillian R. "Environmental Pollutants and Fertility." In *Infertility in the Modern World: Present and Future Prospects.* Eds. Gillian R. Bentley, and N. Mascie-Taylor. New York: Cambridge University Press, 2000.

Berenbaum, Sheri A., and Melissa Hines. "Early Androgens Are Related to Childhood Sex-Typed Toy Preferences." *Psychological Science* 3 (1992): 203–6.

Berger, Patricia J., Norman C. Negus, Edward H. Sanders, and Pete D. Gardner. "6-Methoxybenzoxazolinone: A Plant Derivative That Stimulates Reproduction in Microtus Montanus." *Science* 214 (1981): 67.

Bernhardt, Paul C. "Influences of Serotonin and Testosterone in Aggression and Dominance: Convergence With Social Psychology." *Current Directions in Psychological Science* 6 (1997): 44–48.

Bernhardt, Paul C., James M. Dabbs, Jr., Julie A. Fielden, and Candice Lutter. "Testosterone Changes During Vicarious Experiences of Winning and Losing Among Fans at Sporting Events." *Physiology and Behavior* 65 (1998): 59–62.

Bernstein, Irwin S. "Taboo or Toy." In *Play—Its Role in Development and Evolution.* Eds. Jerome S. Bruner, Alison Jolly, and Kathy Syliva, 194–97. New York: Basic Books, 1976.

Bernstein, Irwin S., Robert M. Rose, and Thomas P. Gordon. "Behavioral and Environmental Events Influencing Primate Testosterone Levels." *Journal of Human Evolution* 3 (1974): 517–25.

Bernstein, Marianne E., and Milciades Martinez-Gustin. "Physical and Psychological Variation and the Sex Ratio." *Journal of Heredity* 52 (1961): 109–12.

Berthold, Arnold A. "Transplantation of Testes (D. P. Quiring, Trans.)." *Bulletin of the History of Medicine* 16 ([1849]1944): 399–401.

Bhasin, Shalender, Thomas W. Storer, Nancy Berman, Carlos Callegari, Brenda Clevenger, Jeffrey Phillips, Thomas J. Bunnell, Ray Tricker, Aida Shirazi, and Richard Casaburi. "The Effects of Supraphysiologic Doses of Testosterone on Muscle Size and Strength in Normal Men." *New England Journal of Medicine* 335 (1996): 1–7.

Biasiotto, J., and A. Ferrardo. "What's the Attraction?" *Muscle and Fitness* (1991): 101 ff.

Blake, Joseph A. "Death by Hand Grenade: Altruistic Suicide in Combat." *Suicide and Life-Threatening Behavior* 8 (1978): 46–59.

Bloom, Amy. "The Body Lies." *The New Yorker,* 18 July 1994, pp. 38–49.

Boissy, A., and M. F. Bouissou. "Effects of Androgen Treatment on Behavioral and Physiological Responses of Heifers to Fear-Eliciting Situations." *Hormones and Behavior* 28 (1994): 66–83.

Booth, A., G. Shelley, A. Mazur, G. Tharp, and R. Kittok. "Testosterone, and Winning and Losing in Human Competition." *Hormones and Behavior* 23 (1989): 555–71.

Booth, Alan, and James M. Dabbs, Jr. "Testoterone and Men's Marriages." *Social Forces* 72 (1993): 463–77.

Booth, Alan, J. N. Edwards, and D. R. Johnson. "Social Integration and Power." *Social Forces* 70 (1971): 207–24.

Booth, Alan, and D. Wayne Osgood. "The Influence of Testosterone on Deviance in Adulthood: Assessing and Explaining the Relationship." *Criminology* 31 (1993): 93–117.

Bouchard, Claude, Jean-Pierre Deprés, Pascale Mauriège, Martine Marcotte, Monique Chagnon, France T. Dionne, and Alain Bélanger. "The Genes in the Constellation of Determinants of Regional Fat Distribtion" *International Journal of Obesity* 15 (1991): 9–18.

Braude, S., Z. Tang-Martinez, and G. T. Taylor. "Stress, Testosterone, and the Immunoredistribution Hypothesis." *Behavorial Ecology* 10 (1999): 345–50.

Braverman, Eric R., and Carl C. Pheiffer. *The Healing Nutrients Within: Facts, Findings, and New Research on Amino Acids,* New Canaan, CT: Keats Publishing, 1987.

Breedlove, S. M. "Sex on the Brain." *Nature* 389 (1997): 801.

Bribiescas, Richard G. "Testosterone Levels Among Ache Hunter/Gatherer Men: A Functional Interpretation of Population Variation Among Adult Males." *Human Nature* 7 (1996): 163–88.

Bronson, F. H. *Mammalian Reproductive Biology.* Chicago: University of Chicago Press, 1989.

Broverman, D. M., I. K. Broverman, W. Vogel, R. D. Palmer, and E. L. Klaiber. "The Automatization of Cognitive Style and Physical Development." *Child Development* 35 (1964): 1343–49.

Brown, R. E., T. Murdoch, P. R. Murphy, and W. H. Moger. "Hormonal Responses of Male Gerbils to Stimuli from Their Mate and Pups." *Hormones and Behavior* 29 (1995): 474–91.

Burke, James Lee. *The Neon Rain.* New York: Pocket Books, 1987.

Burnett, Erin. "Black Males Retrieve a Noble Heritage." *APA Monitor,* June 1999, p. 1 ff.

Buss, David M. "Human Mate Selection." *American Scientist* 73 (1985): 47–51.

_____. *The Evolution of Desire: Strategies of Human Mating.* New York: Basic Books, 1994.

_____. "The Strategies of Human Mating." *American Scientist* 82 (1994): 238–49.

Cacioppo, John T, Richard E. Petty, Jeffrey Feinstein, and Blair Jarvis. "Dispositional Differences in Cognitive Motivation: The Life and Times of Individuals Varying in Need for Cognition." *Psychological Bulletin* 119 (1995): 197–253.

Campbell, Anne. "Staying Alive: Evolution, Culture, and Women's Intrasexual Aggression." *Behavioral and Brain Sciences* 22 (1999): 203–52.

Campbell, Benjamin C., and Paul W. Leslie. "The Reproductive Ecology of Human Males." *Yearbook of Physical Anthropology* 38 (1995): 1–26.

Campbell, Donald T. "On the Conflicts Between Biological and Social Evolution and Between Psychology and Moral Tradition." *American Psychologist* 30 (1975): 1103–26.

Carr, Virginia Spencer. *The Lonely Hunter: A Biography of Carson McCullers.* New York: Carroll & Graf Publishers, 1975.

Cashdan, Elizabeth. "Hormones, Sex, and Status in Women." *Hormones and Behavior* 29 (1995): 354–66.

Cather, Willa. *My Antonia.* New York: Houghton-Mifflin, 1918; New York: Quality Paperback, 1995.

Chance, S. E., R. T. Brown, J. M. Dabbs, Jr, and R. Casey. "Testosterone, Intelligence and Behavior Disorders in Young Boys." *Personality and Individual Differences* 28 (2000): 437–45.

Charney, D. S., G. R. Henninger, J. F. Reinhard, D. E. Sternberg, and K. M. Hdafstead. "The Effect of IV L-Tryptophan on Prolactin, Growth Hormones and Mood in Healthy Subjects." *Psychopharmacology* 78 (1982): 38–45.

Chase, Mary. *Harvey.* New York: Oxford University Press, 1943.

Clark, Mertice M., P. Karbiuk, and B. Galef, Jr. "Hormonally Mediated Inheritance of Acquired Characteristics in Mongolian Gerbils." *Nature* 364 (1993): 712.

Colby, Ann, and William Damon. *Some Do Care: Contemporary Lives of Moral Commitment.* New York: Free Press, 1992.

Collins, Nancy. "Wolf, Man, Jack." *Vanity Fair*, April, 1994, p. 118 ff.

Conroy. *The Great Santini.* Boston: Houghton Mifflin, 1976.

Cooke, B. M., G. Tabibnia, and S. M. Breedlove. "A Brain Sexual Dimorphism Controlled by Adult Circulating Androgens." *Proceedings of the National Academy of Science* 96 (1999): 7538–40.

Courtwright, David. *Violent Land: Single Men and Social Disorder From the Frontier to the Inner City.* Cambridge, MA: Harvard University Press, 1996.

Crook, John H. "The Socio-Ecology of Primates." In *Social Behavior of Birds and Mammals.* Ed. John H. Crook, 103–66. New York: Academic Press, 1970.

Cross, J. A. "Factors Associated With Students' Place Location Knowledge." *Journal of Geography* 86 (1987): 59–63.

Crosset, Todd W., Jeffrey R. Benedict, and Mark A. McDonald. "Male Student-Athletes Reported for Sexual Assault: A Survey of Campus Police Departments and Judicial Affairs Offices." *Journal of Sport and Social Issues* 19 (1995): 126–40.

Culotta, Elizabeth. "St. Louis Meeting Showcases 'Creature Features'." *Science* 267 (1995): 330–331.

Cumming, D. C., M. E. Quigley, and S. S. C Yen. "Acute Suppression of Circulating Testosterone Levels by Cortisol in Men." *Journal of Clinical Endocrinology and Metabolism* 57 (1983): 671–73.

Dabbs, James M., Jr. "Age and Seasonal Variation in Serum Testosterone Concentration Among Men." *Chronobiology International* 7 (1990): 245–49.

_____. "Testosterone and Occupational Achievement." *Social Forces* 70 (1992): 813–24.

_____. "Testosterone, Smiling, and Facial Appearance." *Journal of Nonverbal Behavior* 21 (1997): 45–55.

Dabbs, James M., Jr., Frank J. Bernieri, Rebecca K. Strong, Rhonda Milun, and Rebecca Campo. "Going on Stage: Testosterone in Greetings and Meetings." *Unpublished Manuscript, Georgia State University* (2000).

Dabbs, James M., Jr., Timothy S. Carr, Robert L. Frady, and Jasmine K. Riad. "Testosterone, Crime, and Misbehavior Among 692 Male Prison Inmates." *Personality and Individual Differences* 18 (1995): 627–33.

Dabbs, James M., Jr., and Denise de La Rue. "Salivary Testosterone Measurements Among Women: Relative Magnitude of Daily and Menstrual Cycles." *Hormone Research* 35 (1991): 182–84.

Dabbs, James M., Jr., Denise de La Rue, and Paula Williams. "Testosterone and Occupational Choice: Actors, Ministers, and Other Men." *Journal of Personality and Social Psychology* 59 (1990): 1261–65.

Dabbs, James M., Jr., Robert L. Frady, Timothy S. Carr, and Norma F. Besch. "Saliva Testosterone and Criminal Violence in Young Adult Prison Inmates." *Psychosomatic Medicine* 49 (1987): 174–82.

Dabbs, James M., Jr., and Marian F. Hargrove. "Age, Testosterone, and Behavior Among Female Prison Inmates." *Psychosomatic Medicine* 59 (1997): 477–80.

Dabbs, James M., Jr., Marian F. Hargrove, and Colleen Heusel. "Testosterone Differences Among College Fraternities: Well-Behaved Vs. Rambunctious." *Personality and Individual Differences* 20 (1996): 157–61.

Dabbs, James M., Jr, Charles H. Hopper, and Gregory J. Jurkovic. "Testosterone and Personality Among College Students and Military Veterans." *Personality and Individual Differences* 11 (1990): 1263–69.

Dabbs, James M., Jr., and Alison Mallinger. "High Testosterone Levels Predict Low Voice Pitch Among Males." *Personality and Individual Differences* 27 (1999): 801–4.

Dabbs, James M., Jr., and Suzanne Mohammed. "Male and Female Salivary

Testosterone Concentrations Before and After Sexual Activity." *Physiology and Behavior* 52 (1992): 195–97.

Dabbs, James M., Jr., and Robin Morris. "Testosterone, Social Class, and Antisocial Behavior in a Sample of 4,662 Men." *Psychological Science* 1 (1990): 209–11.

Dabbs, James M., Jr., R. Barry Ruback, Robert L. Frady, Charles H. Hopper, and Demetrios S. Sgoutas. "Saliva Testosterone and Criminal Violence Among Women." *Personality and Individual Differences* 9 (1988): 269–75.

Dabbs, James M., Jr., Rebecca K. Strong, and Rhonda Milun. "Exploring the Mind of Testosterone: A Beeper Study." *Journal of Research in Personality* 31 (1997): 577–87.

Daly, Martin, and Margo Wilson. *Sex, Evolution, and Behavior: Adaptations for Reproduction.* North Scituate, MA: Duxbury Press, 1978.

Davatzikos, C, and S. M. Resnick. "Sex Differences in Anatomic Measures of Interhemispheric Connectivity: Correlations With Cognition in Women but Not in Men." *Cerebral Cortex* 8 (1998): 635–40.

Davidson, Julian M., Carlos A. Camargo, and Erla R. Smith. "Effects of Androgen on Sexual Behavior in Hypogonadal Men." *Journal of Clinical Endocrinology and Metabolism* 48 (1979): 955–58.

Dawkins, Peter. *The Selfish Gene.* New York: Oxford University Press, 1976.

Deal, Terrence E., and Allan A. Kenedy. *Corporate Cultures: The Rites and Rituals of Corporate Life.* Reading, MA: Addison-Wesley, 1982.

Detier, Vincent G. *To Know a Fly.* San Francisco: Holden-Day, 1962.

De Voto, Bernard. *Mark Twain: Letters From the Earth.* Greenwich, CT: Fawcett Publications, 1962.

Diamond, Jared. "The Accidental Conquerer." *Discover,* December 1991, pp. 71–76.

_____. *Guns, Germs, and Steel: The Fates of Human Societies.* New York: W. W. Norton & Co., 1999.

Dickens, Roy. "Ceramic Patterning and Social Structure at Two Late Upper Creek Sites in Alabma." *Paper Presented at 33rd Southeastern Archaeological Conference, Tuscaloosa, AL* (1976).

Dufty, Alfred M., Jr. "Testosterone and Survival: A Cost of Aggressiveness?" *Hormones and Behavior* 23 (1989): 185–93.

Dunn, Katherine. "The Badder, the Better." *Esquire,* February (1995): 94–95.

Durkheim, Emile. *Moral Education: A Study of the Theory and Application of the Sociology of Education.* New York: Free Press, 1961.

Dutton, Donald, and Arthur Aron. "Some Evidence of Heightened Sexual Arousal Under Conditions of High Anxiety." *Journal of Personality and Social Psychology* 30 (1974): 510–517.

Eals, Marion, and Irwin Silverman. "The Hunter-Gatherer Theory of Spatial Sex Differences: Proximate Factors Mediating the Female Advantage in Recall of Object Arrays." *Ethology and Sociobiology* 15 (1994): 95–105.

Ebert, James I. "Ellison's Cow." *Science 81*, December 1981, pp. 68–73.

Ekman, Paul, R. Davidson, and W. V. Friesen. "Emotional Expression and Brain Physiology II: The Duchenne Smile." *Journal of Personality and Social Psychology* 58 (1990): 342–53.

Eliot, T. S. "The Love Song of J. Alfred Prufrock." In *Collected Poems: 1909–1935*. New York: Harcourt, Brace, 1936.

_____. "Little Gitting." In *Four Quartets*, 49–59. New York: Harcourt Brace Javonovich, 1971.

Ellison, Peter T., S. F. Lipson, R. G. Bribiescas, G. R. Bentley, B. C. Campbell, and C. Panter-Brick. "Inter-and Intra-Population Variation in the Pattern of Male Testosterone by Age." *American Journal of Physical Anthropology Supplement* 26 (1998): 80.

Ellison, Peter T. *On Fertile Ground: Ecologyy, Evolution, and Human Reproduction.* Cambridge, MA: Harvard University Press, in press.

Erskine, John. *Galahad: Enough of His Life to Explain His Reputation.* Indianapolis: The Bobbs-Merrill Company, 1926.

Erwin, Roland J., Ruben C. Gur, Raquel E. Gur, Brett Skolnick, Maureen Mawhinney-Hee, and Joseph Smailis. "Facial Emotion Discrimination: I. Task Construction and Behavioral Findings in Normal Subjects." *Psychiatry Research* 42 (1992): 231–40.

Evans, David J., Raymond G. Hoffman, Ronald K. Kalkhoff, and Ahmed H. Kissebah. "Relationship of Androgenic Activity to Body Fat Topography, Fat Cell Morphology, and Metabolic Aberrations in Premenopausal Women." *Journal of Clinical Endocrinology and Metabolism* 57 (1983): 304–10.

Feldman, H. A., I. Goldstein, D. G. Hatzichristou, R. J. Krane, and J. B. McKinlay. "Impotence and Its Medical and Psychosocial Correlates: Results of the Massachusetts Male Aging Study." *Journal of Urology* 151 (1994): 54–61.

Felthous, A. R., and S. R. Kellert. "Childhood Cruelty to Animals and Later Aggression Against People: A Review." *American Journal of Psychiatry* 144 (1987): 710–717.

Fiedler, Leslie. "Montana; or The End of Jean-Jacques Rousseau." In *A Fiedler Reader*, 13–23. New York: Stein and Day, 1977.

Finley, S. K., and Kritzer, "Immunoreactivity for Intracellular Androgen Receptors in Identified Subpopulations of Neurons, Astrocytes and Oligodendrocytes in Primate Prefontal Cortex," *Journal of Neurobiology* 15 (1999): 446–457.

Fischman, Joshua. "Hard Evidence." *Discover* (1992): 44–51.

Fisher, Helen. *The First Sex: The Natural Talents of Women and How They Are Changing the World.* New York: Ballantine Books, 1999.

Fivizzani, A. J., and L. W. Oring. "Plasma Steroid Hormones in Relation to Behavioral Sex Role Reversal in the Spotted Sandpiper, *Actitis Macularia*." *Biological Reproduction* 35 (1986): 1195–201.

Fogelman, Eva, and Valerie Lewis Wiener. "The Few, the Brave, the Noble." *Psychology Today,* August 1985, pp. 61–66.

Frost, Robert. "The Secret Sits." In *The Poetry of Robert Frost.* Ed. Edward Connery Lathem, 362. New York: Holt, Rinehart, and Winston, 1969.

_____. "The Star-Splitter." In *The Poetry of Robert Frost.* Ed. Edward Connery Lathem, 176–79. New York: Holt, Rinehart, and Winston, 1969.

Gage, A. R., J. T. Manning, D. Scutt, M. J. Diver, and W. D. Fraser. "Testosterone, Cortisol and Jaw Size in Men." *Unpublished Manuscript, University of Liverpool* (1999).

Galea, Liisa A. M., and Doreen Kimura. "Sex Differences in Route-Learning." *Personality and Individual Differences* 14 (1993): 53–65.

Gangestad, Steven W., and Jeffry A. Simpson. "The Evolution of Human Mating: Trade-Offs and Strategic Pluralism." *Behavioral and Brain Sciences* (In press).

Gero, Jan M., and Margaret W. Conkey. *Engendering Archaeology: Women in Prehistory.* Oxford: Blackwell, 1991.

Gilligan, Carol. "Remapping the Moral Domain: New Images of Self in Relationship." In *Mapping the Moral Domain: A Contribution of Women's Thinking to Psychological Theory and Education.* Eds. Carol Gilligan, Janie V. Ward, Jill M. Taylor, and Betty Bardige, 3–19. Cambridge, MA: Harvard University Press, 1988.

Gilmore, David D. *Manhood in the Making.* New Haven: Yale University Press, 1990.

Gimbel, Cynthia, and Alan Booth. "Who Fought in Vietnam?" *Social Forces* 74 (1996): 1137–57.

Glickman, S. E., L. G. Frank, S. Pavgi, and P. Licht. "Hormonal Correlates of 'Masculinization' in Female Spotted Hyaenas (*Crocuta Crocuta*). 1. Infancy to Sexual Maturity." *Journal of Reproduction and Fertility* 95 (1992): 451–62.

Glucksmann, Alfred. *Sex Determination and Sexual Dimorphism in Mammals.* London: Wykeham Publication, 1978.

Goldberg, S, and M. Lewis. "Play Behavior in the Year-Old Infant." *Child Development* 40 (1969): 21–31.

Golding, William. *Lord of the Flies.* New York: Coward-McCann, 1962.

Goleman, Daniel. "Brutal Sports and Brutal Fans." *Times,* 13 August 1985, p. 19.

Gould, Stephen J. *Wonderful Life: The Burgess Shale and the Nature of History.* New York: Norton, 1989.

Grafton, Sue. *"F" Is for Fugitive.* New York: Bantam Books, 1990.

Graham, Don. *No Name on the Bullet: A Biography of Audie Murphy.* New York: Penguin, 1989.

Grant, Valerie J. "Maternal Dominance and the Conception of Sons." *British Journal of Medical Psychology* 67 (1994): 343–51.

Gubb-Saba, Louise. "A Painful Tradition." *Newsweek*, 5 July 1999, pp. 32–33.

Gubernick, David J., and Randy J. Nelson. "Prolactin and Paternal Behavior in the Biparental California Mouse, Peromyscus Californicus." *Hormones and Behavior* 23 (1989): 203–210.

Gubernick, David J., Carol M. Worthman, and Joy F. Stallings. "Hormonal Correlates of Fatherhood in Men: A Preliminary Report." *Presented at the International Society for Developmental Psychobiology Meeting, Newport Beach* (1992).

Guttentag, Marcia, and Paul F. Secord. *Too Many Women? The Sex Ratio Question.* Beverly Hills, CA: Sage, 1983.

Hall, Judith A., and G. B. Friedman. "Status, Gender, and Nonverbal Behavior: A Study of Structured Interactions Between Employees of a Company." *Personality and Social Psychology Bulletin* 25 (1999): 1082–91.

Hall, Roberta. *Sexual Dimorphism in Homo Sapiens: A Question of Size.* New York: Praeger, 1982.

Hall, Roberta L., and Henry S. Sharpe. *Wolf and Man: Evolution in Parallel.* New York: Academic Press, 1978.

Hamilton, David. *The Monkey Gland Affair.* London: Chatto and Windus, 1986.

Hamilton, James B., Ruth S. Hamilton, and Gordon E. Mestler. "Duration of Life and Causes of Death in Domestic Cats: Influence of Sex, Gonadectomy, and Inbreeding." *Journal of Gerontology* 24 (1969): 427–37.

Hamilton, James B., and Gordon E. Mestler. "Mortality and Survival: Comparison of Eunuchs With Intact Men and Women in a Mentally Retarded Population." *Journal of Gerontology* 24 (1969): 394–411.

Hammet, Dashiell. *The Maltese Falcon.* New York: Modern Library, 1934.

Hampson, Elizabeth, and Doreen Kimura. "Sex Differences and Hormonal Influences on Cognitive Function in Humans." In *Behavioral Endocrinology.* Eds. Jill B. Becker, S. Marc Breedlove, and David Crews, 357–98. Cambridge, MA: MIT press, 1992.

Harris, J. A., J. P. Rushton, E. Hampson, and D. N. Jackson. "Salivary Testosterone and Self-Report Aggressive and Pro-Social Personality Characteristics in Men and Women." *Aggressive Behavior* 22 (1996): 321–31.

Hassan, Fekri A. *Demographic Archaeology.* New York: Academic Press, 1981.

Hatfield, Elaine, and Richard L. Rapson. *Love, Sex, and Intimacy: Their Psychology, Biology, and History.* New York: Harper Collins, 1993.

Haug, Herbett. "Brain Sizes, Surfaces, and Neuronal Sizes of the Cortex Cerebri: A Stereological Investigation of Man and His Variability and A Comparison With Some Mammals (Primates, Whales, Marsupials, Insec-tivors, and One Elephant)." *American Journal of Anatomy* 180 (1987): 126–42.

Heilman, Madeline E., and Lois R. Saruwatari. "When Beauty If Beastly: The Effects of Appearance and Sex on Evaluations of Job Applicants for Managerial and Nonmanagerial Jobs." *Organizational Behavior and Human Performance* 23 (1979): 360–72.

Hill, Kim, and Hilliard Kaplan. "Tradeoffs in Male and Female Reproductive Stratigies Among the Ache: Part 2." In *Human Reproductive Behavior: A Darwinian Perspective.* Eds. Laura Betzig, Monique Borgerhoff Mulder, and Paul Turke, 291–305. Cambridge: Cambridge University Press, 1988.

Hillerman, Tony. *Listening Woman.* New York: Harper Paperbacks, 1978.

Hines, M., L. Chiu, L. A. McAdams, P. M. Bentler, and J. Lipcamon. "Cognition and the Corpus Callosum: Verbal Fluency, Visuospatial Ability, and Language Lateralization Related to Midsagittal Surface Areas of Callosal Subregions." *Behavioral Neuroscience* 106 (1992): 3–14.

Hines, Melissa. "Gonadal Hormones and Human Cognitive Development." In *Hormones, Brain and Behaviour in Vertebrates. 1. Sexual Differentiation, Neuroanatomical Aspects, Neurotransmitters and Neuropeptides. Comparative Physiology.* Ed. J. Balthazart, 51–63. Basel: Karger, 1990.

Hoberman, John H., and Charles E. Yesalis. "The History of Synthetic Testosterone." *Scientific American* 272 (February 1995): 76–81.

Hunt, K. E., T. P. Hahn, and J. C. Wingfield. "Endocrine Influences on Parental Care During a Short Breeding Season: Testosterone and Male Parental Care in Lapland Longspurs (Calcarius Lapponicus)." *Behavioral Ecology and Sociobiology* 45 (1999): 360–369.

Hurst, Laurence D. "Intragenomic Conflict As an Evolutionary Force." *Proceedings of the Royal Society of London* 248 (1992): 135–40.

Hurst, Laurence D., and William D. Hamilton. "Cytoplasmic Fusion and the Nature of Sexes." *Proceedings of the Royal Society of London* 247 (1992): 189–94.

Huston, Ted L., Gilbert Geis, and Richard Wright. "The Angry Samaritans." *Psychology Today*, June 1976, pp. 61 ff.

Imperato-McGinley, Julianne, Luis Guerrero, Teofilo Gautier, and Ralph E. Peterson. "Steroid 5–Alpha-Reductase Deficiency in Man: An Inherited Form of Male Pseudohermaphroditism." *Science* 186 (1974): 1213–15.

Jacobson, Neil S., John M. Gottman, and Joann Wu Shortt. "The Distinction Between Type-1 and Type-2 Batterers—Further Considerations—Reply to Ornduff Et Al. (1995), Margolin Et Al. (1995) and Walker (1995)." *Journal of Family Psychology* 9 (1995): 272–79.

James, William H. "The Hopothesized Hormonal Control of Human Sex Ratio at Birth—an Update." *Journal of Theoretical Biology* 143 (1990): 555–64.

Jeffcoate, W. J., N. B. Lincoln, C. Selby, and Herbert M. "Correlation Between Anxiety and Serum Prolactin in Humans." *Journal of Psychosomatic Research* 30 (1986): 217–22.

Jewell, Peter A. "Survival and Behaviour of Castrated Soay Sheep (Ovis Aries) in a Feral Island Population on Hirta, St. Kilda, Scotland." *Journal of Zoology* 243 (1997): 623–36.

Josephy, Alvin M., Jr. *500 Nations: An Illustrated History of North American Indians.* New York: Alfred A. Knopf, 1994.

Julian, Teresa, and Patrick C. McKenry. "Relationship of Testosterone to Men's Family Functioning at Mid-Life: A Research Note." *Aggressive Behavior* 15 (1989): 281–89.

Kant, Immanuel. "Eternal Peace." In *Immanuel Kant's Moral and Political Writings.* Ed. Karl J. Frederick, 430–76. New York: Modern Library, 1949.

Kantrowitz, Barbara, and Pat Wingert. "The Science of a Good Marriage." *Newsweek,* 19 April 1999, p. 54.

Kaplan, Justin. *Bartlett's Familiar Quotations.* Boston: Little, Brown, 1992.

Karnow, Stanley. *In Our Image: America's Empire in the Philippines.* New York: Random House, 1989.

Keegan, John. *A History of Warfare.* New York: Alfred A. Knopf, 1993.

Kemper, Theodore D. *Social Structure and Testosterone: Explorations of the Socio-Bio-Social Chain.* New Brunswick, NJ: Rutgers, 1990.

Ketterson, Ellen D., and Val Nolan Jr. "Hormones and Life Histories: An Integrative Approach." *The American Naturalist* 140 (1992): S33–S62.

Kimura, Doreen. *Sex and Cognition.* Cambridge, MA: MIT Press, 1999.

Kirkpatrick, Sue W., P. Samuel Campbell, Rhonda E. Wharry, and Shirley L. Robinson. "Salivary Testosterone in Children With and Without Learning Disabilities." *Physiology and Behavior* 53 (1993): 583–86.

Klein, S. L., and R. J. Nelson. "Adaptive Immune Responses Are Linked to the Mating System of Arvocine Rodents." *American Naturalist* 151 (1998): 59–67.

Knapp, R., J. C. Wingfield, and A. H. Bass. "Steroid Hormones and Paternal Care in the Plainfin Midshipman Fish (Porichthys Notatus)." *Hormones and Behavior* 35 (1999): 81–89.

Krantz, Grover. "The Fossil Record of Sex." In *Sexual Dimorphism in Homo Sapiens: A Question of Size.* Ed. Roberta L. Hall, 85–105. New York: Praeger, 1982.

Kreuz, L. E., R. M. Rose, and R. Jennings. "Suppression of Plasma Testosterone Levels and Psychological Stress." *Archives of General Psychiatry* 26 (1971): 479–82.

Krothiewski, M., and P. Björntorp. "The Effects of Estrogen Treatment of Carcinoma of the Prostate on Regional Adipocyte Size." *Journal of Clinical Investigation* 1 (1978): 365–66.

Kupperman, H. S. "Male Sex Hormones." In *Drill's Pharmacology in Medicine.* Ed. J. R. DiPalma, 1366–86. New York: McGraw-Hill, 1971.

Latané, Bibb, and James M. Dabbs, Jr. "Sex, Group Size, and Helping in Three Cities." *Sociometry* 38 (1975): 180–94.

Lavrakas, P. J. "Female Preference for Male Physiques." *Journal of Research in Personality* 9 (1975): 324–34.

Lemonick, Michael D. "Young, Single, and Out of Control." *Time,* 13 October 1997, p. 68.

Leopold, A. Starker, Michael Erwin, John Oh, and Bruce Browning. "Phytoestrogens: Adverse Effects on Reproduction in California Quail." *Science* 191 (1976): 98–100.

Le Vay, Simon, and D. H. Hamer. "Evidence for a Biological Influence in Male Homosexuality." *Scientific American,* May 1994, pp. 44–49.

Levine, Richard J. "Seasonal Variation in Human Semen Quality." In *Temperature and Environmental Effects on the Testis.* Ed. A. W. Zorgniotti, 89–96. New York: Plenum Press, 1991.

Levy, Steven. "The Roots of Genius? The Odd History of a Famous Old Brain." *Newsweek,* 28 June 1999, p. 32.

Lewis, John, and Michael D'Orso. *Walking With the Wind: A Memoir of the Movement.* New York: Simon & Schuster, 1998.

Lewis, Oscar. "Manly-Hearted Women Among the North Piegan." *American Anthropologist* 43 (1941): 173–87.

Liben, Lynn. "Psychology Meets Geography: Exploring the Gender Gap on the National Georgraphy Bee." *Psychological Science Agenda* 8 (January-February 1995), p. 8–9.

Licht, P., L. G. Frank, S. Pavgi, T. M. Yalcinkaya, P. K. Siiteri, and S. E. Glickman. "Hormonal Correlates of 'Masculinization' in Female Spotted Hyaenas (*Crocuta Crocuta*). 2. Maternal and Fetal Steroids." *Journal of Reproduction and Fertility* 95 (1992): 463–74.

Lieberman, Philip. "Homid Evolution, Supralaryngeal Vocal Tract Physiology, and the Fossil Evidence for Reconstructions." *Brain and Language* 7 (1979): 101–26.

Liou, S. Y., and H. Elliot Albers. "Single Unit Response of Suprachiasmatic Neurons to Arginine Vasopressin (AVP) Is Mediated by a V_1-Like Receptor in the Hamster." *Brain Research* 477 (1989): 336–43.

Lock, Stephen. "'O That I Were Young Again': Yeats and the Steinach Operation." *British Medical Journal* 287 (1983): 1864–68.

London, Perry. "The Rescuers: Motivational Hypotheses About Christians Who Saved Jews From the Nazis." In *Altruism and Helping Behavior.* Ed. Jacqueline R. Macaulay, and Leonard Berkowitz, 241–50. New York: Academic Press, 1970.

Lumsden, Charles J., and Edward O. Wilson. *Genes, Mind, and Culture: The Coevolutionary Process.* Cambridge, MA: Harvard University Press, 1981.

Lutz, D. "The Personality of Physicists Measured." *American Scientist* 82 (1994): 324–25.

Lynn, Richard. "Sex Differences in Intelligence and Brain Size: A Developmental Theory." *Intelligence* 27 (1999): 1–12.

Maccoby, Eleanor E. "Gender and Relationships: A Developmental Account." *American Psychologist* 45 (1990): 513–20.

MacPherson, Myra. *The Power Lovers: An Intimate Look.* New York: G. T. Putnam's Sons, 1975.

Malamud, Daniel, and Lawrence Tabak. *Saliva As a Diagnostic Fluid.* New York: New York Academy of Sciences, 1993.

Margolick, David. "At the Bar." *Times,* 2 November 1990, p. B12.

Markowitz, Jack. *A Walk on the Crust of Hell.* Brattleboro, VT: Stephen Greene Press, 1973.

Marks, Stuart A. *Southern Hunting in Black and White: Nature, History, and Ritual in a Carolina Community.* Princeton, NJ: Princeton University Press, 1991.

Marler, C. A., and Michael C. Moore. "Evolutionary Costs of Aggression Revealed by Testosterone Manipulations in Free-Living Male Lizards." *Behavioral Ecology and Sociobiology* 23 (1988): 21–26.

Martin, Constance R. *Endocrine Physiology.* New York: Oxford University Press, 1985.

Matthiessen, Peter. *The Tree Where Man Was Born.* New York: E. P. Dutton, 1972.

Maurer, David W. *The American Confidence Man.* Springfield, IL: Charles C. Thomas, 1974.

Mazur, Alan, and Joel Michalek. "Marriage, Divorce, and Male Testosterone." *Social Forces* 77 (1998): 315–30.

Mazur, Allan, Alan Booth, and James M. Dabbs, Jr. "Testosterone and Chess Competition." *Social Psychology Quarterly* 55 (1992): 70–77.

Mazur, Allan, Julie Mazur, and Caroline Keating. "Military Rank Attainment of a West Point Class: Effects of Cadet's Physical Features." *American Journal of Sociology* 90 (1984): 125–50.

Mazur, Allan, and Ulrich Meuller. "Channel Modeling: From West Point Cadet to General." *Public Administration Review* 56 (1996): 191–98.

McCarthy, Cormac. *The Crossing.* New York: Random House, 1995.

McCown, Elizabeth R. "Sex Differences: The Female As Baseline for Species Description." In *Sexual Dimorphism in Homo Sapiens: A Question of Size.* Ed. Roberta A. Hall, 37–83. New York: Praeger, 1982.

McDonald, R. Robin. "Despite Heroic Rescue, Heartache." *Atlanta Journal/Constitution,* 2 May 1999, sec. E, p. 9.

_____. "The Happenstance Heroes." Atlanta Journal/Constitution, 30 April 1999, sec C, p1.

McGrath, Joseph E., Joanne Martin, and Richard A. Kulka. "Some Quasi-Rules for Making Judgment Calls in Research." In *Judgment Calls in Research.* Eds. Joseph E. McGrath, Joanne Martin, and Richard A. Kulka, 103–18. Beverly Hills, CA: Sage, 1982.

McLachlan, John A., and Steven F. Arnold. "Environmental Estrogens." *American Scientist* 84 (September–October 1996), p. 452–61.

McLanahan, Sara, and Gary Sandefur. *Growing Up With a Single Parent: What Hurts, What Helps.* Cambridge, MA: Harvard University Press, 1994.

McLanahan, Sarah. "The Consequences of Single Motherhood." *American Prospect* 18 (1994): 48–58.

McMurtry, Larry. *Lonesome Dove.* New York: Pocket Books, 1985.

Meltzoff, A. N., and M. K. Moore. "Imitation of Facial and Manual Gestures by Human Neonates." *Science* 198 (1977): 74–78.

———. "Newborn Infants Imitate Adult Facial Gestures." *Child Development* 54 (1983): 702–9.

Meuser, W., and E. Nieschlag. "Sexualhormone Und Stimmlage Des Mannes." *Deutsche Medizinische Wochenschrift* 102 (1997): 1–4.

Michener, James A. *The Drifters.* New York: Random House, 1971.

Miller, Edward M. "Parental Provisioning Versus Mate Seeking in Human Populations." *Personality and Individual Differences* 17 (1994): 227–55.

Mindell, Earl. *Earl Mindell's Food As Medicine.* New York: Simon & Schuster, 1994.

Mitchell, Joseph. *Up in the Old Hotel, and Other Stories.* New York: Random House, 1992.

Morgan, William W., and Damon C. Herbert. "Elevation of Serum Prolactin Levels After the Inhibition of Serotonin Uptake." *Endocrinology* 103 (1978): 1016–22.

Morris, Naomi M., J. Richard Udry, Firyal Kahy-Dawood, and M. Yusoff Dawood. "Marital Sex Frequency and Midcycle Female Testosterone." *Archives of Sexual Behavior* 16 (1987): 27–37.

Morris, William. *American Heritage Dictionary of the English Language.* New York: Houghton Mifflin, 1969.

Morton, Eugene S., and Jake Page. *Animal Talk: Science and the Voices of Nature.* New York: Random House, 1992.

Moses, Sam. "The Best Man for the Job Is a Woman." *Sports Illustrated,* 22 June 1981, pp. 71–84.

Murdock, George P. "Comparative Data on the Division of Labor by Sex." *Social Forces* 15 (1937): 551–53.

———. "The Common Denominator of Culture." In *The Science of Man in the World Crisis.* Ed. Ralph Linton, 123–42. New York: Columbia University Press, 1945.

Myers, David. *The Pursuit of Happiness.* New York: Avon, 1990.

Myers, David G., and Ed Diener. "Who Is Happy?" *Psychological Science* 6 (1995): 10–19.

Nelson, Randy J. *Introduction to Behavioral Endocrinology.* Sunderland, MA: Sinauer Associates, 1995.

Nesmith, Jeff. "China's Surplus of Bachelors Could Breed Chaos." *Atlanta Journal-Constitution,* 27 January 1995, sec. A, p.12.

Nisbett, Richard E. "Violence and Regional Culture." *American Psychologist* 48 (1993): 441–49.

Noonan, David. "The Lone Ranger Lawyer." *Esquire,* May 1981, pp. 80–87.

Olson, Steve. "Year of the Blue-Collar Guy." *Newsweek,* 6 November 1989, p. 16.

Olweus, Dan, Åke Mattsson, Daisy Shalling, and Hans Löw. "Circulating Testosterone Levels and Aggression in Adolescent Males: A Causal Analysis." *Psychosomatic Medicine* 50 (1986): 261–72.

Osborne, Roxane E., Iwona Niekrasz, David Domek, Yaolong Zhang, Adolfo Garnica, and Thomas W. Seale. "Acute Anxiolytic-Like Behavioral Effects of Testosterone, Its Metabolites, and Related Steoids." *Unpublished Paper From the University of Oklahoma Health Sciences Center* (1995).

Osgood, Charles E., J. G. Suci, and P. E. Tannenbaum. *The Measurement of Meaning.* Urbana, IL: University of Illinois, 1957.

Ott, John N. *Health and Light: The Effects of Natural and Artificial Light on Man and Other Living Things.* Old Greenwich, CT: Devin-Adair, 1973.

Panksepp, Jack. "The Psychobiology of Prosocial Behaviors: Separation Distress, Play, and Altruism." In *Altruism and Aggression.* Eds. Carolyn Zahn-Wexler, E. Mark Cummings, and Ronald Iannotti, 19–57. New York: Cambridge University Press, 1986.

Parkin, Molly. "The Life and Love of a Trans-Sexual." *London Sunday Times,* 7 March 1971.

Pearcey, Sharon M., Karen J. Docherty, and James M. Dabbs, Jr. "Testosterone and Sex Role Identification in Lesbian Couples." *Physiology and Behavior* 60 (1996): 1033–35.

Politoff, Leonidas, Martin Birkhauser, Alfonso Almendral, and Alain Zorn. "New Data Confirming a Circannual Rhythm in Spermatogenesis." *Fertility and Sterility* 52 (1989): 486–89.

Postema, Pam, and Gene Wojciechowski. *You've Got to Have Balls to Make It in This League: My Life As an Umpire.* New York: Simon & Schuster, 1992.

Potter, Stephen. *The Complete Upmanship.* New York: Holt, Rinehart and Winston, 1970.

Potts, Malcolm, and Roger Short. *Ever Since Adam and Eve.* New York: Cambridge University Press, 1999.

Pratto, F., L. M. Stallworth, and J. Sidanius. "The Gender Gap: Differences in Political Attitudes and Social Dominance Orientation." *British Journal of Social Psychology* 36 (1997): 49–68.

Preston, Richard. *American Steel.* New York: Prentice Hall, 1991.

Quindlen, Anna. "Women in Combat." *New York Times,* 8 January 1970, p. A15.

Rahe, Richard H., Samuel Karson, Noel S. Howard, Jr., Robert T. Rubin, and

Russell E. Poland. "Psychological and Physiological Assessments on American Hostages Freed From Captivity in Iran." *Psychosomatic Medicine* 52 (1980): 1–16.

Raleigh, Michael J., and Michael T. McGuire. "Social Influences on Endocrine Function in Male Vervet Monkeys." In *Socioendocrinology of Primate Reproduction.* Eds. Toni E. Ziegler, and Fred B. Bercovitch, 95–111. New York: John Wiley & Sons, 1990.

Raloff, Janet. "The Gender Benders: Are Environmental 'Hormones' Emasculating Wildlife?" *Science News* 145 (1994): 24–27.

_____. "That Feminine Touch: Are Men Suffering From Prenatal or Childhood Exposure to 'Hormonal' Toxicants?" *Science News* 145 (1994): 56–58.

Randall, Walter. "A Statistical Analysis of the Annual Pattern in Births in the USA, 1967 to 1976." *Journal of Interdisciplinary Cycle Research* 18 (1987): 179–81.

Rebuffe-Scrivé, M., P. Marin, and P. Björntorp. "Effect of Testosterone on Abdominal Adipose Tissue in Men." *International Journal of Obesity* 15 (1991): 791–95.

Reid, T. R. *Confucious Lives Next Door.* New York: Viking, 2000.

Rimland, Bernard. "The Altruism Paradox." *Psychological Reports* 51 (1982): 551–52.

Robertson, D. R. "Social Control of Sex Reversal in a Coral-Reef Fish." *Science* 177 (1972): 1007–9.

Rogers, Richard, and Oscar Hammerstein II. *The King and I.* 1951.

Rogers, Stacy J. "The Nexus of Job Satisfaction, Marital Satisfaction and Individual Well-Being: Does Marriage Order Matter?" *Research in the Sociology of Work* 7 (1999): 141–67.

Rosenhan, David. "The Natural Socialization of Altruistic Autonomy." In *Altruism and Helping Behavior.* Eds. Jacqueline Macaulay, and Leonard Berkowitz, 251–68. New York: Academic Press, 1970.

Rosenthal, Gerald A., and Daniel H. Janzen. *Herbivores: Their Interaction With Secondary Plant Metabolites.* New York: Academic Press, 1979.

Ross, Julia. "Clues Sought in Brain's Physiology." *U. S. Medicine,* May 1995, p. 3 ff.

Rothman, D. *The Discovery of the Asylum: Social Order and Disorder in the New Republic.* Boston: Little, Brown, 1971.

Rubin, Robert T., Russell E. Poland, and Ira M. Lesser. "Neuroendocrine Aspects of Primary Endogenous Depression VIII. Pituitary Gonadal Axis Activity in Male Patients and Matched Control Subjects." *Psychoneuroendocrinology* 14 (1991): 217–29.

Rusbult, Caryl E., and John M. Martz. "Remaining in an Abusive Relationship: An Investment Model Analysis of Nonvoluntary Dependence." *Personality and Social Psychology Bulletin* 21 (1995): 558–71.

Sackett, Gene P. "Receiving Severe Aggression Corelates With Fetal Gender in Pregnant Pigtailed Monkeys." *Developmental Psychobiology* 14 (1980): 267–72.

Sagan, Carl, and Ann Druyan. *Shadows of Forgotten Ancestors.* New York: Random House, 1992.

Saint-Exupéry, Antoine de. "Flight to Arras." In *Airman's Oddesy,* 319. New York: Harcourt Brace, 1942.

Saloneimi, Hannu, Kristiinä Wähälä, Päivi Nykänen-Kurki, Karlo Kallela, and Ilkka Staastomoinen. "Phytoestrogen Content and Estrogenic Effect of Legume Fodder." *Proceedings of the Society for Experimental Biology and Medicine* 208 (1995): 13–18.

Sanday, Peggy Reeves. "The Socio-Cultural Context of Rape: A Cross-Cultural Study." *Journal of Social Issues* 37 (1981): 5–27.

_____. *Fraternity Gang Rapes: Sex, Brotherhood, and Privilege on Campus.* New York: New York University Press, 1990.

Schindler, Gail L. "Testosterone Concentration, Personality Patterns, and Occupational Choice in Women." Ph.D. diss., University of Houston, 1979.

Schröder, Fritz H. "Impact of Ethnic, Nutritional, and Environmental Factors on Prostate Cancer." In *Pharmacology, Biology, and Clinical Applications of Androgens: Current Status and Future Prospects.* Eds. Shalender Bhasin, Henry L. Gabelnick, Jeffrey M. Spieler, Ronald S. Swerdloff, and Christina Wang, 121–35. New York: Wiley-Liss, 1996.

Schuett, Gordon W. "Fighting Dynamics of Male Copperheads, Agkistrodon Contortrix (Serpentes, Viperidae): Stress-Induced Inhibition of Sexual Behavior in Losers." *Zoo Biology* 15 (1996): 209–21.

Schuett, Gordon W., H. J. Harlow, J. D. Rose, E. A. Van Kirk, and W. J. Murcoch. "Levels of Plasma Corticosterone and Testosterone in Male Copperheads (Agkistrodon Contortrix) Following Staged Fights." *Hormones and Behavior* 30 (1996): 60–68.

Schuett, Gordon W., H. J. Harlow, J. D. Rose, E. A. Van Kirk, and W. J. Murdoch. "Annual Cycle of Plasma Testosterone in Male Copperheads, Agkistrodon Controtrix (Serpentes, Viperidae): Relationship to Spermatogenesis, Mating, and Agonistic Behavior." *General and Comparative Endocrinology* 105 (1997): 417–24.

Sharpe, Richard M., and Niels E. Skakkebaek. "Are Oestrogens Involved in Falling Sperm Counts and Disorders of the Male Reproductive Tract?" *The Lancet* 341 (1993): 1392–95.

Sheehan, Neil. *A Bright Shining Lie: John Paul Vann and America in Vietnam.* New York: Random House, 1988.

Shermo, Diana Jean. "Classical Music Gender Gap: She Likes It Live, He Likes CDs." *Atlanta Journal / Constitution,* 10 November 1994.

Sherwin, B. B., M. M. Gelfand, and W. Brender. "Androgen Enhances Sexual Motivation in Females: A Prospective, Crossover Study of Sex Steroid Administration in the Surgical Menopause." *Psychosomatic Medicine* 47 (1985): 339–51.

Short, Roger. "Deer: Yesterday, Today, and Tomorrow." *Biology of Deer Production (Royal Society of New Zealand, Bulletin 22)* (1985): 461–69.

Silverman, Irwin, Kastuk, D., Choi, J., and Phillips, K. "Testosterone Levels and Spatial Ability in Men." *Psychoneuroendocrinology* 24 (1999): 813–22.

Simon, Herbert. "A Mechanism for Social Selection and Successful Altruism." *Science* 250 (1990): 1665–68.

Simon, Herbert A. "The Information-Processing Theory of Mind." *American Psychologist* 50 (1995): 507–8.

Singh, Devendra. "Is Thin Really Beautiful and Good? Relationship Between Waist-to-Hip Ratio (WHR) and Female Attractiveness." *Personality and Individual Differences* 16 (1994): 123–32.

Singh, Devendra, Melody Vidaurri, Robert J. Zambarano, and James M. Dabbs, Jr. "Behavioral, Morphological, and Hormonal Correlates of Erotic Role Identification Among Lesbian Women." *Journal of Personality and Social Psychology* 75 (1999): 1025–49.

Smale, Laura, Kay E. Holekamp, Mary Weldele, Laurence G. Frank, and Stephen E. Glickman. "Competition and Cooperation Between Litter-Mates in the Spotted Hyaena, *Crocuta Crocuta*." *Animal Behavior* 50 (1995): 671–682.

Spark, Muriel. "Personal History: Venture into Africa." *The New Yorker* (1992).

Spence, Janet T, and R. L. Helmreich. "Achievement-Related Motives and Behaviors." In *Achievement and Achievement Motives*. Ed. Janet T.Spence, 7–73. San Francisco: Freeman, 1983.

Spencer, Paul. *The Samburu: A Study of Gerontogracy in a Nomadic Tribe.* Berkeley: University of California Press, 1965.

Steiger, A., U. von Bardeleben, K. Wiedemann, and F. Holsboer. "Sleep EEG and Nocturnal Secretion of Testosterone and Cortisol in Patients With Major Endogenous Depression During Acute Phase and After Remission." *Journal of Psychiatric Research* 25 (1991): 169–77.

Stoleru, S., M. C. Gregoire, D. Gerard, J. Decety, E. Lafarge, L. Cinotti, F. Lavenne, D. Le Bars, E. Vernet-Maury, H. Rada, C. Collet, B. Mazoyer, M. G. Forest, F. Magnin, A. Spira, and D. Comar. "Neuroanatomical Correlates of Visually Evoked Sexual Arousal in Human Males." *Archives of Sexual Behavior* 28 (1999): 1–21.

Storey, Anne E., Carolyn J. Walsh, Roma L. Quinton, and Katherine E. Wynne-Edwards. "Hormonal Correlates of Paternal Responsiveness in New and Expectant Fathers." *Evolution and Human Behavior*: in press.

Strack, Fritz, Leonard L. Martin, and Sabine Stepper. "Inhibiting and Facilitating Conditions of the Human Smile: A Nonobtrusive Test of the Facial Feedback Hypothesis." *Journal of Personality and Social Psychology* 54 (1988): 768–77.

Strong, Rebecca K., and James M. Dabbs, Jr. "Testosterone and Behavior in Normal Young Children." *Personality and Individual Differences* 28 (2000): 909–15.

Suojanen, W. W., and N. P. Johannesen. "Leadership and Human Minds." *OE Communique*, no. 4 (1982).

Tajfel, Henri. *Human Groups As Social Categories.* Cambridge: Cambridge University Press, 1981.

Taljapurkar, Shripad, Nan Li, and Marcus W. Feldman. "High Sex Ratios If China's Future." *Science* 267 (1995): 874–76.

Tannen, Deborah. *You Just Don't Understand: Women and Men in Conversation.* New York: Ballantine Books, 1991.

———. *The Argument Culture: Moving From Debate to Dialogue.* New York: Random House, 1998.

Tennyson, Alfred Lord. *Idylls of the King.* New York: New American Library, 1961.

Terkel, Studs. *"The Good War."* New York: Ballantine Books, 1984.

Terrell, Jack, and Ron Martz. *Disposable Patriot: Revelations of a Soldier in America's Secret Wars.* Washington, DC: National Press Books, 1992.

Thiessen, Del. "Hormonal Correlates of Sexual Aggression." In *Crime in Biological, Social and Moral Contexts.* Eds. Lee Ellis, and Harry Hoffman, 153–61. New York: Praeger, 1990.

Thomas, Lewis. "Notes of a Biology Watcher: A Fear of Pheromones." *New England Journal of Medicine* 285 (1971): 292–93.

Thompson, Christopher W., and Michael C. Moore. "Behavioral and Hormonal Correlates of Alternative Reproductive Strategies in a Polygynous Lizard: Tests of the Relative Plasticity and Challenge Hypotheses." *Hormones and Behavior* 26 (1992): 568–85.

Thompson, Wendy M., James M. Dabbs, Jr., and Robert L. Frady. "Changes in Saliva Testoterone Levels During a 90–Day Shock Incarceration Program." *Criminal Justice and Behavior* 17 (1990): 246–52.

Thornhill, Albert R., and A. P. Møller. "Developmental Stability, Disease and Medicine." *Biological Reviews of the Cambridge Philosophical Society* 72 (1997): 497–548.

Thornhill, Randy, and Craig T. Palmer. *A Natural History of Rape: Biological Bases of Sexual Coercion.* Cambridge, MA: MIT Press, 2000.

Tiger, Lionel. *Men in Groups.* New York: Random House, 1969.

Tiwary, Chandra M. "Premature Sexual Development in Children Following the Use of Placenta and/or Estrogen Containing Hair Product(s)." *Pediatric Research* 35, no. 4, part 2 (1994): 108A.

Traweek, Sharon. *Beamtimes and Lifetimes: The World of High Energy Physicists.* Cambridge, MA: Harvard University Press, 1988.

Triandis, Harry C. *Culture and Social Behavior.* New York: McGraw-Hill, 1994.

Tronick, E., H. Als, L. B. Adamson, S. Wise, and T. B. Braselton. "The Infant's Response to Entrapment Between Contradictory Messages in Face-to-Face Interaction." *Journal of the American Academy of Child Psychiatry* 17 (1980): 1–3.

Tuiten, Adriaan, Jack Van Honk, Hans Koppeschaar, Coen Bernaards, Jos Thijssen, and Rien Verbaten. "Time Course of Effects of Testosterone Administration on Sexual Arousal in Women." *Archives of Sexual Behavior* 57 (2000): 149–53.

Tuljapurkar, Shripad, Nan Li, and Marcus W. Feldman. "High Sex Ratios in China Future." *Science* 267 (1995): 874–76.

Turbervile, G. *The Noble Arte of Venerie or Hunting.* Oxford: Clarendon Press, 1908, facsimile 1576 edition.

Udry, J. R., and N. M. Morris. "The Distribution of Events in the Human Menstrual Cycle." *Journal of Reproduction and Fertility* 51 (1977): 419–25.

Udry, J. Richard. "Biosocial Models of Adolescent Problem Behaviors." *Social Biology* 37 (1990): 1–10.

_____. "The Nature of Gender." *Demography* 31 (1994): 561–73.

Udry, J. Richard, Naomi M. Morris, and Judith Kovenock. "Androgen Effects on Women's Gendered Behaviour." *Journal of Biosocial Science* 27 (1995): 359–68.

van Goozen, Stephanie. *Male and Female: Effects of Sex Hormones on Aggression, Cognition, and Sexual Motivation.* Amsterdam: University of Amsterdam, 1994.

van Goozen, Stephanie H. M., Peggy T. Cohen-Ketenis, Louis J. G. Gooren, Nico H. Frijda, and Nanne E. van de Poll. "Activating Effects of Androgens on Cognitive Performance: Causal Evidence in a Group of Female-to-Male Transsexuals." *Neueopsychologia* 32 (1995): 1153–57.

Veldhius, Johannes D., John C. King, Randall J. Urban, Alan D. Rogol, William S. Evans, Lias A. Kolp, and Michael L. Johnson. "Operating Characteristics of the Male Hypothalomo-Pituitary-Gonadal Axis: Pulsatile Release of Testosterone and Follicle-Stimulating Hormone and Their Temporal Coupling With Luteinizing Hormone." *Journal of Clinical Endocrinology and Metabolism* 65 (1987): 929–41.

Vonnegut, Kurt. *Cat's Cradle.* New York: Dell, 1963.

Wade, Nicholas. "Guillemin and Schally: A Race Spurred by Rivalry." *Science* 200 (1978): 510–513.

Wallace, A. *Homicide: The New Social Reality.* Sydney: New South Wales Bureau of Crime Statistics and Research, 1986.

Watson, Neil V., and Doreen Kimura. "Nontrivial Sex Differences in Throwing and Intercepting: Relation to Psychometrically-Defined Spatial Functions." *Personality and Individual Differences* 12 (1991): 375–81.

Webb, Eugene J., and Jerry R. Salancik. "The Interview or the Only Wheel in Town." *Journalism Monographs* (1966).

Weick, Karl. *The Social Psychology of Organizing (2nd Ed.)*. Reading, MA: Addison-Wesley, 1979.

Weintraub, Walter. *Verbal Behavior: Adaptation and Psychopathology*. New York: Springer, 1981.

White, G. F., J. Katz, and K. E. Scarborough. "The Impact of Professional Football Games Upon Violent Assaults on Women." *Violence and Victims* 7 (1992): 157–71.

Whitten, Patricia L., Elizabeth Russell, and Frederick Naftolin. "Effects of a Normal, Human-Concentration, Phytoestrogen Diet on Rat Uterine Growth." *Steroids* 57 (1992): 98–106.

Willerman, Lee, R. Schultz, J. M. Rutledge, and E. D. Bigler. "In Vivo Brain Size and Intelligence." *Intelligence* 15 (1991): 223–28.

Wingfield, John C., Robert E. Hegner, Alfred M. Dufty, Jr., and Gregory F. Ball. "The 'Challenge Hypothesis': Theoretical Implications for Patterns of Testosterone Secretion, Mating Systems, and Breeding Strategies." *American Naturalist* 136 (1990): 829–46.

Winslow, James T., James Ellingboe, and Klaus A. Miczek. "Effects of Alcohol on Aggressive Behavior in Squirrel Monkeys: Influence of Testosterone and Social Context." *Psychopharmacology* 95 (1988): 356–63.

Winslow, James T., Nick Hastings, C. Sue Carter, Carroll R. Harbaugh, and Thomas R. Insel. "A Role for Central Vasopressin in Pair Bonding in Monogamous Prairie Voles." *Nature* 365 (1993): 545–48.

Witelson, Sandra F., Debra L. Kigar, and Thomas Harvey. "The Exceptional Brain of Albert Einstein." *Lancet* 353 (1999): 2149–53.

Wolfe, Tom. *The Right Stuff*. New York: Farrar, Straus and Giroux, 1979.

Worthman, C. M., J. F. Stallings, and D. Gubernick. "Measurement of Hormones in Blood Spots: A Non-Isotopic Assay for Prolactin." *American Journal of Physical Anthropology (Supplement No. 12)* (1991): 186–87.

Yalcinkaya, Tamer M., Pentti K. Siiteri, Jean-Louis Vigne, Paul Licht, Sushama Pavgi, Laurence G. Frank, and Stephen E. Glickman. "A Mechanism for Virilization of Female Spotted Hyenas in Utero." *Science* 260 (1993): 1929–31.

Yochelson, Samuel, and Stanton E. Samenow. *The Criminal Personality*. New York: J. Aronson, 1976.

Zhou, Jiang-Ning, Michel A. Hofman, Louis J. G. Gooren, and Dick F. Swaab. "A Sex Difference and Its Relation to Transsexuality." *Nature* 378 (1995): 68–70.

Zigler, Edward, Cara Taussig, and Kathryn Black. "Early Childhood Intervention: A Promising Prevention for Juvenile Delinquency." *American Psychologist* 47 (1992): 996–1006.

Zillmann, Dolf. "Transfer of Excitation in Emotional Behavior." In *Social Psychophysiology: A Sourcebook*. Eds. John T. Cacioppo, and Richard E. Petty, 215–40. New York: Guilford, 1983.

INDEX

Page numbers of charts, graphs, and illustrations appear in italics.

Women *(cont.)*
  aggression, cultural influence on,
    63, 164
  beauty in, 71–72
  behavior traits and high testos-
    terone, 3–4, 5, 12, 95–96, 111,
    138–139
  bravery, 72, 181–182, 183
  child-bearing role of, 199
  computational ability, 57–58
  conversation patterns, 49
  corpus callosum, size of, 43
  directions, giving and following,
    55–56
  dominance and birth of sons,
    13–14
  estrogen and physical traits, 15,
    32, 64
  evolution of sex-linked behavioral
    characteristics, 31, 32–33, 34
  evolution of sex-linked physical
    characteristics, 31, 32, 34
  fantasy and creativity, 42
  fine motor skills, 42, 57
  flamboyance in, 67
  friendships, 33
  hormone replacement therapy,
    testosterone added to, 87,
    101–102, 166
  ignored by men, 107
  initiation ceremonies, 199–200
  legislators, 50–51
  lesbians and testosterone levels, 121
  libido and testosterone, 87,
    100–103, 166
  longevity, 32
  male occupations, choice of,
    138–139
  masculine traits, 40, 72, 138–139

  masculine traits from *in utero*
    testosterone, 12–15
  menstrual cycles and testosterone
    levels, 100, 105
  photography, preferences in, 54
  pregnancy, and testosterone levels
    in mothers, 12–13, 14–15
  prison inmates, 68, 79–80, 89
  relationships, choice of high-
    testosterone men, 112–116
  reproduction and, 25
  sexual attraction and testos-
    terone, 4
  smiling in, 69, 69n, 157, 158,
    162–163
  spatial skills, 51–58
  testosterone, high- versus low-levels
    in, 57, 61, 139
  testosterone levels across the life
    span, 15–16, *16*
  verbal skills, 42, 47
  waist-to-hip-ratio and testosterone
    level, 14
  web thinking versus step thinking,
    43
Womanhood, 199–200, 206, 211

Xena the Warrior Princess, 5

Yanomomo tribe, 116
Yeager, Chuck, 72
Yeats, William Butler, 99
Yerkes Primate Center, 33, 88
You Just Don't Understand (Tannen),
  37
*You've Got to Have Balls to Make It
  in This League* (Postema), 139

Zigler, Edward, 211

ABOUT THE AUTHOR

Jim Dabbs grew up in South Carolina on his great-great-grandfather's farm. His parents, besides farming, wrote about Southern history and civil rights. He was one of six students in the Mayesville High School Class of 1955. There he learned that individuals are important, an idea reinforced by his parents' civil rights work. Jim earned his Bachelor's Degree at Davidson College and his Ph.D. at Yale University, after which he served two years as an officer in Army Intelligence. From 1965 to 1970, he held research positions at Yale and at the University of Michigan. Since 1970, he has been a teacher/researcher in social psychology at Georgia State University. Often collaborating with students, he has written over a hundred articles on social psychological topics, including social interaction, non-verbal behavior, communication and persuasion, altruism, interpersonal attraction, physiological measures, and testosterone. His work has been supported by the National Science Foundation, the National Institute of Mental Health, and the Spencer and Guggenheim Foundations.

Jim met Mary Godwin in 1962 at a Southern Regional Council meeting, where his father was speaking. Mary was assistant to the editor of *New South*, a civil rights magazine. Jim and Mary have two sons, James and Alan, who provided more than a little inspiration for this book. James is now an engineer, inventor, and entrepreneur, and Alan is an international consultant in ecology, sustainable development, and the rights of indigenous peoples.

Jim, still interested in military intelligence, reads spy stories, real and fictitious. He also enjoys poetry, photography, travel, and being Pop-Pop to granddaughters Haley and Grace.